John Franklin Rowe

History of Reformatory Movements

Resulting in a Restoration of the Apostolic Church....

John Franklin Rowe

History of Reformatory Movements
Resulting in a Restoration of the Apostolic Church....

ISBN/EAN: 9783337161927

Printed in Europe, USA, Canada, Australia, Japan

Cover: Foto ©Lupo / pixelio.de

More available books at **www.hansebooks.com**

HISTORY

OF

REFORMATORY MOVEMENTS,

RESULTING IN A

RESTORATION OF THE APOSTOLIC CHURCH,

WITH A

HISTORY OF THE NINETEEN GENERAL CHURCH COUNCILS.

BY

JOHN F. ROWE,

Author of "The Sketch of the Life of Benjamin Franklin," "Analogies between the Old and the New Institutions," "The Bible versus Infidelity." "The Bible its own Interpreter," "The Unity of the Holy Spirit," etc.

CINCINNATI:
G. W. RICE, PUBLISHER.
1884.

Entered according to Act of Congress, in the year 1884, by

G. W. RICE,

in the Office of the Librarian of Congress at Washington, D. C.

Elm Street Printing Co., 176 and 178 Elm St., Cincinnati.

ELECTROTYPED BY
CAMPBELL & CO., 61 LONGWORTH ST.,
CINCINNATI, OHIO.

PREFACE.

IN preparing this work for the public, we have drawn from the most reliable and distinguished authorities extant. We have prepared the work with much labor and patient research. The present work is the condensation of many volumes. For authorities, we have depended on such standard works as McClintock and Strong's *Encyclopedia*, *Encyclopedia Britannica*, Chambers' *Encyclopedia*, Prof. George P. Fisher's *History of the Reformation*, Philip Schaff's *History of the Christian Church*, Neander's *History of the Christian Religion and Church*, and Prof. R. Richardson's *Memoirs of Alexander Campbell*. In delineating the development of the great apostasy from the original apostolic order of things, in describing the successive Protestant reformations, in setting forth the restoration and identification of the Church of Christ, as accomplished through the labors of Alexander Campbell and his coadjutors, and in giving a brief history of the nineteen Œcumenical Church Councils, we have followed the order of events as closely as it was possible to be done. We have aimed to give places, dates, and authorities, and corroborating testimony from disinterested parties. In a word, if there is any reliability in history, it will be found in the following pages. We have aimed to present a systematic compendium of Reformatory Movements, and as such we ask our readers to receive our work, bating all imperfections, as purely a labor of love.

THE AUTHOR.

INTRODUCTION

For many years the writer has himself felt the pressing need of a work of this character. While young in the ministry, and comparatively poor, in possession of very few books, and having no access to large libraries, he continually felt himself hampered by the absence of books of reference, and felt himself crippled in his public ministrations because he could not find time, in his struggles to live above want, to ransack the pages of history in quest of the desired information. The general reader needs just such a work as this, who, in a moment, by referring to the index, can find what he wants and satisfy himself. The preacher needs it for easy reference, and especially the traveling evangelist, who can not pack a lot of books with him. The author of this work, having frequently desired a help of this kind, which he could carry with him, to aid him both in speaking and writing for the press, came to the conclusion that others might be greatly benefited by the matter contained in it. The author has for a long time had such a work in contemplation. It is not only intended for the Disciples of Christ, but it is also prepared with a view of circulating it among the various denominations, and with the purpose of inciting the independent and untrammeled thinkers in the denominations to investigate the pages of history to see if these things are so.

Within the compass of this work, we have aimed to give a connected view of the Reformatory Movements from Martin Luther down to the times of the great reformer, Alexander Campbell. The reader will discover the fact that while such illustrious reformers as Luther, Zwingli, Melancthon, Calvin, Knox, and Wesley, only aimed at *re*-forming existing abuses and immoralities in the Church, Campbell sought the complete *restoration* of apostolic principles and practices, and, having determined upon a work of that character, did actually raise up a body of people identical with primitive Christians, both in faith and practice. The plan of the work is as follows:

1. A brief statement of the primitive order of things. 2. A sketch of the apostasy from the third century down to the times of Luther, or to the Reformation of the Sixteenth Century. 3. A connected history of the Protestant period, which embraces the efforts made at reformation during the space of three hundred years. 4. The Restoration of the Apostolic Church. 5. A history of the nineteen Œcumenical Church Councils—the study of the proceedings of which is highly instructive and interesting, they serving as a sort of spiritual thermometer of the troublous times of the Church, as the Church was manipulated by princes and priests. The various decrees of successive councils will show how kings and princes were deposed, the rivalries of ambitious men in Church and State, the origin of image worship, auricular confession, penance, the mass, celibacy, purgatory, prayers for the dead, transubstantiation, etc., etc. The subjects we have enumerated should be studied as they are not studied in these days of flashy literature and fast living. There is entirely too much superficial reading done, even by ministers of the gospel, who should be in possession of a general knowledge of Church history, without which they will feel themselves more or less annoyed and crippled in their ministerial work. People who profess to be reformers can not very well progress as reformers unless they have an intelligent view of the situation, as we have outlined it in this work. The general reader, engaged in secular employments, who has not the time to explore the pages of many volumes, and not even time to consult books of reference, will, we feel confident, find this work of great advantage to him, that it will aid him very much in ascertaining the facts of history, and furnish him with facts and data with which to make just comparison between truth and error, between what God has *decreed*, and what man has *invented*, and especially show him the difference between reforming imperfect church organizations and restoring the Church of Christ as founded by the apostles.

INTRODUCTION.

We should probably apologize to the general reader for investing portions of this work with a show of too much learning and too much refined scholarship ; but we found it impossible to prepare a work of this character—which is history condensed—and dress it up in a simple garb of words and terms of speech, without marring more or less the pages of history, and without doing injustice to the subjects treated and to the authors quoted.

If the reader shall derive as much benefit and pleasure in perusing these pages, as the author has derived from the preparation of the work, the author will feel that he has not labored in vain.

CONTENTS.

	PAGE.
Preface,	3
Introduction,	5
Contents,	8

	PAGE
CHAPTER I.—THE PRIMITIVE CHURCH,	11
CHAPTER II.—Union of Church and State,	16
CHAPTER III.—Conflict between Church and State,	19
CHAPTER IV.—Culmination of the Papacy,	22
CHAPTER V.—The Papacy and Episcopacy,	27
CHAPTER VI.—Leo X and Luther,	31
CHAPTER VII.—The Dawn of the Reformation,	34
CHAPTER VIII.—The Mystics,	37
CHAPTER IX.—Luther and the Man of Sin,	40
CHAPTER X.—Origin of the Augsburg Confession,	48
CHAPTER XI.—Reformation in Switzerland,	56
CHAPTER XII.—Origin of the Heidelberg Confession,	59

CONTENTS.

	PAGE.
CHAPTER XIII.—John Calvin and Calvinism,	63
CHAPTER XIV.—Origin of the Church of England,	71
CHAPTER XV.—The Thirty-Nine Articles,	75
CHAPTER XVI.—The Book of Common Prayer,	8
CHAPTER XVII.—Origin of the Westminster Confession of Faith,	87
CHAPTER XVIII.—Origin of Congregationalism,	94
CHAPTER XIX.—American Congregationalism,	97
CHAPTER XX.—Origin of the Baptist Church,	102
CHAPTER XXI.—The Baptist Church in the United States,	112
CHAPTER XXII.—Origin of Methodism,	119
CHAPTER XXIII.—Origin of the Methodist Episcopal Church,	123
CHAPTER XXIV.—Wesley not a Methodist,	128
CHAPTER XXV.—The Reformation of the Nineteenth Century,	136
CHAPTER XXVI.—Attempts at Reformation,	144
CHAPTER XXVII.—The Word of God the Sole Rule of Action,	148
CHAPTER XXVIII.—Attempts at Christian Union,	153
CHAPTER XXIX.—Fundamental Principles,	157
CHAPTER XXX.—The Restoration,	161
CHAPTER XXXI.—The Bible the only Creed,	167
CHAPTER XXXII.—Alexander Campbell Abandons Sectarianism,	171
CHAPTER XXXIII.—A. Campbell Unites with the Baptists,	178
CHAPTER XXXIV.—A Similar Reformation in Kentucky,	186
CHAPTER XXXV.—The Church of Christ Identified,	192
CHAPTER XXXVI.—The Restoration of Apostolic Christianity,	199

	PAGE
HISTORY OF CHURCH COUNCILS,	205
I. Apostolic Council,	207
II. Council of Nice,	208
The Nicene Creed,	212
Councils of Constantinople,	218
General Council of Ephesus,	221
Council of Chalcedon,	223
The Second Council of Nice,	227
Lateran Councils,	231
The Councils of Lyons,	246
Councils of Vienne,	246
Council of Constance,	249
The Council at Basle,	250
Council of Trent,	254
GOSPEL PRINCIPLES.	
Faith and Sight,	261
Reformation of Life,	273
The Good Confession,	280
Immersion,	286
Immersion—Sprinkle—Pour. Which?	299
The Holy Spirit,	306
The Baptism in the Spirit,	312
Impartation of the Holy Spirit by Apostolic Hands,	316
The Word as Revealed by the Holy Spirit,	319
The Confirmation of the Revealed Word,	325
The Gift of the Holy Spirit,	331
The Witness of the Spirit,	339
The Law of the Spirit,	344

HISTORY OF
REFORMATORY MOVEMENTS.

THE PRIMITIVE CHURCH.

ONE essential feature of Protestantism was the abolition of the authority of the hierarchical order. In its mature form, as all history attests, the Reformation of the sixteenth century was a rejection of Papal and priestly authority. As antecedent to the rise of the Reformation, we propose to write several articles on the origin and progressive development of the hierarchical system. The Papacy began by invading the personal rights and prerogatives of the disciples of Christ, who stood upon a common plane of equality, and by instituting a mediatorial priesthood, which, setting aside the office of the great Mediator, assumed to mediate between God and man. It was an invasion of that order of heaven, as recorded in the New Testament, which gave liberty to the soul and direct access to the heavenly Father through the one High Priest of our salvation.

The rise of sacerdotalism destroyed the equality of discipleship. The disciples of Christ, under apostolic teaching, formed a community of brethren, who were associated upon a broad basis of equality, all of them being illuminated and directed and united in the one Spirit. Their organization under Christ, was a marvel of simplicity, and very unlike that hierarchical system which in subsequent times overshadowed the Church of the living God—very dissimilar from the individual congregation where all the members served each other in love and faith.

The New Testament records the fact that all Christians, in a given locality, were united in one society, or *ecclesia*, the old Greek term for an assembly legally called and authorized. In each society there was a board of pastors, indifferently called elders, presbyters—a name taken from the synagogue—or interchangeably styled bishops, overseers, a name given by the Greeks to persons charged with a guiding oversight in civil administration. In the election of these pastors—feeders of the flock—the body of disciples enjoyed a controlling voice, although as long as the apostles remained, their suggestions or appointments would naturally be accepted. These officers did not give up, at first, their secular employments; they were not even, at the outset, intrusted as a peculiar function with the business of teaching, which was free to all and especially imposed upon a class of persons who seemed designated by their various gifts for this work. The elders, with the deacons, whose business it was to look after the poor and to perform kindred duties, were the officers to whom each little separate community committed the lead in the management of its affairs. But, as we approach the close of the second century, we find marked changes;

some of them of a portentous and dangerous character, and as already indicative of the fact that the apostasy had set in. The enlargement of the jurisdiction of bishops by extending it over dependent churches in the neighborhood of the towns and cities, and the multiplying of church officers, were innovations significant of coming evils. By degrees church officers, by assuming powers which did not belong to them, grew into a distinct order, and placed themselves above the "laity" as the appointed medium of conveying to them the grace of God. A church in the capital of a province, with its bishop, easily acquired a precedence over the other churches and bishops in the same district, and thus the metropolitan system grew up. A higher grade of eminence was accorded to the bishops and churches of the principal cities, such as Rome, Alexander and Ephesus; and thus we have the germs of a more extended hierarchical dominion. Even as early as the latter part of the second century, the Church has passed into the condition of a *visible* organized commonwealth. We find Irenæus, who was bishop of Lyons from 177 to 202, uttering the famous dictum that where the Church is— meaning the visible body with its clergy and sacraments —there is the Spirit of God, and where the Spirit of God is there is the Church. To be cut off from this visible Church is to be separated from Christ. By the clergy of that period, this church was made the door of access to the favor of God. We can also readily account for the importance that began to be attached to tradition; for the defenders of the true Church of Christ against the corrupting encroachments of gnosticism, naturally fell back on the historical evidence afforded by the presence and testimony of the leading churches, which the apostles themselves had planted. Irenæus and Tertullian (the latter a presbyter at Carthage, where he died between the years 220 and 240), direct the inquirer to go to Corinth, Rome, Ephesus, to the places where the apostles had taught, and ascertain whether the novel speculations of the time could justly claim the sanction of the first disciples of Christ, or had been transmitted from them.

Says a distinguished author: "It is the pre-eminence of Rome, as the custodian of traditions, that Irenæus means to assert in a noted passage (lib. III. iii. 2) in which he exalts the Church." It was not long until the unity of the Church, as a visible, towering organization, was realized in the unity of the sacerdotal body. It was but a natural and logical sequence to seek and find a head for this traditionized and secularized body; and where should it be found except in mystic Rome, the capital of the world, the seat of the predominating Church, where Paul had suffered martyrdom, and where many believed (but erroneously) that Peter also perished as a martyr. After the sacerdotal order had raised Peter to be chief of the apostles, and when, near the close of the second century, the idea was suggested and became current that Peter had served as bishop of the Roman Church, a strong foundation was laid in the minds of credulous men for a recognition of the primacy of that Church and of its chief pastor. The first mention of Peter as bishop of Rome is found in the *Clementine Homilies,* which were composed in the latter part of the second century. The habit of thus deferring to the see of Rome, as the center of ecclesiastical authority, so far advances upon the credulity of the people, that in the middle of the third century we find Cyprian, whose zeal for episcopal independence would not tolerate the subjection of one bishop to another, still speaking of that see as the chief source of sacerdotal unity. Rome was a mighty and a glorious city. The eyes of all nations were intently fixed upon it, as the metropolis of wealth and splendor and political power. It was an easy thing to transfer this awe and reverence to the Church which had its seat in the eternal City. Leo I., with arrogant pretensions, claimed that the Roman Empire was built with reference to Christianity, and that Rome, for this reason, was chosen for the bishopric of the chief of the apostles. Leo flourished in the fifth century.

UNION OF CHURCH AND STATE.

The accession of Constantine (311) found the Church so firmly organized under its hierarchy that it could not be absolutely merged in the State, as might have been the result had its constitution been different. But under him and his successors, the supremacy of the State, with a large control of ecclesiastical affairs, was maintained by the emperors. General councils, for example, were convoked by them and presided over by their representatives, and conciliary decrees published as laws of the Empire. The Roman bishops felt it to be an honor to be judged only by the emperor. In the closing period of imperial history, the emperors favored the ecclesiastical primacy of the Roman see, as a bond of unity in the Empire. Political disorders and conflicting interests tended to elevate the position of the Roman bishop, especially when he was a person of more than ordinary talents and energy. Leo the Great (440–461), the first, perhaps, who had conferred upon him the title of Pope, proved himself a pillar of strength in the midst of tumult and anarchy. His conspicuous services, as in shielding Rome from the incursions of barbarians and protecting its inhabitants, facilitated the exercise of a spiritual jurisdiction that stretched not only over Italy, but as far as Gaul and Africa. To him was given by Valentinian III. (445) an imperial declaration which made him supreme over the Western Church, or the Church of Rome. We can not follow the alternations of the priestly powers of Rome, nor consume space by depicting the varying fortunes of popes and princes. We can record the fact that in the fifth century the fall of the Western Empire increased the authority of the bishop of Rome; we can speak of the spread of Mohammedanism from Africa and Spain into Europe; of the alliance of the Papacy with the Franks in 750; of the rescue of the Papacy by Pepin and Charlemagne, and of the coronation of the latter by the hands of the Pope, in the Basilica of St. Peter, on Christmas Day, 800. Taking advantage of the conflicts and disorders in the empire of Charlemagne, and seizing the opportunity of his death, which created an era of political strife and unrest, the Roman bishops rapidly began to increase in power. It was in this period that the False or Pseudo Isoderian Decretals appeared. These false decretals introduced principles of ecclesiastical law which made the Church dependent on the State, and elevated the Roman See to a position unknown to preceding ages. The immunity and high prerogatives of bishops, the exaltation of primates, as the servile tools of the popes, above metropolitans who were slavishly dependent upon secular rulers, and the ascription of the highest legislative and judicial functions to the Roman Pontiff, were some of the leading and characteristic features of this spurious collection, which found its way into the codes of the canon law, and which radically modified the ancient ecclesiastical system. These false decretals first appeared about the middle of the ninth century, and they only needed a pope of sufficient talents and energy to give practical effect to such pernicious principles; and such an instrument appeared in the person of Nicholas I, between the years 858 and 867.

Availing himself of a favorable opportunity, he brought Lothair II., king of Lorraine, under the censure of the Church, whom, in a case of matrimony, he compelled to submit to the decrees of the Papacy, while at the same time he deposed the archbishops who had endeavored to thwart his purpose. At the same time, Nicholas humbled Hincmar, the powerful archbishop of Rheims, who had disregarded the appeal which one of his bishops had made to Rome.

According to Baronius, a distinguished Roman Catholic annalist, the anarchical condition into which the empire ultimately fell, left the Papacy, for a century and a half, the prey of Italian factions, by the agency of which the papal office was reduced to a lower point of moral degradation than it ever reached before or since. This period of moral and social debasement—during a considerable portion of which time harlots disposed of the papal office, and their paramours wore the tiara—was interrupted by the intervention of the German sovereigns, Otho I. and Otho II.; with the first of whom the Holy Roman Empire, in the sense in which the name is used in subsequent ages, the secular counterpart of the Papacy, derives its origin. The pontiffs preferred the sway of the emperors to that of the lawless Italian barons, says Von Raumer. This dark period, in which nearly all traces of apostolic usages disappeared, was terminated by Henry III., who appeared in Italy at the head of an army, and, in 1046, at the Synod of Sutri, which he had convoked, dethroned three rival popes, and raised to the vacant office one of his own bishops. The imperial office had passed into the hands of the German kings, and they, like their Carlovingian predecessors, whose acts in history we have purposely omitted, rescued the Papacy from destruction.

CONFLICT BETWEEN CHURCH AND STATE.

When we reach the age of Hildebrand (1073—1085), we find plots and counterplots the order of the day. While this pretended reformer apparently sought a thorough reformation of morals and a restoration of ecclesiastical order and sacerdotal discipline, he undertook at the same time to subordinate the State to the Church, and to subject the Church, such as it was, to the absolute authority of the Pope. The course pursued by Hildebrand and by aspiring pontiffs who succeeded him, in the course of time, resulted in an open conflict between the Papacy and the Empire. Here follows a severe and persistent contest, in which the Papacy gain a decided advantage. That the emperor was commissioned to preside over the temporal affairs of men, while it was left for the Pope to guide and govern them in things spiritual, was a criterion too vague for defining the limits of temporal and spiritual jurisdiction. The co-ordination, the equilibrium of the civil and ecclesiastical powers, was a relation with which, as any one might know, who is conversant with the history of despotic governments, neither party would be content. It was a struggle on both sides for universal monarchy. The apostolic order of things now completely fades out of view. The popes, by continual strategy and rare diplomacy, gained an ascendency over Western Europe, and, for successive years, the Pope everywhere was the acknowledged head of Latin Christianity. Sometimes the Roman pontiffs, when they saw an opportunity of centralizing and consolidating their system of spiritual despotism, became the champions then, as they have frequently since, as suits their base designs, of popular freedom. Acting in the role of Mephistopheles, they can, in turn, become republicans, monarchists, democrats, autocrats and imperialists, if by such transformation they can subserve the interests of the Papacy. The end sanctifies the means. The humiliation of Henry IV. in 1077, whom Hildebrand kept waiting during three winter days, in the garb of a penitent, in the yard of the castle of Canossa, gives evidence of the supremacy of the Papacy in the medieval age. The Worms Concordat which Calixtus II. concluded with Henry V. in 1122, and the acknowledgment which Frederick Barbarossa made of his sin and error to Alexander III. at Venice, in 1177, after a long contest for imperial prerogatives, are facts which furnish evidence of the triumph of the Papacy. The triumph of the Papacy appeared complete when Gregory X. (1271–1276) directed the electoral princes to choose an emperor within a given interval, and threatened, in case they refused compliance with the mandate, to appoint, in conjunction with his cardinals, an emperor for them; and when Rudolph of Hapsburg, whom they proceeded to select, acknowledged in the most unreserved and subservient manner the Pope's supremacy.

These are strange developments of church affairs, compared with the origin of Christianity and primitive gospel simplicity. The facts that we glean and scrap from the Dark Ages, are the full fruitage of the workings of the "mystery of iniquity" alluded to by the apostle Paul. It is impossible to furnish the details of history within our limited space, but it is our purpose to give a connected view of the rise and development of the Papacy, and to represent in as few words as possible the ruin of the ancient Church, and the subsequent growth of an apostate Church. And this we do in order to show the relation which Romanism sustains to Protestantism, and the relation which we sustain to both these in our plea for a perfectly restored Christianity. That there was a remnant of the true worshipers of God found here and there, during the Dark Ages, such as the Nestorians, is a pleasing fact well established in history; but that nearly all traces of the primitive order of things, as established by the apostles of Jesus Christ, are lost sight of in the raging conflicts of rival princes and aspiring ecclesiastics, both of which powers, as they alternated repeatedly between victory and defeat, crushed down the liberties of the people and despoiled them of their personal rights, are facts patent and intelligible to all readers of history. We wish the people of this generation, as well as the people of succeeding generations, to know the reasons why we stand apart from all denominations, Papal and Protestant, and why we propose to stand only upon apostolic ground.

CULMINATION OF THE PAPACY.

FROM the best authorities we have consulted, we learn that it was during the progress of the struggle with the empire that the Papal powers may be said to have culminated. In the period between 1198 and 1216, in which Innocent III. reigned, the Papal despotism shone forth in all its ecclesiastical splendor. The enforcement of celibacy had placed the entire body of the clergy in a closer relation to the sovereign Pontiff. The Vicar of Peter had become the Vicar of God and of Christ. The idea of a Theocracy on earth, in which the Pope should presumptuously rule in this character, fully possessed the mind of Innocent, who, having profited by the boldness, and persistency, and political finesse of Gregory VII., excelled the latter in diplomacy and political strategy. He worked himself up to believe that the two swords of temporal and ecclesiastical power had both been given to Peter and his successors, so that the earthly sovereign derived his prerogative from the great Head of the Church. The Pope was constituted to shine as the great luminary of the world, and the king or civil ruler could only shine from borrowed light. Acting on this theory—the consummation of spiritual despotism—Innocent assumed the position of arbiter in the conflicts of nations, and claimed the right to dethrone kings and princes at his pleasure. We have not space to give examples of his despotism, with which the pages of history are disgraced.

In the Church he assumed the character of universal bishop, based upon the theory that all episcopal power was originally deposited in Peter and in his successors, and communicated through this source to bishops, who were in this manner constituted the only vicars of the Pope, and who might at any time be deposed at the will or beck of the Pope. To him belonged all legislative authority, councils having merely a deliberate power, while the right to convoke them and to ratify or annul their proceedings belonged exclusively to him. He alone, in the role of an absolute autocrat, was exempt from all law, and might dispense with them in the case of others. Even the doctrine of Papal infallibility, which brought forth its legitimate fruit in the reign of Pope Pius IX., was discovered in the writings of Thomas Aquinas, the most eminent theologian of that age. As the feudal system gradually gave way to political monarchy, so the independency of the churches was absorbed and concentrated in the Pope. The right to confirm the appointment of all bishops, the right even to nominate bishops and to dispose of all benefices, the exclusive right of absolution, canonization and dispensation, the right to assess the churches—such were some of the iniquitous prerogatives, for the enforcement of which Papal legates, clothed with limitless powers, were commissioned to penetrate all the countries of Europe, in order to override the authority of bishops and of local ecclesiastical tribunals. About this time originated the famous mendicant orders of St. Francis and St. Dominic, from which beggarly institutions there came forth a swarm of itinerant preachers, who, as the pets of the Pope, were very intimately associated with his pontifical Highness, and who were ever ready, as pliant tools, to defend Papal prerogatives and Papal extortions against whatever opposition might arise from the secular clergy. Insinuating themselves, serpent-like, within the walls of the universities of Europe, they defined and defended, in lectures replete with subtilties and sophistries, and by a pretended array of scholastic wisdom, all the usurpations of the Papacy.

Conflicts between popes and temporal princes continued. The Papal assertions in regard to the two swords, the supremacy of the ecclesiastical over the secular power, and the subjection of every living soul to the Pope, who judges all and is judged by none, were met by a united and determined resistance on the part of the French people. When Boniface VIII. summoned the French clergy to Rome to sit in judgment on the acts of the king, the summons aroused a storm of indignation. The Papal Bull, snatched from the hand of the legate, was publicly burned in Notre Dame, on the 11th of February, 1302. The insulted clergy of France flatly denied the proposition that in secular affairs, the Pope stands above the king. The prestige of the Papacy now began to wane rapidly. There was an expansion of knowledge in every direction. Political reformers came to the front. Literature began to spread, and poets and jurists, of learning and distinction, began to exert a powerful influence in the direction of civil and religious liberty. There comes the period of the Babylonian captivity, or the long residence of the Pope at Avignon — called the Babylonian captivity, because it continued about as long as the captivity of the Jews in ancient Babylon — and the period of the great schism, when, during a great part of this period, the Papacy was enslaved to France, and served the behests of the French court. Various forms of ecclesiastical oppression followed, which involved Germany, England, and other countries in humiliation. The revenues of the court at Avignon were supplied by means of extortions and usurpations which had hitherto been without parallel. Every form of extortion was resorted to for replenishing the Papal treasury. France was willing, as long as the Papacy remained her tool, to indulge the popes in extravagant assumptions of authority. Avignon became the headquarters of an extremely luxurious and profligate court—a cesspool of vice—the boundless immorality of which has been vividly depicted by Petrarch, who himself was an eye-witness to the shameful abominations. Then arose the great battle of the fourteenth century, between the Monarchists and the Papists, when such celebrated writers as Marsilius of Padua, William of Occam, and Dante, as the defenders of the "Monarchists," vigorously denounced the presumptions of the Papacy. "These bold writings attacked the collective hierarchy in all its fundamental principles; they inquired, with a sharpness of criticism before unknown, into the nature of the priestly office; they restricted the notion of heresy, to which the Church had given so wide an extension; they appealed, finally, to the Holy Scriptures, as the only valid authority in matters of faith. As fervent monarchists, these theologians subjected the Church to the State. Their heretical tendencies announced a new process in the minds of men, in which the unity of the Catholic Church went down."

During the schism which ensued upon the election of Urban VI., in 1378, there was presented before Christendom the spectacle of rival popes imprecating curses upon each other; each with his court to be maintained by taxes and contributions, which had to be largely increased on account of the division. When men were compelled to choose between rival claimants of the office, it was inevitable that there should arise a still deeper investigation into the origin and grounds of Papal authority. Inquirers reverted to the earlier ages of the Church, in order to find both the causes and the cure of the dreadful evils under which Christian society was suffering. More than one jurist and theologian called attention to the ambition of the popes for secular rule and to their oppressive domination over the Church, as the prime fountain of this frightful disorder. (*History of the Reformation*, by George P. Fisher.)

THE PAPACY AND EPISCOPACY.

A FRUITLESS attempt was made, at about this period, to reform the Church "in head and members." Princes interposed to make peace between popes, as popes had before interposed to produce peace between princes. According to Laurent (*La Reforme*), it is the era of the Reforming councils of Pisa, Constance, and Basel, when, largely under the leadership of the Paris theologians (1409-1443) a reformation in the morals and administration of the Church was sought through the agency of these great assemblies. It was now a conflict for supremacy between Papacy and Episcopacy. The Pope was regarded as primate of the Church, but at the same time it was asserted that bishops derived their grace and authority for the discharge of their office, not from the Pope, but from the same source as that from which he derived his powers. It was held that the Church, when convened by its representatives in a general council, is the supreme council, to which the Pope himself is subordinate and responsible. "Their aim," says Prof. Fisher, "was to reduce him to the rank of a constitutional instead of an absolute monarch. The Gallican theologians held to an infallibility residing somewhere in the Church; most of them, and ultimately all of them, placing this infallibility in œcumenical councils. The flattering hopes under which the Council of Pisa opened its proceedings, were doomed to disappointment, in consequence of the reluctance of the reformers to push through their measures without a pope, and the failure of Alexander V. to redeem the pledges which he had made them prior to his election. Moreover, the schism continued, with three popes in the room of two. The Council of Constance began under the fairest auspices. The resolve to vote by nations was a significant sign of a new order of things, and crushed the design of the flagitious Pope, John XXIII., to control the assembly by the preponderance of Italian votes. Solemn declarations of the supremacy and authority of the Council were adopted, and were carried out in the actual deposition of the infamous Pope. But the plans of reform were mostly wrecked on the same rock on which they had broken at Pisa. A pope must be elected; and Martin V., once chosen, by skillful management and by separate arrangements with different princes, was unable to undo, to a great extent, the salutary work of the Council, and even before its adjournment to reassert the very doctrine of Papal superiority which the Council had repudiated. The substantial failure of this Council, the most august ecclesiastical assemblage of the Middle Ages, to achieve reforms which thoughtful and good men everywhere deemed indispensable, was a proof that some more radical means of reformation would have to be adopted. But another grand effort in the same direction was put forth; and the Council of Basel, notwithstanding that it adopted numerous measures of a beneficent character, which were acceptable to the Catholic nations, had, at last, no better issue: for most of the advantages that were granted to them, and the concessions that were made by the popes, especially to Germany, they contrived afterward, by adroit diplomacy, to recall."

History gives abundant evidence of the fact that no good ever came from human councils, which undertook to interfere with and modify the doctrine and government of the Church of Christ. Only evil, and unmitigated evil, ever emanated from such a source. The fifteenth century was characterized by national rivalries, and by the plots and counterplots of aspiring princes, who served the Papal cause, or compelled the Papacy to serve them, as self-interest might dictate. It is difficult to tell which exercised the most chicanery, and which practiced the most intrigue, or which sank to the lowest depths to gain power—the civil or ecclesiastical powers. One thing is certain, and that is, that selfishness reigned supreme. In illustration of this statement, it is recorded that Innocent VIII., besides advancing the fortunes of seven illegitimate children, and waging two wars with Naples, received an annual tribute from the Sultan for detaining his brother and rival in prison, instead of sending him to lead a force against the Turks, the enemies and despoilers of Christendom. Alexander VI., whose deep depravity recalls the dark days of the Papacy in the tenth century, busied himself in founding a principality for his favorite son, that monster of iniquity, Cæsar Borgia, and in amassing treasures, by base and cruel means, for the support of the licentious Roman Court. He is said to have died of the poison which he had caused to be prepared for a wealthy cardinal, who bribed the head cook to set it before the Pope himself. If Julius II. satisfied the extortionate demands of his relatives in a more peaceable way, he still found his enjoyment in carnal war and savage conquest, and made it his chief occupation to the States of the Church. According to the testimony of Gieseler, the eminent German historian, he organized alliances and defeated one enemy after another, forcing Venice to submit to his outrages, and not hesitating, old man as he was, to take the field himself, in the time of winter. In 1510, having brought in the French, and having joined the league of Cambray for the sake of subduing Venice, he called to his aid the Venetians for the expulsion of the French. The Church, and especially the priesthood of Rome, had become thoroughly demoralized; and this was the condition of things on the eve of the reformation of the sixteenth century.

LEO X. AND LUTHER.

AT the opening of the Reformation, Leo X. was made a cardinal at the age of thirteen, and elected Pope at the age of thirty-seven. He was more "familiar with the fables of Greece, and the delights of the poets, than with the history of the Church and the doctrine of the Fathers." He indulged in profane studies, and gave much of his time to hunting, jesting and pageants. He sported in a gay and luxurious court, and made religion subordinate to the fascinations of literature, art and music. Vast sums of money, which his religious subjects were obliged to contribute, were lavished upon his relatives, and the historian Ranke has characterized his habits of life as "a sort of intellectual sensuality." Luther began his Reformation in the reign of this cold-hearted Pope. "During the Middle Ages," says Coleridge, "the Papacy was another name for a confederation of learned men in the west of Europe against the barbarians and ignorance of the times. The Pope was the chief of this confederacy; and, so long as he retained that character, his power was just and irresistible. It was the principal means of preserving for us and for all posterity all that we now have of the illumination of past ages. But as soon as the Pope made a separation between his character as premier clerk in Christendom and as a secular prince—as soon as he began to squabble for towns and castles—then he at once broke the charm and gave birth to a revolution. Everywhere, but especially throughout the North of Europe, the breach of feeling and sympathy went on widening; so that all Germany, England, Scotland and other countries, started, like giants out of their sleep, at the first blast of Luther's trumpet." (*Table Talk*, July 24, 1832.)

Coleridge may have seen a special providence in the rise of the Papacy, as a "confederation of learned men in the west of Europe;" but we can not see the special providence. We see the Papacy, with all its worldly wisdom, sagacity, duplicity, diplomacy; with all its arrogance, assumption of power, corruptions and abominations. We also see its downfall at the approach of Bible knowledge, apostolic teaching and popular education.

The age immediately preceding the Lutheran Reformation was characterized by the dogmatic system, as elaborated by the schoolmen from the abundant materials furnished by tradition and sanctioned by the mongrel Church; which constituted a vast body of mystic and scholastic doctrine, and which every man of the least religious pretensions was bound to accept in all particulars, or come under the ban of excommunication. The polity of the mongrel Church lodged all ecclesiastical rule in the hands of a superior class, the besotted priesthood, who were commissioned as the indispensable almoners of divine grace. The worship centered in the sacrifice of the mass, a constantly repeated miracle wrought by the hands of the wily and winsome priest. Justification by meritorious works, without respect to character and a godly life, was stereotyped into a wicked dogma, which was eating out the vitals of all religious life. Human merit was substituted for the mercy of God. A religion of external performances, which consisted in quantity rather than in quality, and various modes of pretentious abstinences, with the institution of monasticism and the celibacy of the priesthood, were prominent features in the existing order of things. According to Ullman (*Reformatoren von der Reformation*) the masses, pilgrimages, fastings, flagellations, prayers to saints, homage to their relics and images and similar features so prominent in medieval mysticism, which passed as piety, illustrate the essential character of the times.

The forerunners of the Reformation have been properly divided," says Prof. Fisher, quoting from Dr. Ullman, "into two classes. The first of them consists of the men who, in the quiet path of theological research and teaching, or by practical exertions in behalf of a contemplative, spiritual tone of piety, were undermining the traditional system. The second embraces names who are better known, for the reason that they attempted to carry out their ideas practically in the way of effecting ecclesiastical changes. The first class are more obscure, but were not less influential in preparing the ground for the Reformation. Protestantism was a return to the Scriptures as the authentic source of Christian knowledge, and to the principle that salvation, that inward peace, is not from the Church or from human works, ethical or ceremonial, but through Christ alone, received by the soul in an act of trust. Whoever, whether in the chair of theology, in the pulpit, through the devotional treatise, or by fostering the study of languages and of history, or in perilous combat with ecclesiastical abuses, drew the minds of men to the Scriptures and to a more spiritual conception of religion, was, in a greater or less measure, a reformer before the Reformation.

THE DAWN OF THE REFORMATION.

From the twelfth century down to the dawn of the Reformation, there were found here and there, especially in Southern France and Northern Italy, "anti-sacerdotal sects," who indulged in vehement invectives against the shameful immoralities of the priesthood and their baneful usurpations of power. Among these sects in Southern France, we may mention the noted Albigenses, who vigorously opposed the authority of ecclesiastical tradition and of the hierarchy, but who were finally crushed out of existence by means of a bloody and heartless crusade, instigated by Innocent III., and which, through his agency, was followed up by the iniquitous Inquisition, which here had its origin. "Catharists" was a general name applied to these anti-sacerdotal sects. Succeeding the Albigenses, there appear in 1170, the Waldenses, under the leadership of Peter Waldo, of Lyons. Because of their attachment to the Scriptures, and of their fiery opposition to clerical usurpation and profligacy, they also became forerunners of the Reformation. Disaffection and unrest, and a stubborn resistance against the aggressions of the priesthood, were experienced in all quarters, especially among the poor and dependent classes.

The Inquisition had done its bloody work in the extirpation of all such heretics as the Albigenses and the Waldenses. More radical and influential reformers have now moved to the front, such as Huss, Jerome of Prague and John Wickliffe. But the theologians of Paris made themselves infamous and almost outstripped their Papal antagonists, during the sessions of the Council of Constance, in their violent treatment of Huss, and in the alacrity with which they condemned him and Jerome to the stake. One hundred and fifty years before the days of Luther, Wickliffe proved himself a formidable antagonist to the pretensions of the Papacy. He anticipated the grand reformation with a knowledge of the religious situation, with a perspicuity of genius, and by apostolic blows of radical reform, that shook the very foundations of the Papal edifice. He set aside Papal decrees by a direct appeal to the Holy Scriptures. He denies transubstantiation; he boldly asserts that in the primitive Church there were only two classes of church officers; denies that there is scriptural authority for the rites of confirmation and extreme unction; advocates non-interference on the part of the clergy with civil affairs and temporal authority; condemns auricular confession; holds that the exercise of the power to bind and loose is of no effect, unless it conforms to the doctrine of Christ; is opposed to the multiplied ranks of the clergy — popes, cardinals, patriarchs, monks, canons, *et. al.*; repudiates the doctrine of indulgences and supererogatory merits, the doctrine of the excellence of poverty, as that was held and as it lay at the foundation of the mendicant orders; and he sets himself against artificial church music, pictures in worship, consecration with the use of oil and salt, canonization, pilgrimages, church asylums for criminals, and the celibacy of the clergy. These facts are all clearly authenticated by reliable historians. The followers of Wickliffe were called Lollards. It is a remarkable fact that Wickliffe predicted that from the monks themselves there would arise men who would abandon their false interpretations of Scriptures, and, returning to the apostolic order of things, would reconstruct the Church in the spirit of Paul. The work of reform as inaugurated by Wickliffe, we may remark, in passing, presents many features resembling the work of reform as inaugurated by Thomas and Alexander Campbell. The latter was an ardent admirer of the illustrious Wickliffe. It was in the Council of Constance that Huss asserted the right of private judgment. This was going behind the Council; and for his temerity he was commanded to retract his avowals of opinion, which he refused to do until he could be convinced by argument and by citations from the Scriptures, that his sentiments were erroneous. The right of private judgment became one of the prominent and distinctive principles of Protestantism. Other reformers sprung up, whom we can not mention, such as the distinguished and eloquent Savonarola, who lived at Florence, where he carried on his work of moral reform, until his death in 1498. He exposed the demoralized condition of the mongrel Church, and for laying bare the rottenness of the Papal system, he forfeited his life under the flagitious Alexander VI., but predicted a coming reformation.

THE MYSTICS.

THE Reformation of the sixteenth century was preceded by a school of men, called *Mystics*, of whom the noted Anselm was the father. The characteristic of the Mystics is the sensation of feeling, rather than of believing; the preference of intuition to logic, the quest for knowledge through light imparted to feeling, rather than by processes of the intellect; the indwelling of God in the soul, elevated to a holy calm by the consciousness of his presence; absolute self-renunciation and the absorption of the human will into the divine; silent meditation and the ecstatic mood. The characteristic spirit of this mystical school, which was a recoil from dogmatic theology, and from the extravagant use of outward sacraments and ceremonies, was illustrated by Thomas à Kempis, in his celebrated work, entitled "The Imitation of Christ," which it is said has probably had a larger circulation than any other book except the Bible. Luther himself was more or less influenced by the doctrines of the Mystics, especially by the writings of John Tauler and Thomas à Kempis.

The Reformation was preceded by a revival of learning—a new era of intellectual culture—in which three eminent writers—Dante, Petrarch and Boccaccio—made themselves distinguished. Scholasticism, which for several hundred years had been dominant in the medieval ages, gradually gave way as books began to multiply, and as the Scriptures continued to be translated into the native languages of the people. The Schoolmen and the Mystics began to retire to the background immediately upon the introduction of the art of printing, and as distinguished scholars, coming to the front, began to test the doctrinal and ecclesiastical system of that age by a translation of the Old and New Testament from the original, the original fountain of truth having been oppressed by the Papacy, and the mass of the people deprived of the key of knowledge. The gigantic fabric of Latin Christianity, that vast receptacle of idolatry and Pagan superstition, began to quake at the near approach of intelligent faith and reason, and of civil and religious liberty. The Papacy could no longer endure the light of investigation. But the revival of literature in Italy was, to a considerable extent, the revival of Paganism. "Even an Epicurean infidelity," says Prof. Fisher in his *History of the Reformation*, "as to the foundation of religion, which was caught from Lucretius and from the dialogues of Cicero, infected a wide circle of literary men. Preachers, in a strain of florid rhetoric, would associate the names of Greek and Roman heroes with those of the apostles and saints, and with the name of the Savior himself. If an example of distinguished piety was required, reference would be made to Numa Pompilius. So prevalent was disbelief respecting the fundamental truths of natural religion that the Council of the Lateran, under Leo X., felt called upon to affirm the immortality and individuality of the soul." It appeared as if the gods of the old mythology had risen from the dead, if we may judge by the sentiments of the poets and rhetoricians of that literary revival, "while in the minds of thinking men Plato and Plotinus had supplanted Paul and Isaiah."

The influence of the classic school upon the Church in Italy, as described by Guizot (*History of Civilization*, lect. xi.), is fearful to contemplate. As a specimen of his delineation of the crookedness of the times, he says that the Church in Italy "gave herself up to all the pleasures of an indolent, elegant, licentious civilization; to a taste for letters, the arts, and social and physical enjoyments."

On the principle that like causes produce like effects, may not the study of the same classics revive a love for Pagan literature in our times; and is it not now the tendency of pulpit rhetoricians, as they come from our colleges dripping with the distillations of Pagan philosophy, to supplant Paul and Isaiah by the introduction of Plato and Plotinus? And how often do we hear college fledglings, and some older ones, who consider themselves "advanced thinkers," associating the names of Greek and Roman heroes with those of the apostles and saints, and even with the name of the Savior himself.

The religious condition of things in Germany, at the outbreak of the Reformation, was far different from that of Italy. Reuchlin and Erasmus, two of the most eminent scholars of the age, taking advantage of the revival of literature, made it contribute to the purification of the morals of the people, and to an earnest and vigorous investigation of the Scriptures. These were the men who furnished Luther, the great champion of the Reformation, with the literary munitions of war that crushed the dominion of the Papacy, and which liberated the masses from ignorance and foul superstition.

LUTHER AND THE MAN OF SIN.

The people of this generation have a just right to know why we propose, and strenuously labor for, a thorough restoration of the apostolic order of things, and why, religiously, we reject all human authority and accept only the law and authority of Jesus the Christ. For more than a half century we have kept this grand proposition before the eyes of all men. It is due to the rising generation—doubly due to our own children—that we should furnish the most substantial reasons for having inaugurated a movement as radical and far-reaching as that which was inaugurated by Christ and his apostles. We propose more than a *reformation of reformations*. We go back of all reformations, and plant ourselves upon apostolic ground. It is a fact patent to all men acquainted with ecclesiastical history, that there is not a Protestant denomination in existence that has entirely emerged from the great apostasy, of 1260 years' continuance, and that has effectively cleared itself of the mystic influences of Spiritual Babylon. No denomination, however respectable it may appear in the eyes of the world, can claim identity with the Church of Christ, as founded by his apostles, as long as it countenances human dogmas, substitutes theories for facts, supplants the law and authority of Christ by laws of expediency, changes the ordinances of the Church, mystifies the design of the ordinances, bears titles which the Spirit never authorized, and carnalizes the worship of the true and living God.

It is our purpose, in these essays, to show the origin and drift of the several reformations from the days of Luther down to the present time, and to show also, in tracing out these events, that not one of the so-called reformatory movements ever resulted in the full restoration of Apostolic Christianity. We write for those who neither read nor investigate, but who ought to read and investigate. Many of our own people, which statement includes many of our own preachers, are not posted on these questions as they ought to be, while professing at the same time to stand upon the only true and tenable ground.

Luther was a great power in crushing the Man of Sin, but he did not succeed in grinding him to powder. Luther was first aroused by the visible presence of a corrupt priesthood. The origin of the Reformation of the sixteenth century was quite humble and somewhat indefinite. Pope Leo X. had arranged for a very extensive sale of indulgences. He gave out as a pretext for the outrage that the proceeds of the sale were intended for a war against the Turks and the erection of St. Peter's Church. It was quite generally believed that the real destination of the money was to defray the exorbitant expenditures of the Pope's court and to serve as a marriage dowry of his sister. Archbishop Albert, of Mentz, a man whose character was no better than that of Leo X., authorized the sale in Germany on condition that fifty per cent. should flow into his own pocket. Tetzel, a Dominican friar, carried on the trade with such a dash of effrontery as to outrage the sentiments of thousands of honest and sincere people. Luther, then a young monk in an Augustinian convent,

4

was among the first to rise against this profanation of pure religion, and to conscientiously protest against the abomination. When a young student, he had been driven by his anxiety for the salvation of his soul into the seclusion of a convent. After long doubts and many mental troubles, he had derived from a profound study of the Scriptures, and of the writings of Augustine and Tauler, the consolatory belief that man is to be saved, not by his own works of righteousness, but by faith in God through Jesus Christ. As an earnest Christian man, who had taken upon himself a solemn obligation to teach a pure religion, and who, as we have reason to believe, sincerely believed in the Christianity of the Holy Scriptures, he felt himself impelled to enter an energetic protest against the daring deeds of Tetzel. In accordance with the principles of the Church of Rome, he addressed himself to several neighboring bishops, urging them to stop the sale of indulgences; but, not heeding his appeal, he resolved to act upon his own account.

It was on the eve of All-Saints' Day, October 31, 1517, that he affixed to the Castle Church of Wittenberg the celebrated ninety-five theses, which bold act has generally been regarded as the beginning of the Lutheran Reformation. But both Papal and Protestant writers are agreed that these theses involved by no means, on Luther's part, a conscious renunciation of the Roman Catholic doctrine. Luther himself made this manifestly clear by his subsequent appeal to the Pope, and also by the fact that he was attempting the *reformation* and not the *disorganization* of the Church. His opposition to the corruptions of Rome was but a reflex of public opinion, which, by this time, had become wide-spread. The Pope became alarmed, and was startled, as by an electric shock, when he discovered finally that the humble and obscure monk, whom he at first feigned to despise, had sent an impulse all over the religious world. Immediate steps were taken to arrest, if possible, the progress of Luther's revolutionary movement. At first the Pope summoned Luther to Rome; but at the request of the University of Wittenberg, and the elector of Saxony, the concession was made that the Papal legate, Thomas de Vio (better known in history as Cajetanus), should examine Luther in a paternal and conciliatory manner. Luther's characteristic line of defense was the rejection of the arguments as taken from the Fathers and the scholastics, and the demand to be refuted by arguments cited from the Bible. After hearing that the Pope had issued a fresh Papal bull in behalf of indulgences, Luther changed his appeal to an ecumenical council. Soon after this the court of Rome found it expedient to change its policy with Luther, and to win him back by compromise and kindliness. The Papal Chamberlain, Karl Von Miltitz, a native of Saxony, was so far successful that Luther promised to write letters in which he would admonish all persons to be obedient and respectful to the Church of Rome, and to write to the Pope to assure him that he had never thought of infringing upon the rights and privileges of the Mother Church. History informs us that the letter was actually indited; its language is replete with expressions of condescension, and it exalts the Roman Church above every thing but Christ himself. He also promised to discontinue the controversy if his opponents would agree to do the same. But only a brief period elapsed before he was drawn into the Disputation of Leipsic (continuing from June 27 to July 15, 1519), which the vain glorified Dr. Eck had originally arranged with Carlstadt.

History awards to Dr. Eck the glory of having proved himself the more able disputant, but Luther's cause was nevertheless greatly benefited by the discussion. The arguments of his fiery opponents drove Luther onward to a more decided rejection of Romish innovations. He was led by degrees to assert boldly that the Pope was not by divine right the universal Bishop of the Church, to entertain doubts of the infallibility of councils, and to believe that not all the Hussite doctrines were heretical.

Great men soon came to the support of Luther, and among others, Dr. Melancthon, one of the greatest scholars of the age. The conflict between Rome and Luther now became one of life and death. Dr. Eck returned from a journey to Rome with a Papal bull, which declared Luther a heretic, and which ordered the burning of his writings. Luther, on the other hand, systematized his views in three works, all of which appeared in 1520, viz.: *To his Imperial Majesty and the Christian Nobility of the German Nation—On the Babylonian Captivity of the Church—Sermon on the Freedom of a Christian Man.* The culmination finally came, when (December 10, 1520) Luther publicly burnt the Papal bull with the Papal canon law. The Pope succeeded in prevailing upon the German emperor and the German Diet of Worms (1521) to proceed against the great heretic; and when Luther firmly refused to recant and persistently avowed that he could yield to nothing but the Holy Scriptures and sound argument, he was placed under the ban of the empire; but so great was the discontent in Germany with corrupt Rome, that the same assembly which condemned Luther for opposing the faith of their ancestors, presented 101 articles of complaint against the Roman See. As the ban of the empire against

Luther imperiled his life, he was persuaded by his friends to seclude himself in the Castle of Wartburg. Placed beyond the turmoil of political agitation, he found time to issue several powerful polemical essays against auricular confession, against monastic vows, against masses for the dead, and against the new idol of the Archbishop of Mentz. After his return from Wartburg, Luther gave his chief attention to the continuation of his translation of the Bible in German, which was completed in 1534, and which was a master production for that age of the world, while Melancthon, in his celebrated work on theological science, gave to the theological leaders of the new order of things *a hand-book of doctrine.* Then came the Augsburg Confession, by which every man was to be measured; and, having adopted this as the theological measure of every man, then the Bible became once more a sealed book, then a cessation of Bible investigation, and finally the imposition of human dogmas and ecclesiastical contraction, in which condition of stagnation the Lutheran Reformation has stood ever since, but with an expansion of many millions of nominal members, all of whom were made members of the Lutheran Church in infancy, without faith and knowledge, and without liberty of choice. At the Diet of Worms, 1521, before the Augsburg Confession was formulated into a creed, when Luther was peremptorily called upon to recant, he replied in Latin: "Unless I shall be convinced by the testimonies of the Scriptures or by evident reason (for I believe neither Pope nor councils alone, since it is manifest they have often erred and contradicted themselves), I am bound by the Scriptures I have quoted, and my conscience is held captive by the Word of God; and as it is neither safe nor right to act against conscience, I can not and will not retract anything." He added in German: *"Here I stand; I can not otherwise; God help me. Amen."*

Memorable words, if only he had adhered to them. But subsequently he took an active part in forming the constitution of the Consistories. He was, in conjunction with other ecclesiastics, the author of the Marburg Articles and Schwabach Articles (1529), which furnished the basis, and to a large extent, the material, both doctrinal and verbal, of the Augsburg Confession, in 1530, during its direct preparation and presentation. During his conflicts with the powers of Rome, he exhorted his friends not to call themselves Lutherans, but Christians, and he also told them that he was not writing his tracts to bring them to him, but to bring them to the Bible. In dissolving Church and State, and in procuring the civil liberties of the German people, as well as the liberties of the people of other States, the Lutheran Reformation accomplished great and lasting good; but, religiously, as soon as the Augsburg Confession was made to occupy the place of the Bible, reformation ceased, and there has been but little progress in that direction since. Luther never attempted the complete restoration of Apostolic Christianity. He never comprehended such a question, which is made the more evident by the fact that the Augsburg Confession contains doctrines and dogmas which are purely of Papal origin, notably the dogma of Transubstantiation, on account of which, as well as on account of other Romish dogmas, Zwingli and other reformers, in Switzerland, separated from him, as we shall show in our next article. Though the great reformer freed himself from the fetters of Papal ecclesiasticism, and severed his connection with the despotism of Rome, it is nevertheless a fact that he never divested himself entirely of the mysticism of the dark ages, and never thoroughly rid himself of the traditions of Rome. Hence the necessity of succeeding reformatory movements, not one of which effected a restoration of the apostolic order of things, neither in doctrine nor in practice, as we shall discover in our future investigations. We accept the good that preceding reformers have accomplished, and honor those who have rescued the Bible from the grasp of a despotic hierarchy, but whatever they taught contrary to God's word, we reject. What the early reformers left undone, we propose to complete; by which we mean an entire restoration of the ancient order of things, in faith and practice, in doctrine and discipline.

ORIGIN OF THE AUGSBURG CONFESSION.

Having in a previous number given the origin and a brief outline of the Lutheran Reformation, we next proceed to present a history of the Augsburg Confession, which we derive from the most reliable standard authorities:

After Charles V. had concluded a peace with France, he summoned a German Diet to meet at Augsburg, April 8, 1530. The decree of invitation called for aid against the Turks, who, in 1529, had besieged Vienna; it also promised a discussion of the religious questions of the time, and such a settlement of them as both to abolish existing abuses and to satisfy the demands of the Pope. Elector John, of Saxony, who received this decree, March 11, directed (March 14) Luther, Jonas, Bugenhagen and Melancthon to meet in Torgau, and draw up a summary of the most important and necessary articles of faith, in support of which the evangelical princes and states should combine. These theologians, as we shall term them, drew up a profession of their faith, the ground-work of which they found in the seventeen articles which had been prepared by Luther for the convention at Schwalbach, and fifteen other articles, which had been drawn up at the theological conference at Marburg, and subsequently presented to the Saxon elector John at Torgau. The first draft made by the four theologians, in seventeen articles, was at once published, and elicited a joint reply from Wimpina, Mensing, Redœrfer and Dr. Elgers, which Luther immediately answered. The subject of the controversy had thus become generally known. Luther, Jonas and Melancthon were invited by the Saxon elector to accompany him to Augsburg. However, subsequently, it was deemed best for Luther's safety to leave him behind. Melancthon, soon after his arrival at Augsburg, completed the Confession, and gave to it the title *Apologia*. On the 11th of May he sent it to Luther, who was then at Coburg, and on the 15th of May he received from Luther an answer of approval. Several alterations were suggested to Melancthon in his conference with Jonas, the Saxon Chancellor Brück, the conciliatory Bishop Stadion of Augsburg, and the Imperial Secretary Valdes. To the latter, upon his request, seventeen articles were handed by Melancthon, with the consent of the Saxon elector, and he was to have a preliminary discussion concerning them with the Papal legate Pimpinelli. Upon the opening of the Diet, June 20, the so-called evangelical theologians who were present—Melancthon, Jonas, Agricola, Brenz, Schnepf and others—presented the Confession to the elector. The latter, on June 23, had it signed by the evangelical princes and representatives of cities who were present, viz: John, elector of Saxony; Gerge, margrave of Brandenburg; Enerst, duke of Lunenburg; Philip, landgrave of Hesse; John Frederick, duke of Saxe; Francis, duke of Lunenburg; Wolfgang, prince of Anhalt; and the magistrates of Nuremberg and Reutlinger.

The emperor had ordered the Confession to be presented to him at the next session, June 24: but when the evangelical princes asked for permission to read it,

5

their petition was refused, and efforts were made to prevent the public reading of the document altogether. The evangelical princes declared, however, that they would not part with the Confession until its reading should be allowed. The 25th of the month was then fixed as the day of its presentation. In order to exclude the people, the little chapel of the Episcopal Palace was appointed in the place of the spacious City Hall, where the meetings of the Diet were held. In this chapel the Protestant princes assembled on the appointed day, June 25, 1530. The Saxon Chancellor Brück, held in his hands the Latin, Dr. Christian Bayer, the German copy. They stepped into the middle of the august assembly, and all the Protestant princes rose from their seats, but were instantly commanded to sit down. The emperor wished to hear the Latin copy read first, but the elector replied that they were on German ground: whereupon the emperor consented to the reading of the German copy, which was done by Dr. Bayer. The reading lasted from four to six o'clock. The reading being completed, the emperor ordered both copies to be given to him. The German copy he handed to the Archbishop of Mayence, the Latin he carried with him to Brussels. Neither of these copies is now extant. The emperor promised to take this "highly important matter" into serious consideration, and make known his decision; in the meanwhile the Confession was not to be printed without imperial permission. The Protestant princes promised to comply with this wish; but when, soon after the reading, an erroneous edition of the Confession appeared, it became necessary to have both the German and the Latin texts published, which work was done through Melancthon. On June 27 the Confession was given, in the presence of the whole assembly, to the Roman Catholic theologians to be refuted. The most prominent among them were Eck, Faber, Wimpina, Cochlæus and Dietenberger. Before they got through with their work a letter was received from Erasmus, who had been asked for his opinion by Cardinal Campegius, recommending caution, and the concession of the Protestant demands concerning the marriage of the priests, monastic vows and the Lord's Supper.

On July 12 the Roman Catholic "Confutation" was presented, which so displeased the emperor that "of 280 leaves, only 12 remained whole." A new "Confutation" was therefore prepared and read to the Diet, August 3, by the imperial secretary Schweiss. No copy of it was given to the "evangelical members" of the Diet, and it was not published until 1573, by Fabricius. Immediately after the reading of the Confutation, the Protestants were *commanded* to conform to it. Negotiations for effecting a compromise were begun by both parties, but led to no practical result. Negotiations between the Lutherans and the Zwinglians were equally fruitless. Zwinglias—anglicized Zwingle—had sent to the emperor a memorial, dated July 4, and Bucer, Capito and Hedio had drawn up, in the name of the cities of Strasburg, Constance, Memmingen and Lindau, the *Confessio Tetrapolitana*, which was presented to the emperor July 11. Neither of these two Confessions was read, and both were rejected.

Melancthon, at the request of the "evangelical princes" and cities, prepared an "Apology of the Confession" in opposition to the Roman Catholic "Confutation," which was presented by the Chancellor Brück, September 22, to the emperor, who refused to receive it. Subsequently Melancthon received a copy of the "Confutation," which led to many alterations in the first draft of the Apology. It was then published in Latin, and in a German translation by Jonas (Wittenberg, 1531). A controversy subsequently arose, in consequence of which Melancthon, after 1540, made considerable alterations in the original Augsburg Confession, altering, especially in Article X., the statement of the doctrine of the Lord's Supper in favor of the view of the Reformers. Melancthon, who had already been charged with "crypto-Calvinism" (concealed Calvinism), was severely attacked on account of these alterations; yet the "*Confessio Variata*" remained in the ascendency until 1580, when the *Confessio Invariata* was put into the "*Concordienbuch*" in its place, and thus the unaltered Confession has come to be generally regarded as the standard of the Lutheran churches. It is but just to say, however, that the altered Confession has not ceased to find advocates, and several branches of the Lutheran Church have even abrogated the authoritative character of the Confession, and do not demand from their clergy a belief in all its doctrines.

And this is how the Augsburg Confession struggled into existence. The following table of the contents of the Confession and of the Apology will give the reader an idea of a religious system of things that, at this time, probably wields an influence, directly and indirectly, over 40,000,000 people.

Part I. 1. Acknowledges four œcumenical councils: 2. Declares original sin to consist wholly in concupiscence: 3. Contains the substance of the Apostles' Creed: 4. Declares that justification is the effect of faith, exclusive of good works: 5. Declares the word of God and the sacraments to be the means of conveying the Holy Spirit, but never without faith: 6. That faith must produce good works purely in obedience to

God, and not in order to the meriting justification: 7. The true church consists of the godly only: 8. Allows the validity of the sacraments, though administered by the evil one: 9. Declares the necessity of infant baptism: 10. Declares the real presence in the Eucharist continued with the elements only during the period of receiving: 11. Declares absolution to be necessary, but not so particular confession: 12. Declares against the Anabaptists: 13. Requires actual faith in all who receive the sacraments: 14. Forbids to teach in the church, or to administer the sacraments, without being lawfully called: 15. Orders the observance of the holy days and ceremonies of the church: 16. Of civil matters and marriage: 17. Of the resurrection, last judgment, heaven and hell: 18. Of free will: 19. That God is not the author of sin: 20. That good works are not altogether unprofitable: 21. Forbids the invocation of saints.

PART II. 1. Enjoins communion in both kinds, and forbids the procession of the holy sacrament: 2. Condemns the law of celibacy of priests: 3. Condemns private masses, and enjoins that some of the congregation shall communicate with the priest: 4. Against the necessity of auricular confession: 5. Against tradition and human ceremonies: 6. Condemns monastic vows: 7. Discriminates between civil and religious power, and declares the power of the church to consist only in preaching and administering the sacraments.

These are briefly the facts which show the origin, gestation and birth of the Augsburg Confession. The intelligent Bible reader can easily tell how much of this theological medley is Papal, how much Protestant, how much tradition, how much human speculation, and how much apostolic teaching. To say nothing of the sinfulness of making the creed, many of its doctrines are positive contradictions of the word of God, and wholly subversive of Bible teaching. The reader will have noticed, in the history of the Confession just given, that civil rulers had about as much to do in producing the creed as the reformers themselves. The formation of this Augsburg Confession cut off all further investigation of the Scriptures, and forever stereotyped the faith of its adherents. By the doctrines of this Confession it will be seen that Luther remained partly a Roman Catholic as long as he lived, and it was because of this fact that Zwingle, as we shall see further on, with other reformers in Switzerland, separated from Luther, and framed another confession in harmony with their belief. Creedism, as the reader will have perceived, *began* at the very point where reformation *ceased*. And hence as long as creeds exist, and as long as men prefer creeds in lieu of the word of God, there can be no Christian union upon the basis of the Scriptures, so far as creed lovers are concerned.

REFORMATION IN SWITZERLAND.

ULRICH ZWINGLE was the founder of Protestantism in Switzerland. He was a man of fine education and of extensive learning. He was educated in the Roman Catholic Church. He possessed a bright intellect, was a great lover of literature, was early in life distinguished for his love of truth, and devoted himself intensely to an investigation of the Scriptures. Like Luther, witnessing the corruptions of the clergy, and discovering dogmas and traditions not found in the Word of God, such as the worship of the Virgin Mary and the hideous doctrine of indulgences, he attempted a work of reform in the bosom of the Church. He was soon charged with preaching heresy, which the Papal powers regarded as subversive of the established order of things. In a conference held at Zurich, called at his own request, January 29, 1523, in the presence of an assembly of more than six hundred men, he defended sixty-seven propositions, which were leveled against the system of Romanism. In his defense against the charge of heresy, he substituted the authority of the gospel for the authority of the Church; he declared the Church to be the communion of the faithful, who have no head but Christ; he maintained that salvation is through faith in Christ as the only priest and intercessor; he rejected the Papacy and the mass, the invocation of saints, justification by works, fasts. festivals, pilgrimages, monastic orders and the priesthood, auricular confession, absolution, indulgences, penances, purgatory and indeed all the characteristic peculiarities of the Romish Church. In another disputation, before a much larger assembly, on the 26th of October following, he obtained a decree of the council against the use of images and the sacrifice of the mass.

By these statements it will be seen that Zwingle, as a clear-headed reformer, and as one capable of making clean-cut distinctions between the teaching of the Bible and the Traditions of Rome, was in advance of Luther. In 1525, he published his chief work, entitled a "Commentary on True and False Religion," and also a treatise on original sin. The tenets he published are subtantially the same as those adopted by the Protestant Churches generally. In his philosophy he was a predestinarian of an extreme type, transcending both Augustine and Calvin. He did not confine the illumination of the Spirit within the circle of revealed religion, nor do his adherents of the present age, or to those who receive the word of God and the "sacraments." He held that the virtues of heathen sages and heroes are due to the presence of divine grace, and asserted, for example, that Socrates was more pious and holy than all Dominicans and Franciscans. "He had busied himself," says Neander, "with the study of antiquity, for which he had a predilection, and had not the right criterion for distinguishing the ethical standing-point of Christianity from that of the ancients." From Zurich the Reformation spread, and in a short time Zwingle found in Œcolampadius as great a counselor and leader, as Luther had found in the distinguished and scholarly Melancthon. The authority of the Papal system never had the same deep-set hold upon Zwingle as it had upon

Luther, a question, however, which is not necessary to discuss here, as we are only aiming to present a historical connection of things and events. When Luther was put under the ban of the Church, Zwingle, as we learn from Ranke, the German historian, was still the recipient of a pension from the Pope. When Luther at the Diet of Worms, in the face of Papal princes and the legates of Rome, refused to submit to the authority of the Pope, Zwingle had not yet been seriously molested. As late as 1523 he received a complimentary letter from Pope Adrian VI.—facts which go to show that the reformations effected in the sixteenth century were only partial, and of course incomplete, and a fact which we desire our contemporaries to understand, in view of the work in which we are engaged.

Finally there broke out the great controversy on the dogma of Transubstantiation between the Lutheran and Swiss reformers. Luther did not obtain this dogma from the apostolic record, but from theologians of the Latin Church—from Radbert, of the ninth century, from the leading schoolmen of the thirteenth century, which was made an article of faith by the fourth Lateran Council, in 1215, under Innocent III. The reformers, as a class, with one consent, denied this dogma, "together with the associated doctrine of the sacrificial character of the Eucharist." But Luther stoutly affirmed the actual, corporate presence of the glorified body and blood of Christ, in connection with the bread and wine, so that the body and blood, in some mysterious way, are received by the communicant, whether he be a believer or an unbeliever. Luther did not hold that the heavenly body of Christ, which is offered and received in the "sacrament," occupies space; yet it is received by all who partake of the bread and wine—not a portion of the body, but the entire Christ by each communicant. It is received, in some proper sense, with the mouth. We have quoted from De Wette, with the German before us. Zwingle denied that the body of Christ is present, in any sense, in the "sacrament," but, with his followers, he was more and more disposed to attach importance to a *spiritual* presence in the institution. This belief Calvin emphasized and added the positive assertion of a direct influence upon the believing communicant, which flows from Christ through the medium or instrumentality of his human nature. "The Word and the Sacraments Luther had made the criteria of the Church. On upholding them in their just place, everything that distinguished his reform from enthusiasm or rationalism depended. He had never thought of forsaking the dogmatic system of Latin Christianity in its earlier and purer days, and he looked with alarm on what struck him as a rationalistic innovation." At the Conference of Marburg, in 1529, which was called with a view of reconciling the disaffected parties, when the theologians sat by a table, the Saxons on one side and Swiss on the opposite side, Luther wrote upon the table with chalk his text: "*Hoc est meum corpus*" (this is my body), and resolutely refused to budge an iota from the literal sense.

ORIGIN OF THE HEIDELBERG CONFESSION.

As a result of the controversy between the Lutheran reformers and the Swiss reformers, we have the Heidelberg Catechism, the property of the Reformed Church. Its name is derived from the city in which it was compiled and first printed. It is also sometimes styled the Palatinate Catechism, from the territory (the Palatinate) of the Prince (Frederick III.) under whose auspices it was prepared. Soon after the introduction of Protestantism into the Palatinate in 1546, the controversy between Lutherans and Calvinists broke out, and for years, especially under the Elector Otto Heinrich (1556–59), it raged with great violence in Heidelberg. Frederick III. who came into power in 1559, adopted the Calvinistic view of the Lord's Supper, and favored that side of the question with all his princely power. He reorganized the Sapienz College (founded by his predecessor) as a theological school, and placed at its head (1562) Zacharias Ursinus, a pupil and friend of Melancthon, who had adopted the Reformed opinions. In order to put an end to religious disputes in his dominions, he determined to put forth a Catechism, a Confession of Faith, and laid the responsibility of preparing it upon Ursinus and Caspar Olevianus, for a time professor in the University of Heidelberg, then court-preacher to Frederick III. They made use of the catechetical literature then in existence, especially of the catechisms of Calvin and John à Lasco. Each prepared sketches or drafts, and "the final preparation was the work of both these theologians, with the constant co-operation of Frederick III. Ursinus has always been regarded as the chief author, as he was afterwards the principal defender and interpreter of the Catechism; still, it would appear that the nervous German style, the division into three parts (as distinguished from the five parts in the Catechism of Calvin, and the previous draft of Ursinus), and the genial warmth and unction of the whole work, are chiefly due to Olevianus." (Schaff, in *Am. Pres. Rev.* July, 1863, p. 379.) Philip Schaff, of New York, is the acknowledged leader of the Reformed Church in America. When the Catechism was completed, Frederick laid it before a synod of the superintendents of the Palatinate, December, 1562, and after a careful examination it was duly approved. Dr. Schaff observes, in the same *Review* from which we have already quoted, that "the Catechism is a true expression of the convictions of its authors, but it communicates only so much of these as is in harmony with the public faith of the Church, and observes a certain reticence or reservation and moderation on such doctrines (as the *twofold* predestination), which belong rather to scientific theology and private conviction than to a public Church confession and the instruction of youth."

The Heidelberg Catechism contains substantially the same tenets, dogmas, traditions, speculations and private opinions that are found in all Protestant creeds, except in governmental affairs. In common with all creeds, whether Romanist or Protestant, it teaches infant baptism and sprinkling. The body of people which it represents, is called the Reformed Church, and this Reformed Church is regarded by its theologians and admirers as a decided improvement upon the Lutheran Church; that is to say, there is not as much *Romanism* in the Heidelberg Catechism as there is in the Augsburg Confession. The theologians and princes of Germany and Switzerland began reformation with the Bible, and ended their work by the substitution of Creeds—Confessions of Faith—Symbols of Faith—Church Standards, etc. Taking the Bible as their guide, they beat a retreat from the mystic realms of Papal Babylon, but had not gone far until the leaders commanded a halt, when they went to work, while still under the potent influence of Rome, and formulated Confessions of Faith; and, wedded to these human inventions, as their supporters now are, they still dwell within the confines of old Babylon. If not ecclesiastically under the power of the "Mother Church," they are religiously and spiritually of the same affinities. None of these creeds, whether Catholic or Protestant, tells a man how to become a Christian. They tell a man how he may become a Catholic, a Lutheran, a Reformer, an Episcopalian, a Presbyterian, a Methodist, a Baptist, perchance. There is not a Confession of Faith in existence that ever saved a soul. As human compositions, one is just as full of light and knowledge as another, and just as efficacious in the salvation of the soul. They all originated in the councils of men; they were digested in the heat of human passions; they were concocted and planned by envious and rival theologians; they became the symbols—the insignia—of rival princes; they have always engendered strife, hatred, malice, bigotry, intolerance and persecution, and will continue to do so until the end of time. There is no Christian love in them; there is nothing in them that will unite the people of God, and make them one people. The mind of God is not found in them, and the spirit of

Christ does not breathe through them. They confuse the human mind; they divide the counsels of Christians; they paralyze the power of truth; they make a fable of the gospel; they mock the prayers of the Savior; they make void the law of God; they infuse the spirit of sectarianism; they cramp the human intellect; they place insuperable barriers between those seeking love and unity upon the basis of the Bible.

In view of these facts, and many more yet to be produced, let our brethren understand that our mission is not yet ended, but, on the contrary, only fairly begun. We have no human creed to defend. The Bible, and the Bible only, is our rule of faith and practice. The word of God only is the man of our counsel. All creeds must be crushed under the weight of divine authority. "The unity of the Spirit in the bond of peace," must destroy all sectism. There must be but one fold and one Shepherd. We are set for the defense of the gospel of the Son of God, and we propose to walk in the old paths. We propose the restoration of the apostolic order of things. To this work we consecrate our life's blood. Upon this altar we lay our all. We trust that all those who have been called into this marvelous light, will stand firm, and work, and contend for the faith, and show themselves men in the highest sense of the word, and never, never, yield an iota of the truth.

JOHN CALVIN AND CALVINISM.

It is not our purpose, nor is it necessary to the end we have in view, to trace the Lutheran Reformation as it spread all through the Scandinavian kingdom, penetrated the Slavonic nations, and took Hungary captive. We shall next have something to say about John Calvin and his theology.

In French Switzerland, the reformatory movement began in 1526, in the French parts of the cantons Berne and Biel, where the principles of reform were preached by William Farel, a native of France. In 1530, he established the Reformation in Neufchâtel. A beginning was made in Geneva as early as 1528; in 1534, after a religious conference held at the suggestion of the people of Berne, in which Farel defended the Reformation, public worship was granted to those who belonged to the Reformed branch; rapid progress was then made through the zeal of Farel, Froment and Viret; and in 1535, after another disputation, the Papacy was abolished by the council and the doctrines of the Reformation adopted. In 1536 John Calvin arrived in Geneva, and was induced by Farel to remain in the city and to aid him in his struggle against a party of free-thinkers, who called themselves *Spirituals*. In October of the same year he took part with Farel and Viret in a religious disputation held at Lausanne, which resulted in gaining over the Pays-de-Vaud to the cause of the

Reformation. In 1538 both Farel and Calvin were banished by the council, which had taken offense at the very strict Church discipline introduced by the reformers. Soon, however, the friends of the Reformation regained the ascendency, and Calvin was recalled in 1541, while Farel remained in Neufchâtel. For several years Calvin was put under the necessity of sustaining a desperate struggle against his opponents, but in 1555 they were finally subdued in an insurrection incited by one Ami Perrin. From that time forward the reformatory ideas of Calvin were carried through in both Church and State with a consistency as rigid as iron, and Geneva became a center whence reformatory influences spread to the remotest parts of Europe. By an extensive correspondence and numerous theological theses, he exerted a powerful personal influence upon a certain class of mind far beyond the boundaries of Switzerland. The theological academy of Geneva, founded in 1588, supplied the churches of many foreign countries, especially France, with preachers trained in the spirit of Calvin. When Calvin died, in 1564, the continuation of his work devolved upon the learned Theodore Beza. Calvin disagreed in many points with Zwingle, whose views gradually lost ground as those of Calvin advanced. The Second Helvetic Confession, the most important among the symbolical books of the Reformed Church, which was compiled by Bullinger in Zurich, published in 1566, and recognized in all Reformed countries, completed, we are told, the superiority of Calvin's reformatory notions over those of Zwingle.

Calvin was only eight years old when Luther posted his famous theses upon the door of the Cathedral in Wittenberg. He was born at Noyon, in Picardy, on the 10th of July, 1509. He was well provided for by families of nobility, who assisted him in obtaining a splendid education in the best colleges of Paris. His physical constitution was not strong, but early in life he developed extraordinary intellectual power. He was raised in affluence, and was never subjected to penury and rough discipline, as were the German and Swiss reformers. In college he surpassed his companions in severe mental application, and in a natural aptitude to learn. He spent most of his time by himself, and from his serious and severe turn of mind, he was nicknamed by his companions, "The Accusative Case." At the age of eighteen he received the tonsure, and preached occasionally, but had not taken orders, as his father, changing his plan, concluded to qualify him for the profession of a jurist. He studied under the most celebrated teachers. Before long, however, his attention was directed to the study of the Scriptures through the influence of Protestant relatives. Little is known of his public career until about 1532, soon after which he gives an account of his "sudden conversion." "Calvin had hesitated about becoming a Protestant, out of reverence for the Church. But he so modified his conception of the Church as to perceive that the change did not involve a renunciation of it. Membership in the true Church was consistent with renouncing the rule of the Roman Catholic prelacy; for the Church, in its essence invisible, exists in a true form wherever the gospel is faithfully preached and the sacraments administered conformably to the directions of Christ." So says George P. Fisher, D. D., in his *History of the Reformation*, p. 195-6.

Calvin, by his great learning, by the rare acuteness of his intellect, and by his extensive acquaintance with the contents of the Bible, became an acknowledged leader of the Protestant party in France. Speaking of Calvin's characteristics as a writer and a man, Prof. Fisher says: "His direct influence was predominantly and almost exclusively upon the higher classes of society. He and his system acted powerfully upon the people, but indirectly through the agency of others. He was a patrician in his temperament. By his early associations, and as an effect of his culture, he acquired a certain refinement and decided affinities for the class elevated by birth or education. This was one of his points of dissimilarity to Luther: he was not fitted, like the German reformer, to come home to the 'business and bosoms' of common men. He had not the popular eloquence of Luther, nor had he the genius that left its impress on the words and works of the Saxon reformer; but he was a more exact and finished scholar than Luther." Melancthon greeted Calvin as "the theologian," and by the enemies of Protestantism his work was styled "the Koran of the heretics." A contemporary writer thus spoke of him:

> "Some think on Calvin heaven's own mantle fell,
> While others deemed him an instrument of hell."

Professedly he adopted the Bible as the sole standard of doctrine, while at the same time he made his peculiar speculation of Predestination to overshadow the whole Bible, and to render nugatory the revealed plan of salvation. While his "Institutes" show him to be a very acute critic and a profound exegetical writer, yet at the same time it is apparent that by his theocratic interpretations of Scripture he renders the gospel of Christ a myth. While he scouts the doctrine that the truth of the Bible rests on the authority of the Church, and holds that the divine authority of the Bible can be established by reason, he at the same time maintains that a spiritual insight of gospel truth is imparted directly by the Holy Spirit. While he professes little esteem for the fathers of the Church, and while he stigmatizes the dogmas and rites of the Papacy as the "impious inventions of men," without warrant from the Word of God, yet at the same time, unlike the other reformers, he frequently pays deference to the Church. Believing in a *Church Invisible*, composed of true believers, and also believing in the *Church Visible*, the criteria of which are the proper administration of the Sacraments and the teaching of the Word, and theoretically demanding positive submission to the model of the New Testament, he at the same time fails to identify the apostolic Church in its complete restoration and purity. The smell of the Papacy tinges much of his writings. Prof. Fisher thus summarizes the peculiar theological tenets of Calvin:

Predestination to him is the correlate of human dependence; the counterpart of the doctrine of grace; the antithesis to salvation by merit; the implied consequences of man's complete bondage to sin. In election, it is involved that man's salvation is not his own work, but, wholly, the work of the grace of God; and in election, also, there is laid a sure foundation for the believer's security under all the assaults of temptation. It is practical interest which Calvin is sedulous to guard; he clings to the doctrine for what he considers its religious value; and it is no more than justice to him to remember that he habitually styles the tenet, which proved to be so obnoxious, an unfathomable mystery, an abyss into which no mortal mind can descend. And, whether consistently or not, there is the most earnest assertion of the moral and responsible nature of man. Augustine held that in the fall of Adam, the entire race were involved in a common act and a common catastrophe. The will is not destroyed; it is still free to sin, but is utterly disabled as regards holiness. Out of the mass of mankind, all of whom are alike guilty, God chooses a part to be the recipients of his mercy, whom he purifies by an irresistible influence, but leaves the rest to suffer the penalty which they have justly brought upon themselves. In the "Institutes," Calvin does what Luther had done in his book against Erasmus; he makes the Fall itself, the primal transgression, the object of an efficient decree. In this particular he goes beyond Augustine, and apparently affords a sanction to the extreme, or supralapsarian type of theology, which afterwards found numerous defenders—which traces sin to the direct agency of God, and even founds the distinction of right and wrong ultimately on his omnipotent will. [Inst. 3, xxiii. 6, seq.] But when Calvin was called upon to define his doctrine more carefully, as in the *Consensus Genevensis*, he confines himself to the assertion of a permissive decree—a volitive permission—in the case of the first sin. In other words, he does not overstep the Augustinian position. He explicitly avers that every decree of the Almighty springs from reasons which, though hidden from us, are good and sufficient; that is to say, he founds will upon right, and not right upon will. He differs, however, both from Augustine and Luther, in affirming that none who are once converted fall from a state of grace, the number of believers being coextensive with the number of the elect.

Calvin lives in history as a scholar and a theologian, but not as a reformer. He rendered valuable service as an interpreter and expounder of Scriptures, but, like Luther, Zwingle and Knox, he failed to restore the primitive apostolic order of things. His speculations, theologically known as Predestination, Total Hereditary Depravity, Particular Election, Reprobation, Final Perseverance and the Eternal Decrees, have only served the purpose of dividing the people of God instead of uniting them—have only perplexed and confused the human mind instead of making plain the simplicity of the gospel. It is said of Calvin by his biographers, that at times he was so carried away by gusts of passion, that he lost all self-control. He had tried in vain, he says, to "tame the wild beast of his anger;" and on his death-bed he asked pardon of the Senate of Geneva for outbursts of passion, while at the same time he thanked them for their forbearance.

Calvin, by instinct and choice, was better fitted for the rigid Theocracy of Moses than for the liberty of the gospel. He had a stronger inclination toward Mosaic legislation than toward a system of divine truth which makes the individual free. He ruled with a rod of iron in the city of Geneva, where he directed civil as well as ecclesiastical affairs. "In 1568, under the stern code which was established under the auspices of Calvin, a child was beheaded for striking its father and mother. A child sixteen years old, for *attempting* to strike its mother, was sentenced to death; but, on account of its youth, the sentence was commuted, and having been publicly whipped, with a cord about its neck, it was banished from the city. In 1565 a woman was chastised with rods for singing songs to the melody of the Psalms." And other inflictions are recorded too numerous to mention. The expulsion of Castellio from Geneva, a highly cultivated scholar whom Calvin had brought from Strasburg, to take charge of the Geneva school—an expulsion caused by the influence of Calvin himself—and the death of Servetus, instigated by Calvin, and executed by those directly under his influence, because Servetus wrote a book entitled "Errors of the Trinity," which contradicted the opinions of Calvin,—these heartless acts indicate the temper of Calvin's spirit, these show the character of his cold intellect, these demonstrate the rigidity and inflexibility of his will power. The powerful intellect of such a man may excite the admiration of cold-hearted theologians, and overawe the ignorant and superstitious with amazement, but such a disposition can never command the love and affection of the "common people." In our opinion, there is nothing in Calvinism but the defeat of Christianity—there is nothing in it on which a sinful and helpless world can lean for support. There is not a gleam of hope in it. It is a death-dealing system.

ORIGIN OF THE CHURCH OF ENGLAND.

WE headed this series of articles *Reformatory Movements*. It may become evident before we conclude, that this series should have been designated *A History of the Protestant Denominations*, for the reason that many of them do not contain the elements of religious reformation at all.

The principles of the Lutheran Reformation swept across the English Channel, and seized the people of the British Empire. But, as might have been expected, the heresies of Luther and of Wycliffe met with intense and malicious opposition from the start. King Henry VIII., at the outbreak of the politico-religious revolution, became a conspicuous opponent of Luther, as well as a champion of the Papal cause. For writing a polemical book against Luther upon the Seven Sacraments, Leo X. conferred upon the King the title "Defender of the Faith" (*Defensor Fidei*). This took place in 1521. Henry also addressed a letter to the emperor of Germany, in which he demanded the extirpation of the heretics. But the doctrines of Luther found ardent adherents even at the English universities, and an English translation of the Bible, by Frith and Tyndale, members of the University of Cambridge, produced a decisive and salutary effect. It was not long, however, until King Henry had a quarrel with the Pope, because the latter refused to annul Henry's marriage with Catharine, of Aragon, the niece of the Emperor Charles V. Henry, who represented that his marriage with Catharine, his brother's widow, was open to objections, laid the matter, by advice of Thomas Cranmer, before the universities of Europe, "not abstaining, however, from the use of bribery abroad, and of menaces at home;" but when replies came back declaring the marriage with a brother's wife null and void, the King separated from Catharine, married Anne Boleyn, and, as a consequence, fell under the Papal ban.

Through the conniving of Henry, the English Parliament was induced to sunder the connection between England and Rome, and to recognize the King as head of the new Church. It became the fixed purpose of Henry to destroy, if possible, the influence of the Pope over the Church of England, with a desire at the same time to preserve its Catholic character. As a revenge upon the Pope, he subjected the cloisters to a searching investigation in 1535, and in the following year he totally abolished them. In 1538, the Bible was diffused in the mother tongue as the only source of doctrine; "but the statute of 1539 imposed distinct limits upon the Reformation, and, in particular, confirmed transubstantiation, priestly celibacy, masses for the dead, and auricular confession." After the Pope's authority was abolished in England, Parliament passed the Act of Supremacy, "That the King, our sovereign lord, his heirs and successors, Kings of this realm, shall be taken, accepted, and reputed the only supreme head in earth of the Church of England, called the Anglicana Ecclesia."

And this was the origin of the Episcopal Church! Up to this memorable event, the Pope of Rome was recognized as head of the Church of England: now Henry VIII. becomes head of the Church, and the ecclesiastical are brought into subjection to the civil powers. Many of those who refused to submit to the new order of things in England, were executed, and their goods confiscated by the loyal but servile minions of the English King. It is evident that while Henry was a Protestant in form, he was a Romanist in heart. A powerful party, headed by Thomas Cranmer, afterwards Archbishop of Canterbury, and Thomas Cromwell, royal vicar-general in ecclesiastical affairs, exerted a silent influence towards the Reformed churches of continental Europe. They met with little success during the reign of Henry, but gained a temporary ascendency in the regency which ruled England during the minority of Edward VI. Certain parties, including Peter Martyr, Bucer and Fagius, were invited to England to aid Cranmer in establishing the Reformation. The basis was laid in the Book of Homilies (1547), the new English Liturgy (the Book of Common Prayer, 1548), and the Forty-two Articles, 1552; but the labors of Cranmer were interrupted by the death of Edward VI. in 1553. His successor, Queen Mary, the daughter of Henry and Catharine of Aragon, was, as the intelligent reader knows, a devoted partisan of the Church of Rome, during whose bloody reign Cranmer and from three hundred to four hundred other persons were executed on account of their religious views. A Papal nuncio appeared in England, and an obsequious Parliament sanctioned the reunion with Rome; but the affections of the people were not regained, and the early death of Mary, in 1558, put an end to the official restoration of the Papal Church. Queen Elizabeth, the daughter of Henry and Anne Boleyn, whose birth, in consequence of the Papal decision, was regarded by the Roman Catholics as illegitimate, resumed the work of her father, and completed the English Reformation, as a work distinct both from the Church of Rome and the Reformation of Germany and Switzerland.

THE THIRTY-NINE ARTICLES.

The Book of Common Prayer, which had been adopted under Edward VI., was so changed as to be less offensive to the Romish party; and by the Act of Uniformity, June, 1559, it was made binding on all the churches of the kingdom. Most of the subjects of the Pope conformed. The Confession of Faith, which had been formulated under Edward, in forty-two articles, was reduced to Thirty-nine Articles, and in this form it was adopted by a convocation of the clergy, at London, in 1562, and by Parliament made, in 1571, the rule of faith for all the clergy of the realm. According to the Thirty-nine Articles, the Scriptures contain, so they tell us, everything necessary to salvation. We are further informed that justification is through faith alone, which Article, we presume, was intended as an offset to the Romish doctrine of justification by works alone, or the doctrine of indulgences; but works acceptable to God are the necessary fruit of this faith. Of course, neither Christ nor his apostles were consulted, when the English Parliament declared that supreme power over the Church is vested in the English crown, though limited by the statutes. Bishops continued to be the highest ecclesiastical officers and the first barons of the realm, which, it must be confessed, does not resemble the simplicity of the primitive order. Subscription to the Articles was made binding on the clergy; freedom of conscience was granted to the laity. The adoption of the Thirty-nine Articles completed, substantially, the constitution of the Episcopal Church of England. Some parts of the Church government and the Liturgy, especially the retaining of sacerdotal vestments, gave great offense to a number of zealous people, of a radical turn of mind, who had suffered persecution during the reign of Mary, and, while exiles, had become strongly attached to the extreme dogmas of Calvinism. They demanded a greater purity of the Church (hence the origin of the term "Puritans"), a simple, spiritual form of worship, a strict church discipline, and a Presbyterian form of government. The Act of Uniformity, in 1559, threatened all Non-conformists with fines and imprisonment, and their ministers with deposition and banishment. When the provisions of the Act began to be enforced, a number of the Non-conformist ministers formed separate congregations in connection with Presbyteries, subsequent to 1572, and a considerable portion of the ministers and laity of the Established Church sympathized with them. The rupture between the parties was widened, when, in 1592, by an act of Parliament it was decreed that all who obstinately refused to attend public worship, or induced others to do so, should be imprisoned and submit, or after three months be banished; and again, in 1595, when the Presbyterians applied the Mosaic Sabbath laws to the Lord's day, and when Calvin's doctrines respecting Predestination excited bitter and lengthy disputes.

Thus far, by the aid of history, we have learned that Henry VIII., a very dissolute king, was constituted head of the English Church, or the Episcopal Church, called so by the fact that all church government is lodged in a bench of lordly Bishops, that the Book of

Prayer was adopted, which was patterned after the Roman Catholic Missal, and that the Thirty-nine Articles, which it is not necessary to insert here, became the Creed of the English Church. On the general character of the Anglican or English Church, George P. Fisher, Professor of Ecclesiastical History in Yale College, has this to say:

As head of the Church, the King could make and deprive bishops, as he could appoint and degrade all other officers in the kingdom. The Episcopal polity was retained, partly because the bishops generally fell in with the proceedings of Henry VIII. and Edward for the reform of the Church, and on account of the compact organization of the Monarchy, in consequence of which the nation acted as one body. But in the first age of the Reformation, and until the rise of Puritanism as a distinct party, there was little controversy among Protestants in relation to Episcopacy. Not only was Melancthon willing to allow bishops with a *jure humano* authority, but Luther and Calvin were also of the same mind. The Episcopal constitution of the English Church for a long period put no barrier in the way of the most free and fraternal relations between that body and the Protestant Churches on the continent. As we have seen, Cranmer placed foreign divines in very responsible places in the English Church. Ministers who had received Presbyterian ordination were admitted to take charge of English parishes without a question as to the validity of their orders. (*History of the Reformation*, p. 332-33.)

"The feature," says Prof. Fisher, "that distinguished the English Church from the Reformed Churches on the continent, was the retention in its polity and worship of so much that had belonged to the Catholic system." And the Episcopal Church is to this day essentially Catholic. The English Church owes its existence more to a stroke of political policy (*coup d'etat*) than to a deep conviction of the supremacy of truth. The supremacy of the King himself was deemed of vastly more importance than the supremacy of apostolic truth. In all these controversies the Church of Christ, as founded by the apostles, was not once thoroughly and distinctively identified. No plan of salvation is defined. The Bible is translated, which, for the times, was a memorable event, and one fraught with far-reaching consequences. The translation of the Bible into the vernacular of the people was the harbinger of both the civil and religious liberty of modern times. Great revolutionary principles were abstracted from the Bible, and many proof-texts from the Bible furnished matter for divisive and contradictory creeds, but the Bible itself as an infallible guide, and as containing the divine system of salvation, was laid upon the shelf as a useless piece of lumber. The controversialists of that period scarcely ever make an appeal to the Word of God in their efforts to sustain their respective dogmas and theories. While they all acknowledged the supremacy of the Scriptures, and in a general way deferred to them, yet the facts go to show that the truth of the Bible was nullified and the power of the gospel paralyzed by savage and ceaseless controversies—by controversies between the defenders of the Augsburg Confession and the advocates of the Heidelberg Catechism—by polemical struggles between Luther and Zwingle—by angry disputes between the King of England and the Pope of Rome, and by repeated wrangles of opposing Councils. Dogmas were popularized, creeds were stereotyped, human opinions were consecrated, metaphysical speculations furnished food for the common mind, and doctrinal statements, essentially dead, and wholly inoperative, were made to occupy the place of a living Bible.

Why did not the "Reformers" of the sixteenth century continue as they had begun? Who authorized them to make creeds and catechisms, and to formulate Church standards? Why did they occupy more time in discussing Transubstantiation and Predestination—both metaphysical and untaught questions, and not comprehensible by the common people—and on which no man's salvation depends—than they spent in preaching and teaching just what the apostles preached and taught? The followers of the Reformers of the sixteenth century have had 350 years in which to follow up the apostles, but up to this time they have not found them.

THE BOOK OF COMMON PRAYER.

A HISTORY of the origin and development of Church Creeds is indeed a curious and entertaining, if not a profitable, study. The history of Creeds is not a history of genuine reformation, but in the manufacture of those tests of church fellowship we discover the mental and spiritual portraits of uninspired men. God "breathed into man the breath of lives," but creed-mongers have breathed into creeds the putrid breath of sectaries, dogmatists, humanists, traditionists, sciolists, scholastics, opinionists, purists, transcendentalists, metaphysicians, and so forth. God made the Bible, but men made creeds. The trail of the serpent is found in every human creed. The hope of the world is to be found in the Bible; the hope of prelates and of priests —the glowing hope of all sectarian leaders—can be found in diverse Symbols of Faith, in the figments and fancies of creed architects, in Church Standards which divide the people of one common Lord, and in every form of "Systematic Theology," which furnishes employment to as many theologians, and to as many distinct parties, as are represented by these varying systems. In short, the history of creed-making is the history of human passion, human prejudice, human bigotry, superstition, ignorance of God's Word, human ambition, of plots and counterplots, of partisans, of strife, of theological tournaments, and of cunning craftiness. They are the product of ingenious men, intellectually acute, skilled in the art of dialectics, and powerful as polemics.

The history of the incubation and birth of the English Prayer Book, or Book of Common Prayer, is a study that will tire any mind, and discourage any heart, if one had no other object in view except the mere reading of its history. It is but just to say that the men, as a class, who inflicted creeds upon the world, were better in spirit and character than the creeds they made; and that whatever of goodness and greatness they possessed, and that whatever of purity and nobility of life they manifested, they derived directly from the Word of God and from the Fountain of Life: which fact, by itself alone, is a crushing argument against all creeds—even against "Revised Creeds," as at present proposed by the orthodox world.

Before the Reformation of Luther, the Missals, Breviaries, etc., of the Church of Rome, were in use in England. In 1537, the Convocation put forth in English, "*The godly and pious Institution of a Christian Man*," containing the Lord's Prayer, the Creed, the Commandments, and the Ave Maria. In 1547, in the reign of Edward VI., a committee was appointed to draw up a Liturgy in English, free from Popish errors. Cranmer, Ridley, and other eminent reformers, composed this committee, and their book was confirmed by Parliament in 1548. This is known as the *first Prayer-book of Edward VI.* A large portion of it was taken from the old services used in England before the Reformation; but the labors of Melancthon and Bucer helped to give the book its Protestant form. "About the end of the year 1550 exceptions were taken against some parts of this book, and Archbishop Cranmer proposed a new review. The principal alterations occasioned by this second review were the addition of the *Sentences, Exhortations, Confession and Absolution,* at the beginning of the morning and evening services, which in the first Common Prayer-book began with the Lord's Prayer; the addition of the *Commandments* at the beginning of the communion office; the removing of some rights and ceremonies retained in the former book, such as the use of oil in confirmation, the unction of the sick, prayers for the departed souls, the invocation of the Holy Ghost at the consecration of the Eucharist, and the prayer of oblation that used to follow it; the omitting the rubric that ordered water to be mixed with the wine, with several other less material variations. The habits, likewise, which were prescribed in the former book were in this laid aside; and, lastly, a rubric was added at the end of the communion office to explain the reason of kneeling at the Sacrament." (Hook.) The Liturgy, thus revised and altered, was again confirmed by Parliament in 1551, and is cited as the *second Prayer-book of Edward VI.* Queen Mary, on her accession, repealed the acts of Edward, and restored, through the influence of her Papal advisers, the Romanist prayer-book. "On the accession of Elizabeth to the English throne, this repeal, however, was reversed, and the second book of Edward VI. with several alterations and emendations, was re-established. This Liturgy continued in use during the long reign of Elizabeth, and received further additions and improvements." (*Eadie Eccles. Enc.*)

Early in the reign of James I. the Prayer Book was again revised, but the "improvements" suggested by James were not ratified by Parliament. In 1661, the year after the restoration of Charles II., the commissioners, both Episcopal and Presbyterian, who had assembled at the Savoy to revise the Liturgy, having come to no agreement, the Convocation agreed to certain "alterations and additions." The whole book, being finished, passed both houses of Convocation; it was subscribed to by bishops and clergy, and was ratified by act of Parliament, and received the royal assent May 19, 1662. This was the last revisal of the Book of Common Prayer in which any alteration was made by public authority. Several attempts have been made to revise the book since 1665, but without success. The first attempt was made in the reign of William III. encouraged by Tillotson and Stillingfleet, who in 1668 had united with Bates, Manton and Baxter, in preparing a bill for the "comprehension of Dissenters." Failing then, as well as in 1681, the scheme was resumed after the Revolution, and in 1689 a commission was formed to revise the Prayer-book. A number of alterations were suggested, in order, if possible, to gratify the Dissenters, but the attempt proved abortive. There is at the present time a *Liturgical Revision Society* in England, which, in its *Declaration of Principles and Objects*, proposes to bring the Book of Common Prayer "into closer conformity with the written word of God and the principles of the Reformation, by excluding all those expressions which have been assumed to countenance Romanizing doctrine or practice."

After the American Revolution, the "Protestant Episcopal Church" was established as an organization separate from the Church of England, in 1784. In 1786, a committee was appointed to adapt the English Liturgy to use in America, and they prepared a book, which, however, never came into general use.

At the General Convention in October, 1789, the

whole subject of the Liturgy was thrown open by appointing committees on the different portions of the Prayer-book, whose several reports, with the action of the two houses thereupon, were consolidated in the Book of Common Prayer, etc., as it is now in use, the whole book being ratified and set forth by a vote of the Convention on the sixteenth of October, 1789, its use being prescribed from and after the first day of October, 1790. The American Liturgy retains all that is excellent in the English service, omits several of its really objectionable features, brings some of the offices (the communion, for example) nearer to the primitive pattern, modifies others to suit our peculiar institutions, and, on the whole, is a noble monument to the wisdom, prudence, piety and churchmanship of the fathers of the American Church. By the forty-fifth canon of 1832, it is required that every minister shall, before all sermons and lectures, and all other occasions of public worship, use the Book of Common Prayer, as the same is or may be established by the authority of the General Convention of this Church. And in performing said service, no other prayers shall be used than those prescribed by the said book. (Hook, *Church Dictionary*, Am. Ed.)

We ask, where is the scriptural authority for all this priestly jugglery and ecclesiastical legislation? There is no scriptural authority, and the creed-mongers do not pretend to give any. The whole question rests upon assumptions. Why, instead of working over three hundred years to bring the Book of Common Prayer "*into conformity with the written word of God*," did they not take the "written word of God," and stand upon it, and stay there? Why have they been shuffling around these many years? If it is reform they are after, and they are truly seeking the unity of God's people, and if they are really desirous of discovering and identifying the Apostolic Church, why not accept the teaching of inspired apostles, and follow the teaching of the apostles, and pattern after the model Church as established by those holy men of God? We answer, because if they were to do so, they would be shorn of ecclesiastical power; bishops could no longer legislate for the "laity;" distinctive titles of honor would have to be given up; bishops could not live sumptuously every day, and there would be a heavy decrease in their stipends; they could no longer lord it over God's heritage, and all chances for clerical and prelatical promotion would be cut off. Liturgies, and "Church standards," and Confessions of Faith, are changed from time to time, so as to be adapted to the people and to the times. This is worldly wisdom, but not the wisdom that comes from above. These ecclesiastical vandals dare not change the Bible to suit times and places, and the people; but they will assume to create a creed, and then assume to change it with the changing times. Did Christ and his apostles leave instructions to the effect that the gospel and the plan of salvation should, in successive ages, be so changed as to harmonize with every form of society, and with the varying forms of civil goverment? God intended that the truths of the Bible and the doctrine of the gospel should educate and mold society and civil governments, and not that ecclesiastics and civil governments should transform the word of God into Creeds and Symbols of Faith. Why not as well undertake to change the immutable laws of nature as to presume to alter or modify the constitutional laws of the kingdom of God?

What kind of an infallible guide is that to the human soul, that "omits objectionable features," and modifies others to suit our "peculiar institutions," in order to bring the people "*nearer to the primitive pattern?*" Why not take the "primitive pattern" itself, and lay aside all makeshifts and counterfeits? Can we not understand the "primitive pattern"—God's own workmanship —far easier than all human imitations? Creeds do not contain the principles of reform, much less the light and the knowledge that lead to a complete restoration of apostolic Christianity. If men are wiser and better, it is because their love of God and their love of Bible truths has made them so. They are good in spite of their lifeless creeds. Creeds have not revolutionized the world, and set up the right and torn down the wrong, but the spirit of Christ and the power of the gospel have done it.

ORIGIN OF THE WESTMINSTER CONFESSION OF FAITH.

WE now come to speak of the origin of the Presbyterian Church and of the formation of the Westminster Confession of Faith. A joint resolution of the houses of the English Parliament, without the sanction of King Charles I., was passed June 12, 1643, which convoked a Synod "for settling the government and liturgy of the Church of England, and for vindicating and clearing of the doctrine of said Church from false aspersions and interpretations," and, furthermore, for bringing about a more perfect reformation of the Church than was obtained under Edward VI. and Elizabeth, by which a closer union of sentiment with the Church of Scotland and the Reformed churches of the continent might be secured. Parliament appointed to membership in this Synod 121 clergymen, taken from the various shires of England, ten members of the House of Lords, and twenty members from the House of Commons. The General Synod of Scotland, August 19, 1643, elected five clergymen and three lay elders as commissioners to the Westminster Synod. About twenty of the members originally summoned were clergymen of the Church of England, and several of them afterwards bishops; but few of the Episcopal members took their seats. The bishops of the English Church never acknowledged its claims, and the King condemned its sessions under extreme penalties, June 22, 1643. The Synod, however, contrary to the will of the King, convened July 1, 1643, in Westminster Abbey (hence the name, Westminster Confession of Faith), in the presence of both houses of Parliament. The average attendance of clerical members during the sessions was between sixty and eighty. The great body of the members, both clerical and lay, were Presbyterians; ten or twelve were Independents, or, as now styled, Congregationalists; and five or six called themselves Erastians. The great majority were Calvinistic in faith.

The purposes for which this august Assembly of divines was convoked, as already intimated, were to vindicate the doctrine of the Church of England, and to recommend such further reformation of her discipline, liturgy and government as might "be agreeable to God's holy word, and most apt to procure and preserve the peace of the Church at home, and nearer agreement with the Church of Scotland and other Reformed churches abroad." But the Parliament, feeling their need of Scottish aid, acceded to the Solemn League and Covenant, and urged the Scotch to send their deputies to the Assembly. Its objects were extended; and, in order to carry out the covenanted uniformity, it was empowered to prepare a new Confession of Faith and Catechism, as well as directories for public worship and church government, which might be adopted by all the Churches represented. The Church of Scotland threw all its influence in favor of strict Calvinism and Presbyterianism. Before electing delegates to the Westminster Assembly, in compliance with the request of Parliament, it adopted, August 17, 1643, the so-called "Solemn League and Covenant," which bound the Scottish nation to the defense of the Reformed religion in Scotland, the furtherance of the Reformation in England and Ireland in doctrine, worship, church organization and discipline; the establishing of ecclesiastical and religious uniformity in the three realms; the extirpation of papacy and prelacy, of heresy and all ungodliness; and the support of all the rights of Parliament and of the rightful authority of the King. This document was immediately transmitted to Parliament, and thence to the Westminster Assembly, and was formally endorsed by each of these bodies, but was condemned by the King. The Assembly sought to gain the fraternal sympathies of the Reformed churches on the continent also, and to that end addressed to them circular letters which elicited more or less favorable responses, and which the King endeavored to neutralize by issuing a manifesto in Latin and English, in which he denied the intention charged upon him of re-establishing the Papal power in his realm. The Solemn League and Covenant, binding the ecclesiastical bodies of the two nations into a union, had been passed in Scotland, August 17, was subsequently accepted by the Westminster Assembly, and ordered by the English Parliament to be printed, September 21, and subscribed September 25, when the House of Commons, with the Scottish Commissioners and the Westminster Assembly, met in the Church of St. Margaret, Westminster. The House of Lords took the "Covenant," October 15.

"The question of church government occasioned the most difficulty, and seemed for a time impossible to be settled. Many of the most learned divines who were entirely on the side of the Parliament were yet in favor of what they termed primitive episcopacy, or the system in which the presbyters and their president governed the churches in common. Then there were the Scottish commissioners and the more radical Puritans, who were at the opposite extreme; and, in order to reach a conclusion, these differences must be reconciled. It was accomplished after much discussion and long delay by the adoption of the Presbyterian form of government."

A committee, consisting of about twenty-five members, was appointed by the Assembly "to prepare matter for a joint Confession of Faith," about August 20, 1644. The matter was prepared, in part, at least, by this committee, and the digesting of it into a formal draught was intrusted to a smaller committee on May 12, 1645. The debating of the separate articles began July 7, 1645, and the following day a committee of three (afterwards increased to five) was appointed to "take care of the wording of the Confession," as the article should be adopted in the Assembly. On July 16, the committee reported the heads of the Confession, and these were distributed to the three large committees to be elaborated and prepared for discussion. All were repeatedly read and debated in the most thorough manner possible in the Assembly. On September 25, 1646, a part of the Confession was finally passed, and on December 4, the remainder received the sanction of the Assembly, when the entire document was presented to the Parliament. That body ordered the printing of 600 copies for the use of members of Parliament and of the Assembly, and that Scripture proofs should be added to the Confession, which was accordingly done. In 1647, the Confession was approved by the Church of Scotland in the form in which it passed the Assembly, and it was afterwards ratified by the Scotch Parliament. It was passed by the English Parliament in 1648, under the title of *Articles of Christian Religion*, but with certain changes.

The basis of the Confession, says the historian, is doubtless those Calvinistic articles which are supposed to have been prepared by Usher, and in 1615, were adopted by the Convocation of the Irish Church. In the formation of this Presbyterian "Symbol" the Assembly at first undertook to revise the Thirty-nine Articles of the Anglican Church, and proceeded with that work until fifteen articles had been revamped with elements of a more pronounced Calvinistic character and provided with Scripture proofs. The only important change made in this process was the omission of Article VIII., concerning the authority of the three œcumenical symbols. The intention of the Synod was to ground every statement directly on Scripture as the only rule of faith, while the Church of England, under Edward VI. and Elizabeth, conceded to Catholic tradition, "if not in conflict with Scripture, a regulative authority." The Scottish delegates, however, induced the Assembly to undertake the formation of an entirely "new Symbol."

The Confession, under the title of *"The Humble Advice of the Assembly of Divines, now by Authority of Parliament sitting at Westminster, concerning a Confession of Faith,"* etc., was printed in London in December, 1646, without proofs, and in May, 1647, with proofs, for the use of the houses of Parliament and the Assembly. A copy of this last edition was taken to Scotland by the commissioners, and from it 300 copies were printed for the use of the General Assembly there. After being approved by that body, it was published in Scotland with the title of *"The Confession of Faith Agreed upon by the Assembly of Divines,"* etc., and while the House of Commons were still considering it, a London bookseller brought it out under the same title in 1648. In the same year it was, with the omission of parts of certain chapters, and with some minute verbal alterations, approved by the two houses, and published under the title, "*Articles of Christian Religion, Approved and Passed by both Houses of Parliament after Advice had with the Assembly of Divines.*" But the latter form is not common, and the Confession continues to be printed in the form in which it was drawn by the Assembly and approved by the Church of Scotland. The last of the Scotch commissioners left the Assembly November 9, 1647. On February 22, 1649, after the Assembly had held 1163 sittings, lasting each from nine o'clock A. M. to 2 P. M., the Parliament, by an ordinance, changed what remained of the Assembly into a committee for trying and examining ministers, and in this form it continued to hold weekly sittings until the dissolution of the "Long Parliament," April 20, 1653. The *Larger Catechism* was sent to the House of Commons October 22, 1647; the *Shorter Catechism*, November 25, the same year. In the autumn of 1648 both houses of Parliament ordered the printing and publishing of the *Shorter Catechism*, but the House of the Lords was discontinued before it had acted on the *Larger Catechism*.

And thus, in the midst of such politico ecclesiastical throes as we have described, the Westminster Confession of Faith was born into the world. We have seen that the civil powers had as much to do in the manufacture of this abstruse, recondite, metaphysical document as the Church "Divines." It is the creation of State craft and priest craft. It is a compromise between Romanism and Episcopacy—a sort of hybrid, begotten of the Papacy and born of Protestantism. Facts go to show that Episcopacy and Presbyterianism, as well as Romanism, would now, as then, make civil government subservient to the ecclesiastical authorities. It is but just to say that through the instrumentality of the Reformers of the sixteenth century the Papacy received a fatal blow. But let it be understood that it was not the formulation and publication of Confessions of Faith, nor the influence of the abstract propositions they contained, that paralyzed the arm of the Pope, and that gave impulse to the Reformatory movements of that eventful age. On the contrary, it was the translation of the Scriptures into the language of the common people, and the faithful proclamation of God's word, that effectually and fatally weakened the despotism of Rome. It was Luther and Zwingle, exposing the rottenness of the priesthood of Rome, and Calvin, by the word of God, striking at the false theology of Romish prelates, and Knox, by the same word of God, before creeds took on form, demolishing the governmental usurpations of the Papal See, that, combined and co-operating, wrought the mighty work, the impulse of which revolution still moves among modern reformers. As a Bible people, we accept the Bible principles of reform, as advocated and applied by the reformers of the sixteenth century, but we reject their Creeds *in toto*, as being the product of fallible and uninspired men, and as being the prolific and chief source of sectarianism and a divided Church, with all their concomitants of sectarian rivalry, sectarian bigotry and sectarian pride.

We have our mission, and we know our mission, which is the repudiation of all Symbols of Faith, all Church Standards, and all bodies that presume to legislate for the Church in the stead of Christ, while at the same time we shall elevate the Bible above all the works of men, and persistently plead for complete restoration of apostolic teaching and practice.

ORIGIN OF CONGREGATIONALISM.

We now come to the origin and development of Congregationalism, which forms an integral and interesting chapter in reformatory movements. As contrasted with Romanism and Episcopacy, and as contrasted also with Presbyterianism, we shall find Congregationalism, as a system of "Church polity," far in advance of those ecclesiastical systems, but, in some features, as falling short of the apostolic order of things. We are free to admit that Congregationalism makes a nearer approach to the primitive order than any of the "Orthodox Churches." They claim that their system is only a substantial return to the order and practice of the apostolic churches, which had been corrupted by the tendencies that culminated in the Papacy; and that traces of dissent from the episcopal power are found in every age. (See Punchard's *History of Congregationalism*.) The origin of modern Congregationalism may be traced to the early developments of the Reformation in England, an account of which we have already given. From the beginning of the protest against Romanism, some of the principal distinctive opinions, afterwards developed into Congregational polity, especially the identity of "bishop" and "presbyter," and notably the independent right of each congregation to chose its own "pastor" and exercise discipline, without the interposition of council or bishop, found decided advocates and unflinching adherents. While Henry VIII., after repudiating the Romish supremacy, which we have already noted, adhered to the essential features of Romish theology, and in part to Papal polity and practice, the advancement of enlightened reason continued in the opposite direction. When the reforms conducted by Edward VI., already noted in previous chapters of this series, were peremptorily brought to a standstill by Mary, Queen of Scotland, dissenting congregations, the forecast substantially of modern Congregationalism, came immediately, though privately, into existence in various places, as, for instance, in London in 1555. Their existence is learned almost entirely from persecutions to which their members were subjected, but of which few particulars are preserved in history.

Among the Congregational martyrs were Barrowe, Greenwood and Penry, executed in 1593. Of the Congregational Church formed in London in 1592, of which Francis Johnson was "pastor," and John Greenwood "teacher," fifty-six members were seized and imprisoned. Many of them eventually found their way to Amsterdam, where they re-organized under the same pastor. Robert Brown's publication, in 1582, of "A Book which showeth the Life and Manners of all true Christians," etc., presents the earliest full development of the Independent side of Congregationalism. While at first only Puritans, many became Separatists, in despair of securing complete reformation in the Church of England. About the year 1602 a congregation was organized in Gainesborough in Lincolnshire, Rev. John Smyth pastor. In 1606 another congregation was formed at Scrooby, Nottinghamshire, Richard Clyton pastor, which met at the house of William Brewster. Of that congregation John Robinson was a member, and afterwards associate pastor. In 1606 Mr. Smyth and his friends removed to Amsterdam. In the following year Mr. Clyton and many of his church members, after enduring great persecution, also escaped to Amsterdam, and in 1608 the majority of the remaining members of the Scrooby congregation followed. After the lapse of about a year the church removed to Leyden. But owing to the disadvantage of residing in a country of different language and customs from their own, they resolved to emigrate to America, and consequently a portion of the Leyden Church, with Elder William Brewster, after many tedious trials, landed at Plymouth, Massachusetts, Dec. 21, 1620 (N. S.), while Robinson, with a portion of the congregation, remained at Leyden. In 1616 a Congregational Church was established at Southwark, London, under the care of Henry Jacob, who had been confirmed in Congregational principles by conference with John Robinson at Leyden. This congregation, organized after Mr. Jacob had conferred with leading Puritans, probably gathered together some of the scattered members of Mr. Johnson's congregation.

Though sometimes called "the first Independent Church in England," there had been in existence secret organizations in the reign of Mary, and the congregations of Gainesborough and Scrooby, and, it is said, one at Duckenfield, Cheshire Co. About 1624 Rev. John Lathrop became pastor of the Southwark congregation. In 1632 he was imprisoned, with forty others of its members. In 1634 Mr. Lathrop, having been released, removed to America, with about thirty of his flock, and in that year organized the congregation in Scituate, Massachusetts, where he continued till 1639, when the majority removed to West Barnstable, where that congregation is still existing.

AMERICAN CONGREGATIONALISM.

THE history of the American Congregationalists is pretty well known. The Plymouth settlement was distinct in origin and government from that of Massachusetts Bay, the Pilgrim settlers being distinctively known as the "Pilgrims." The persecutions under Laud, in the Old Country, drove many Puritans into the resolution to emigrate. Endicott and his companions began the colony at Salem, Mass., in 1628, and 1630, John Winthrop, their governor, with other emigrants, occupied Boston and the surrounding towns. Settlements were made at Hartford and Saybrook, in Connecticut, in 1635, and in 1638, Davenport and his associates founded the New Haven colony, while in 1633 a distinct company reinforced the colonies on the Piscataqua River. The Plymouth congregation had come out fully organized; in the other settlements congregations were immediately formed. None except the Plymouth people had come to America as Separatists; the others declared that they did not separate from the Church of England, but that, on the contrary, they only desired to expurgate its corruptions. But, having colonized in a strange and far-away country, removed from all ecclesiastical establishments, and searching the Scriptures as the basis of their ecclesiastical order, they all adopted the Congregational Church polity. Most of their ministers had been regularly ordained in the

Church of England, and, as is well known, were a highly educated class of men, as (*e. g.*) Cotton and Wilson, of Boston; Mather, of Dorchester; Hooker and Stone, of Hartford; Davenport and Hooke, of New Haven.

American Congregationalism proper received its religious form, essentially, in the early religious history of New England. If traced to the writings of any one person, it would be to those of John Robinson, of Leyden; those of John Cotton and Thomas Hooker, in America, being next in importance. Robert Brown was never acknowledged as a leader, he being a strict and severe Independent, and, finally, returning to the communion of the Church of England; but, at the same time, it is conceded that his writings did undoubtedly incite many minds to examine and reject the claims of Episcopacy. The system, can not, however, be satisfactorily traced to any one man, but rather to the united sentiment of the early emigrants, who agreed in carrying into practice the opinion that every congregation is, according to the Scriptures, confined to the limits of a single or individual congregation, and that it must be democratic in government; while, at the same time, all congregations are regarded as in fellowship with one another. Hence the term "the Congregational Church" is never used to denote the denomination, but "the Congregational churches."

Congregationalists are generally Calvinistic in theology, although in the United States there is an advanced party who repudiate distinctive Calvinism. Congregationalists, as a class, hold to a system of church government which embraces these two fundamental principles, viz., (1) that every local congregation of believers, united for worship, and for observing the "sacraments," and for the enforcement of discipline, is a complete church within itself, and can not be subjected in governmental affairs to any ecclesiastical authority outside of itself; and (2) that all such local congregations are in communion with one another, and are under moral obligations to fulfill all the duties involved in such fellowship. The system is distinguished from Presbyterianism by the first, and from Independency by the second. It involves the equal right of all the members to vote in all governmental affairs; and the parity of all ministers, the ministers being set apart by the congregations, and who, as ministers, are not invested with any power of government, but who have official power only in the congregations by which they may be chosen pastors. It is seen that in regard to the independency (autonomy) of the congregations, the Congregationalists occupy nearly the same position as that which is held by the Disciples of Christ, or by those people who have in reality identified the Church of Christ as established by the apostles. But the Congregationalists are not only wrong in name, viewed from the angle of apostolic teaching, but they are wrong in doctrine, which is made clear by the fact that they have, in common with all pedobaptists, substituted aspersion and rantism for immersion, and practice infant baptism, in respect to which practices they are not a whit in advance of the Romish Church, from which these violations of the law of God have descended. They are right in discarding councils, Synods, Conferences and Presbyteries, and right in denying all ecclesiastical authority beyond the individual congregation, but they are decidedly wrong in changing the ordinances of Jesus Christ. As means of regeneration, they are right in denying the alleged spiritual influence of dreams, and visions, and psychological impressions, and all hallucinations of the imagination, but as an exponent of the true Apostolic Church, in all the constituent elements of the one body, the Congregational Church is materially defective. It is not built exclusively upon the basis of God's Word, and hence never can form the nucleus of Christian unity, because, if a system is found to be defective in one or more parts, it must be rejected as a whole. A system of things which presumes to represent the divine model, and at the same time incorporates tradition and false dogmas, professedly on the principle of human expediency, and with a view of conciliating the captious and unregenerated world, can never hope to restore, unimpaired, the apostolic order of things.

Hence the necessity of the existence of the people known as the Disciples of Christ, who, repudiating all ecclesiastical authority outside of the government of Christ, and who, rejecting all the creeds and dogmas of contradictory and self-consuming sects, plant themselves exclusively upon the inspired Scriptures, as their only reliable and infallible guide, and as their only rule of faith and practice. Their tocsin of war is the avowed destruction of all sectism, and the motto of the banner they bear is "one Lord, one Faith and one Baptism." They regard the divisions of Christendom as a positive sin, and also as the prolific source of infidelity. They assume that "the unity of the Spirit" can only secure "the bond of peace"—a permanent and lasting peace—by an appeal to the Holy Scriptures, as the only source of information and authority. They constantly keep before their eyes the last intercessory prayer of our Lord: "Neither pray I for these alone [the apostles]; but for them also who shall believe on me *through their word:* that they all may be one, as thou, Father, art in me, and I in thee; that they also may be one in us: that the world may believe that thou hast sent me." We hold that sinners can only be saved, and church unity accomplished, through the words of the apostles; for Christ said to the apostles: "Whoever hears you, hears me; and whoever hears me, hears him who sent me." And to the Corinthians (2 Cor. v. 20) Paul writes: "Now then we are ambassadors *for Christ*, as though God did beseech you *by us;* we pray you in Christ's stead, be you reconciled to God." Paul said to Timothy, "*Preach the Word,*" which excludes the preaching of dogmas, theories, opinions, Church polities, human Creeds and "Church Standards."

ORIGIN OF THE BAPTIST CHURCH.

The origin of the Baptist Church is confessedly obscure. It is a difficult and involved history to trace. The Baptist Church, distinctively, can not be traced beyond the sixteenth century. It is purely a creation of circumstances. Its incipient developments are found in the religious chaos of the sixteenth century. In the midst of all the diversities of opinion that existed in the Reformation of that eventful period, it was constantly maintained by Protestants that "Holy Scripture containeth all things necessary to salvation, so that whatsoever is neither read therein nor may be proved thereby, although it be some time received of the faithful as godly and profitable for an order and comeliness, yet no man ought to be constrained to believe it as an article of faith or repute it requisite to the necessity of salvation." (Articles of King Edward VI.) The operation of this broad principle of toleration and private judgment was denied by the Church of Rome, and, consequently, those who adopted this principle, manifestly so fair and equitable, suffered the anathemas of the Papal powers. Each separate body of Protestants claimed the privilege of standing on the basis of the Scriptures, and was prepared to resist alike the tyranny of Rome and what it considered the license of other Protestant sects. Thus it came to pass that the Baptists, or, as their opponents called them, the Anabaptists (or, as Zwingle names them, Catabaptists), were strenuously opposed by all other sects of Protestantism, and it was regarded by nearly all the early reformers to be the duty of the civil magistrates to punish them with fine and imprisonment, and even with death, as an abundance of historical documents attest. A writer in the *Encyclopædia Britannica* says: "There was, no doubt, some justification for this severity in the fact that the fanaticism which burst forth in the early times of the Reformation frequently led to insurrection and revolt, and in particular that the leader of the 'peasant war' in Saxony, Thomas Münzer, and probably many of his followers, were Anabaptists both on the continent and in this country (England) are very few and meagre. Almost all that is currently known of them comes to us from their opponents."

There is, however, much valuable information, together with detailed accounts of their sufferings, in the Dutch Martyrology of Van Braght, himself a Baptist, which bears the title *Martalaers Spiegel der Doopsgesinde* (2d ed. fol., 1685), an English translation of the latter half of which was published in two vols., 8vo., London, 1850-53, edited by Dr. Underhill, now Secretary of the Baptist Missionary Society. Probably the earliest confession of faith of any Baptist community is that given by Zwingle in the second part of his *Elenchus contra Catabaptistas*, published in 1527. Zwingle professes to give it entire, translating it, as he says, *ad verbum* into Latin. He upbraids his opponents with not having published these articles, but declares that there is scarcely any one of them that has not a written (*descriptum*) copy of these laws which have been so well concealed. The articles are in all seven. The first, which we give in full, relates to baptism:

Baptism ought to be given to all who have been taught repentance and change of life, and who in truth, believe that through Christ their sins are blotted out (*abotila*), and the sins of all who are willing (*volunt*) to walk in the resurrection of Jesus Christ, and who are willing to be buried with him into death (not very good Baptist doctrine in the present age) that they may rise again with him. To all, therefore, who in this manner seek baptism, and of themselves ask us, we will give it. By this rule are excluded all baptism of infants, the great abomination of the Roman pontiff. For this article we have the testimony and strength of Scripture, we have also the practice of the apostles; which things we simply and also steadfastly will observe, for we are assured of them.

The second article, we are told by the same writer, relates to withdrawment (*abstentio*) or excommunication, and declares that all who have given themselves to the Lord and have been *baptized into the one body of Christ* should, if they lapse into sin, be excommunicated. (The Baptists of the present day baptize into the Baptist Church, not "into the one body of Christ," as the Disciples of Christ teach). The third article relates to the breaking of bread; in this it is declared that they who break the one bread in commemoration of the broken body of Christ, and drink of the one cup in commemoration of his blood poured out, must first be *united together into the one body of Christ*, that is, into the Church of God—which is not the Baptist Church of the present day. The fourth article asserts the duty of separation from the world and its abominations, among which are included all papistical and semi-papistical works. The fifth relates to pastors of the congregation. They assert that the pastor should be some one of the flock who has a good report from those who are without. "His office is to read, admonish, teach, learn, exhort, correct, or excommunicate in the church, and to preside well over all the brethren and sisters, both in prayer and in the breaking of bread; and in all things that relate to the body of Christ, to watch that it may be established and increased so that the name of God may by us be glorified and praised, and that the mouth of blasphemers may be stopped." The sixth article relates to the power of the sword. "The sword," they say, "is the ordinance of God outside the perfection of Christ, by which the bad is punished and slain, and the good is defended." They further declare that a Christian ought not to decide or give sentence in secular matters, and that he ought not to exercise the office of magistrate. The seventh article relates to oaths, which they declare are forbidden of Christ.

It is here proper to state, for the benefit of the general reader, that the name "Anabaptist" means one baptism upon another baptism, or the immersion of those who have been sprinkled. There is no doubt of the fact that the Anabaptists suffered terrible persecution, and that all sorts of epithets of abuse and calumny were heaped upon their devoted heads. Zwingle styles them as "fanatical, stolid, audacious, impious." To us, at the present day, who enjoy personal liberty and religious toleration, it appears as shocking as it is wonderful, that the Protestant council of Zürich, which had with great difficulty won its own liberty, should pass a decree, as Zwingle himself reports, that any person who administers anabaptism should be drowned; and still more shocking that, at the time when Zwingle wrote, this cruel decree should have been carried into effect against one of the leaders of the Anabaptists, Felix Mantz, who himself had been associated with

Zwingle, not only as a student, but also at the beginning of the Reformation. In this base and contemptible persecution, the reformers of the sixteenth century have very little to be proud of, and such persecution on the part of the reformers only goes to show that the blight of Romanism still clung to them, as it still does to their descendants of the present day. In 1537 Menno Simonis united with the Anabaptists and soon distinguished himself as their acknowledged leader. His moderation and piety, according to Mosheim, held in check the turbulent spirit of the more fanatical among them. He died in 1561, after a life passed amid continual dangers and conflicts. His name remains as the ecclesiastical designation of the Mennonites, who eventually settled in the Netherlands under the protection of William the Silent, Prince of Orange, many of them emigrating to the United States, and settling in the Middle and Western States, where their descendants have been largely absorbed by the various denominations, though some remain in separate bands, here and there, who have become wholly indifferent to immersion.

The *Encyclopædia Britannica* says that "of the introduction of Baptist views into England we have no certain knowledge." Fox relates "that the registers of London make mention of certain Dutchmen counted for Anabaptists, of whom ten were put to death in sundry places in the realm, *anno* 1535; the other ten repented and were saved." In 1536 Henry VIII., as "in earth supreme head of the Church of England," issued a proclamation together with articles concerning faith agreed upon by Convocation, in which the clergy are told to instruct the people that they ought to repute and take "the Anabaptists' opinions for detestable heresies and to be utterly condemned." The document is given *in extenso* by Fuller, who further tells us from Stow's *Chronicles* that, in the year 1538, "four Anabaptists, three men and one woman, all Dutch, bare fagots at Paul's Cross, and three days after a man and woman of their sect were burnt in Smithfield." The Anabaptists united in communities separate from the Established Church. Latimer, in 1552, speaks of them as segregating themselves from the company of other men. We have not space to follow the history of the persecutions which the Anabaptists endured in England for opinion's sake. About the beginning of the seventeenth century the severe laws against the Puritans led many dissenters to emigrate to Holland. Some of these were Baptists, and an English Baptist Church was formed in Amsterdam about the year 1609. In 1611 this church published "a declaration of faith of English people remaining at Amsterdam, in Holland." The article relating to baptism is as follows: "That every church is to receive in all their members by the confession of their faith and sins [Modern Baptists do not teach this apostolic practice, but the disciples of Christ do, mark that], wrought by the preaching of the gospel according to the primitive institution and practice. And therefore, churches constituted after any other manner [mark that too], or of any other persons, are not according to Christ's testament. That baptism or washing with water is the outward manifestation of dying unto sin and walking in newness of life; and therefore in nowise appertaineth to infants." Many members of the Brownist or Independent denomination held baptist views. An Independent congregation in London, gathered in the year 1616, included several such persons, and as the congregation was larger than could conveniently meet together in times of persecution, they agreed to allow these persons to constitute a distinct congregation, which was formed on the 12th of September, 1633; and upon this the majority, if not all, of the new congregation were baptized. Another Baptist Church was formed in London, in 1639. These churches were "Particular" or Calvinistic Baptists. The church formed in 1609 at Amsterdam, held Arminian views. In 1644 a Confession of Faith was published in the names of seven congregations in London, "commonly (though falsely) called Anabaptists," in which were included the two congregations just mentioned. The article on baptism is as follows: "That baptism is an ordinance of the New Testament given by Christ to be dispensed only upon persons professing faith, or that are disciples, or taught, who, upon a profession of faith [not the recital of a dreamy "experience," as modern Baptists hold], ought to be baptized." "The way and manner of dispensing this ordinance the Scripture holds out to be dipping or plunging the whole body under water." They made a clear distinction between the rights of conscience and the rights of the civil magistrates.

After showing their willingness to yield "subjection and obedience" to the magistrates, as unto the Lord, and after indulging the hope that God would "incline the magistrates' hearts so far to tender our consciences as that we might be protected by them from wrong, injury, oppression, and molestation," they proceed to say: "But if God withhold the magistrates' allowance and furtherance herein, yet we must, notwithstanding, proceed together in Christian communion, not daring to give place to suspend our practice, but to walk in obedience to Christ in the profession and holding forth this faith before mentioned, even in the midst of all trials and afflictions, not accounting our goods, lands, wives, children, fathers, mothers, brethren, sisters, yea, and our own lives, dear unto us, so that we may finish our course with joy; remembering always that we ought to obey God rather than men." They close their Confession thus: "If any take this that we have said to be heresy, then do we with the apostle freely confess, that after the way which they call heresy worship we the God of our fathers, believing all things which are written in the Law and in the Prophets and Apostles, desiring from our souls to disclaim all heresies and opinions which are not after Christ, and to be steadfast, immovable, always abounding in the work of the Lord, as knowing our labor shall not be in vain in the Lord." This breathing spell, however, was not of long continuance, for soon after the Restoration, in 1660, the meetings of Nonconformists were continually disturbed by the constables, and their preachers were carried before the magistrates and fined or imprisoned, of which numerous instances could be given.

The history of the persecution of Baptists, as well as of other Protestant dissenters, ceases with the Revolution of 1688, and the passing of the Act of Toleration in 1689. The removal of the remaining disabilities, such as those imposed by the Test and Corporation Acts repealed in 1828, has no special bearing on Baptists more than on other Nonconformists. The ministers of the "three denominations of dissenters"— Presbyterians, Independents and Baptists—resident in London and the neighborhood, had the privilege accorded to them of presenting on proper occasions an address to the sovereign in state, a privilege which they still enjoy.

It is unfortunate that modern Baptists have not carried out the principles of reform as proclaimed by the Baptists of the seventeenth century, who verged very close upon apostolic restoration; for we see in the history of the early Baptists that they, upon profession of faith, baptized believers into the one body of Christ, and that, too, without postponement. The early Baptists depended upon the word of God as the source of enlightenment, regeneration and sanctification, and not on a "Christian experience"—not on special illumination without the word of God—not on the mystic and twistic operations of an abstract Spirit, out of which theory of conversion have come, in the modern Baptist Church, illusions, hallucinations, sensuistic impressions, ecstasies, dreams and many other vagaries. The Baptists of the seventeenth century had a clearer perception of apostolic teaching, had a more comprehensive view or grasp of the scheme of redemption, and approximated more nearly the New Testament order of things, than the modern school of Baptists, who have been spoiled by contact with pedobaptist "orthodoxy"—by contact with "Evangelical Churches"—whose smiles they court, and whose ill-will they seek to propitiate. The earlier Baptists did not baptize into the Baptist Church, as is the modern practice, but they baptized believing penitents "into the one body of Christ," which sounds exactly like apostolic teaching. We read of no monthly meetings called for the examination of converts who gave an "experience" of something that never occurred, except in the imagination of the convert; nor do we read that their "experience," wrought by the strivings of a "still small voice," was taken as an evidence of pardon; nor do we read of sinners being pardoned before immersion into the one body; nor do we learn from the records that they held monthly communion seasons, instead of communing on every first day of the week.

THE BAPTIST CHURCH IN THE UNITED STATES.

We continue our observations upon the origin and history of the Baptist Church. Some writers (as, for instance, Orchard, in his *History of Foreign Baptists*, London, 1838) have attempted to trace an *uninterrupted succession* of Baptist churches from the time of the apostles down to the present. He gives as the summing up of his researches, that "all Christian communities during the first three centuries were of the Baptist denomination in constitution and practice. In the middle of the third century the Novation Baptists established separate and independent societies, which continued until the end of the sixth age, when these communities were succeeded by the Paterines, which continued until the Reformation (1517). The Oriental Baptist churches with their successors, the Paulicians, continued in their purity until the tenth century, when they visited France, resuscitating and extending the Christian profession in Languedoc, where they flourished till the crusading army scattered, or drowned in blood, one million of unoffending professors. The Baptists in Piedmont and Germany are exhibited as existing under different names down to the Reformation. These churches, with their genuine successors, the Mennonites of Holland, are connectedly and chronologically detailed to the present period."

We showed in a previous article that the Baptist

Church could not be traced beyond the sixteenth century, and that the Church, or sect rather, had its rise among the Anabaptists. As a contradiction of Orchard's assumptions THE CHRISTIAN REVIEW (January, 1855, p. 23), the leading Baptist Quarterly of America, speaks as follows:

"We know of no assumption more arrogant, and more destitute of proper historic support, than that which claims to be able to trace the distinct and unbroken existence of a church substantially Baptist from the time of the apostles down to our own." Thus also Cutting (*Historic Vindications*, Boston, 1859, p. 14) remarks on such attempts: "I have little confidence in the results of any attempt of that kind which have met my notice, and I attach little value to inquiries pursued for the predetermined purpose of such a demonstration."

The Baptist churches in the United States owe their origin to Roger Williams, who, before his immersion, was an Episcopalian minister. He was persecuted for opposing the authority of the State in ecclesiastical affairs and for principles which "tended to Anabaptism." In 1639 he was immersed by Ezekiel Holliman, and in turn immersed Holliman and ten others, who with him organized a Baptist Church at Providence, Rhode Island. A few years before (1635), though unknown to Williams, a Baptist preacher of England, Hansard Knollys, had settled in New Hampshire and taken charge of a church in Dover: but he resigned in 1639 and returned to England. Williams obtained in 1644, a charter for the colony which he and his associates had founded in Rhode Island, with full and entire freedom of conscience. Rhode Island thus became the first Christian State which ever granted full religious liberty. In other British colonies the persecution against the Baptists continued a long time. Massachusetts issued laws against them in 1644, imprisoned several Baptists in 1651, and banished others in 1669. In 1680, the doors of a Baptist meeting-house were nailed up. In New York laws were issued against them in 1662, in Virginia in 1664. With the beginning of the eighteenth century the persecution greatly abated. They were released from tithes in 1727 in Massachusetts, in 1729 in New Hampshire and Connecticut, but not before 1785 in Virginia. The spread of their principles was greatly hindered by these persecutions, especially in the South, where in 1776 they counted about one hundred societies. After the Revolution they spread with extraordinary rapidity, especially in the South and Southwest, and were inferior in this respect only to the Methodists. In 1817, a triennial general convention was organized, which, however, has since been discontinued. In 1845, the discussion of the slavery question led to a division of the Northern and Southern Baptists. The destruction of slavery, in consequence of the failure of the Great Rebellion and the adoption of the constitutional amendment in 1865, led to efforts to reunite the societies of the Northern and Southern States. The Northern associations generally expressed a desire to corporate again with the Southern brethren in the fellowship of Christian labor, but they demanded from the Southern associations a profession of loyalty to the United States Government, and they themselves deemed it necessary to repeat the testimony which, during the war, they had, at each annual meeting, borne against slavery. The Southern associations that met during the year 1865, were unanimously in favor of continuing their former separate societies, and against fraternizing with the Northern societies. They censured the American Baptist Home Missionary Society for proposing, without consultation or co-operation with the churches, associations, conventions or organized Boards of the Southern States, to appoint ministers and missionaries to preach and raise churches within the bounds of the Southern associations. Some of the Southern associations, like that of Virginia, consequently advised the churches "to decline any co-operation or fellowship with any of the missionaries, ministers, or agents of the American Baptist Home Mission Society." A number of negro Baptist churches in the Southern States separated from the Southern associations, and either connected themselves with those of the North, or organized, with the co-operation of the Northern missionaries, independent associations. (McClintock and Strong's *Bib. Theo., and Ec. Enc.*, vol. i. p. 654).

In the United States the Baptist family is divided into the "Regular Baptists," or Missionary Baptists, Seventh-day Baptists, Anti-mission Baptists, Free-Will Baptists, and Six Principle Baptists. The *Free* or *Open Communion Baptists*, who were organized about 1810, united in 1841 with the Free-Will Baptists.

The Baptists have no standard Confession of Faith. The congregation being independent as to governmental affairs, each adopts its own articles of belief. In England the "Old Connection" are chiefly Socinians; the "New Connection," evangelical Arminians; the "Particular Baptists," Calvinists of various shades. In the United States, the Regular Baptists are for the most part Calvinists. The Baptists generally form "Associations," which, however, exercise no jurisdiction over the churches. They recognize no higher church officers than pastors and deacons. Elders are sometimes ordained as evangelists and missionaries. Though Regular Baptists accept of no authority other than the Bible for their faith and practice, yet nearly all of the societies have a confession of faith in pamphlet form for distribution among its members. The "New Hampshire Confession of Faith," which contains nineteen Articles, is more generally used among the societies in the North and East, while the "Philadelphia Confession of Faith," which embodies twenty-five Articles, is the one generally adopted in the South. The American

Baptist churches are more rigid on the question of "close communion" than are the British Baptist churches. The German Baptists of America, commonly known as Dunkers, but who denominate themselves Brethren, originated at Schwarzenau, in Germany, in 1708, were driven by persecution to America, between the years 1719 and 1729. They purposely neglect any record of their proceedings, and are opposed to statistics, which they believe to foster pride. They originally settled in Pennsylvania, but are now most numerous in Ohio and Indiana.

The regular Baptists, unlike most of the Protestant denominations, have no distinctive creed which is made a test of fellowship. They have, however, a "visible church" and an "invisible church," which duplex order of things, unlike the Church of Christ as founded by his apostles, is the source of much confusion and mysticism. The spiritual birth, as taught by Baptists, brings sinners into the "invisible church," while, at the same time, regenerated sinners in the "invisible church," can not come into the "visible church"—into the Baptist Church—until they are immersed! To say the least, this is not New Testament teaching. Though Baptists may not intend it, this is a practical denial that baptism, as the consummating act in the divine process, is for the remission of sins—a positive contradiction of the words of the apostle Peter on the day of Pentecost. Baptists teach that sinners are directly illuminated and regenerated by the special and mystic influence of the Holy Spirit, without the mediation of the Word of God, and that a special grace, not revealed in the gospel, is necessary to convict and convert the sinner. This is a practical nullification of "the gospel" as "the power of God unto salvation to all them who believe." They claim that by the direct regenerating influence of the Spirit, the convicted sinner is made *conscious*, without the testimony of God's word, of the forgiveness of sins, and of justification, and of adoption into the family of God—into the "invisible church." He is called upon to give a "Christian experience," of what he *saw and felt*, as an evidence of pardon, thus setting aside the Word of God, or the law of pardon in the gospel, as the only revealed evidence. The convert tells what the Lord has done for him through the strivings of the Spirit, and instead of relying on the testimonies of God's word for evidence of pardon, such as was preached by the apostles, he revels in dreams and fancies, and substitutes his *feelings*, called a "Christian experience," for the law of pardon, as proclaimed by the apostles in the name of Jesus Christ.

According to such mystical teaching, the sinner is regenerated, born of God, saved, justified, sanctified, adopted, and made a child of God without the birth of baptism! And yet this alleged child of God—directly regenerated by the Holy Spirit, saved from his sins, justified, sanctified and adopted—can not enter the Baptist Church—the "visible church"—until he is immersed! Here is the startling disclosure made that immersion is a "*non-essential*" in constituting a sinner a child of God—a citizen of the "invisible kingdom"—but that in order to become a child in the Baptist family—a member in the "visible church"—immersion is made very *essential!* Such mystical teaching did not obtain in the apostolic church, and hence we have good reason for rejecting it. As neither Christ nor the apostles ever founded a Baptist Church, nor taught the *direct* agency of the Holy Spirit in the conversion of sinners, nor appointed "monthly meetings" where converts might give the "experience" of their *feelings* as an evidence of pardon, nor appointed the celebration of the Lord's Supper but once a month, we reject all such theology as unscriptural and non-apostolic. By such dreamy speculation, and with no other evidence but the *feelings* of the misguided sinner, the Baptists contradict (through ignorance of the plan of salvation, it may be) the doctrine that the *Word of God is the "sword of the Spirit,"* which "kills and makes alive." Surely with such evidence before us, we dare not say that the Baptist Church is identical with the Church of Christ, which the apostles founded, and who made immersion into the name of the Father, and of the Son, and of the Holy Spirit, essential to salvation, a doctrine which the Baptist Church ignores.

ORIGIN OF METHODISM.

JOHN WESLEY, the founder of Methodism, was born at Epworth, Lincolnshire, England, June 17, 1703. He was raised in the Church of England, was ordained a priest in 1728, by Bishop Potter, and died an Episcopalian. At the age of thirty-five he was scarcely known beyond the academic circles of Oxford. From childhood he was deeply devout and religious and conscientious, which characteristics he inherited from a mother of superior endowments and of rare excellency of character. His love of learning was very strong, and he was very studious at college, but "his poverty held him back from the costly vices which enslaved many of his college companions." It is said by one of his biographers that his uncommonly fine traits of character, and his narrow, not to say marvelous, escape from the burning rectory when he was six years of age, gave birth in the mind of his mother to an impression that this child was destined to an extraordinary career. She therefore consecrated him to God with special solemnity, resolving "to be more particularly careful . . to instill into his mind the principles of religion and virtue." He received some of his first religious impressions while reading the *Christian's Pattern*, by Thomas à Kempis. The perusal of Law's *Christian Perfection* and *Serious Call* deepened these convictions, "and led him to devote himself, soul, body and substance, to the service of

God." "But, owing to his failure to comprehend the scriptural doctrine of salvation by faith only, he groped in the dark through thirteen years of ascetic self-denial, ritualistic observances, unceasing prayer, and works of charity, before he gained an assurance that God, for Christ's sake, had pardoned his sins." And his change of heart, "through those long, wearisome, comfortless years of seeking God without finding him," is thus related:

And when, on his voyage to Savannah (Ga.), he saw some pious Moravians rejoicing, while he was shaken with fears of death, amid the fury of a storm which apparently was driving them into the jaws of destruction, he did not suspect that his fear was the fruit of his erroneous views. He talked much with some of the Moravian brethren after his arrival in Savannah; but it was not until after his return to England in 1738, that Peter Bohler, a Moravian preacher in London, after much conversation, aided by the testimonies of several living witnesses, convinced him that to gain peace of mind he must renounce that dependence upon his own works which had hitherto been the bane of his experience, and replace it with a full reliance on the blood of Christ shed for *him*. To gain this faith he strove with all possible earnestness. And at a Moravian Society meeting in Aldersgate Street, while one was reading Luther's statement of the change which God works in the heart through faith, Wesley says, "I felt my heart strangely warmed. I felt I did trust in Christ, Christ alone, for salvation; and an assurance was given me that he had taken away *my* sins, even *mine*, and saved *me* from the law of sin and death." (Rev. D. Wise, D. D., in *McClintock and Strong's Enc.*, Vol. VI., p. 913.)

In November, 1729, the Wesley brothers, Whitefield and their associates, about a dozen young men, students of Oxford University—formed themselves into a society for purposes of mutual moral and spiritual improvement. As members of the Church of England, which had lost all love of souls and all desire for spiritual life through formalism and ritualism, these young men sought to excite new life into a dead body, and to stimulate piety among a people where none existed. In view of the corrupt and lifeless condition of the Church of England, they voluntarily abandoned themselves to a life of self-denial and personal consecration. By instructing the children of the neglected poor; by visiting the sick and the inmates of prisons and almshouses; by a strict observance of the fasts appointed by the Church, and by scrupulous exactness in their attendance upon public worship, they became objects of general notice. They were severely criticised and treated with contempt by their formalistic contemporaries, and, as is usual in such cases, their sincerity called in question by mockers and scoffers. Even by their fellow-students they were called in turn, *Sacramentarians, Bible-bigots, Bible-moths, the Godly Club.* One, a student of Christ-Church College, with greater reverence than his fellows, and more learning, observed, in regard to their *methodical* manner of life, that a new sect of METHODISTS had sprung up, alluding to the ancient school of physicians known by that name. The appellation obtained currency, and although the title is still sometimes used reproachfully as expressive of enthusiasm, or undue religious strictness, it has become the acknowledged designation of one of the largest bodies of religious people of modern times.

" Wesley's idea at this time, and for many years afterwards," says Keats (*History of the Free Churches of England*, p. 363), "was merely to revive the state of religion in the Church; but he knew enough of the condition of society in England, and of human nature, to be aware that unless those who had been brought under the awakening influence of the gospel met together, and assisted each other in keeping alive the fire which had been lit in their hearts, it must, in many instances, seriously diminish, if not altogether die out." By this fact it will be seen that it was no part of the design of Wesley and his associates to found a new religious sect. "*He* considered them all members of the Church of England — zealous for her welfare, and loyal to her legitimate authorities." So says a Methodist authority, because such are the facts of history.

ORIGIN OF THE METHODIST EPISCOPAL CHURCH.

THE Methodist Episcopal Church of the United States received its official title, as a distinct body, at what is historically known as the "Christian Conference," which began its sessions in Baltimore, on Friday, December 24, 1784. The first Methodist service in America is supposed to have been held in the year 1766, in the city of New York, by Philip Embury, an Irish emigrant and local preacher, a carpenter by trade, who was moved thereto by the stirring appeals of Barbara Heck, an Irish woman, whose name is illustrious in the annals of the denomination. In the course of a year or two, their numbers had considerably increased, and they wrote to John Wesley requesting him to send them out some competent preachers. Two at once offered themselves for the work, Richard Boardman and Joseph Pilmoor, who were followed in 1771 by Francis Asbury and Richard Wright. The agitations preceding the War of Independence, which soon afterwards broke out, interrupted the labors of the English Methodist preachers in America, all of whom, with the exception of Asbury, returned to England before the close of the year 1777; but their place appears to have been supplied by others of native origin, and they continued to prosper, so that, at the termination of the Revolutionary struggle, they numbered forty-three preachers and 13,740 members.

Up to this time, the American Wesleyan Methodists had laid no claim to being a distinct religious organization. Like Wesley himself, they regarded themselves as members of the English Episcopal Church, or rather of that branch of it then existing in this country, and their preachers as a body of irregular auxiliaries to the ordained clergy. It is said that "Episcopal churches are still standing in New York (or were but a few years since) and elsewhere, at whose altars Embury, Pilmoor, Boardman, Strawbridge, Asbury and Rankin, the earliest Methodist preachers, received the holy communion." But the recognition of the United States as an independent country, and the difference of feeling and interests that necessarily sprung up between the congregations in America and those in England, rendered the formation of an independent society inevitable. Wesley became conscious of this, and met the emergency in a manner as bold as it was unexpected. Himself only a presbyter in the Church of England, he persuaded himself that in the primitive Church a presbyter and a bishop were one and the same order, differing only as to their official function, he, assuming the office of the latter, and, with the assistance of some other presbyters who had joined his movement, set apart and ordained Rev. Thomas Coke, D. C. L., of Oxford University, bishop of the infant church, September 2, 1784. Coke immediately sailed for America, and appeared, with his credentials, at the Conference held at Baltimore, December 25th, of the same year. He was unanimously recognized by the assembly of preachers, appointed Asbury coadjutor bishop, and ordained several preachers to the offices of deacon and elder. Wesley also granted the preachers permission (which shows the extensive ecclesiastical power he wielded) to organize a separate and independent church under the Episcopal form of government: hence arose the "Methodist Episcopal Church in the United States of America."

To facilitate the work of Coke and Asbury, Wesley furnished them with a "Sunday Service," or liturgy, a collection of songs and hymns, and also "The Articles of Religion," twenty-four of them, which he selected from the Thirty-nine Articles of the Book of Prayer, and which he revised for the benefit of the churches in the United States. Upon the arrival of Coke in America, accompanied by his ordained elders and deacons (he being ordained by Wesley "superintendent"— afterwards tortured into *bishop*), a special conference or convention of the itinerant preachers was summoned, and on the 24th of December, sixty of them assembled in the Lovely Lane Chapel in the city of Baltimore. Dr. Coke took the chair, and presented the following letter from Wesley, written eight days after the ordinations, and tersely stating the grounds of what he had done and advised. As this letter contains the pith of Episcopal Methodism, we give it entire:

To Dr. Coke, Mr. Asbury, and our Brethren in North America:

By a very numerous train of providences, many of the provinces of North America are totally disjoined from their mother country, and erected into independent States. The English government has no authority over them, either civil or ecclesiastical, any more than over the States of Holland. A civil authority is exercised over them, partly by the Congress and partly by the provincial assemblies; but no one either exercises or claims any ecclesiastical authority at all. In this peculiar situation, some thousands of the inhabitants of these States desire my advice; and in compliance with their desire, I have drawn up a little sketch.

Lord King's account of the Primitive Church, convinced me, many years ago, that bishops and presbyters are of the same order, and consequently have the same right to ordain. For many years I have been importuned, from time to time, to exercise this right, by ordaining part of our traveling preachers. But I have still refused, not only for peace' sake, but because I was determined as little as possible to violate the established order of the National Church, to which I belonged.

But the case is widely different between England and North America. Here there are bishops who have a legal jurisdiction. In America there are none, neither any parish ministers: so that for some hundred miles together there is none either to baptize or to administer the Lord's Supper. Here, therefore, my scruples are at an end, and I conceive myself at full liberty, as I violate no order and invade no man's right, by appointing and sending laborers into the harvest.

I have accordingly appointed Dr. Coke and Mr. Francis Asbury to be joint superintendents over our brethren in North America, as also Richard Whatcoat and Thomas Vasey to act as elders among them, by baptizing and administering the Lord's Supper. And I prepared a liturgy little differing from that of the Church of England (I think, the best constituted national church in the world), which I advise all the traveling preachers to use on the Lord's Day in all the congregations, reading the litany only on Wednesdays and Fridays, and praying extempore on all other days. I also advise the the elders to administer the Supper of the Lord on every Lord's Day.

If any one will point out a more rational and scriptural way of feeding and guiding those poor sheep in the wilderness, I will gladly embrace it. At present I can not see any better method than I have taken.

It has, indeed, been proposed to desire the English bishops to ordain part of our preachers for America; but to this I object: (1) I desired the bishop of London to ordain only one; but could not prevail. (2) If they consented, we know the slowness of their proceedings; but the matter admits of no delay. (3) If they would ordain them now, they would likewise expect to govern them; and how grievously would this entangle us! (4) As our American brethren are now totally disentangled, both from the State and the English hierarchy, we dare not entangle them again, either with the one or the other. They are now at full liberty simply to follow the Scriptures and the Primitive Church. And we judge it best that they should stand in that liberty wherewith God has so strangely made them free.

After the reading and consideration of this document, it was, without a single dissenting voice, regularly and formally "agreed to form a Methodist Episcopal Church, in which the liturgy (as presented by Rev. John Wesley) should be read, and the sacraments be administered by a superintendent, elders and deacons, who shall be ordained by a Presbytery, using the Episcopal form, as prescribed in Rev. Mr. Wesley's Prayer-book;" or, in the language of the Minutes of the Conference, "following the counsel of Mr. John Wesley, who recommended the Episcopal mode of government, we thought it best to become an Episcopal Church, making the Episcopal office elective, and the elected superintendent or bishop amenable to the body of ministers and preachers."

Wesley was an Episcopalian, and thoroughly believed in the Episcopal form of church government. "I firmly believe," he said, "I am a scriptural *Episcopos*, as much as any man in England or in Europe;" but he did not believe in an "uninterrupted succession." When he ordained Coke a "superintendent," he ordained him a bishop. He objected to the title as it was used in the English Church, but did not object to the thing itself. He was opposed to the abuse of the office, not the use of it. At any rate, the Episcopacy of the English Church was incorporated into the Methodist Church of America, with three orders of clergy, viz.: bishops, elders and deacons.

WESLEY NOT A METHODIST.

LIKE Luther, Zwingle, Calvin and Knox, Wesley never made any attempt to return to apostolic practice, nor did either of these reformers even suggest the idea of reproducing the Church of Christ as established by the apostles. They simply aimed to *re-form* existing ecclesiastical institutions. As to Wesley, he desired to *re-form* the Church of England by vitalizing and spiritualizing its priesthood, and by arousing the activities of its membership; and, as respected his work in America, as we have already seen, it is very evident that he sought, with the tact and diplomacy of a crafty statesman, to adjust the Church of England to the peculiar political condition of the government of the United States—to a republican form of government as contrasted with a kingly government. He was a shrewd manager in politico-ecclesiastical affairs. He was a proficient in the study of adaptations of means to the consummation of proposed measures, and it is a noteworthy fact that, up to this day, the same spirit of diplomacy—the same spirit of accommodation to surrounding influences—pervades the entire fabric of the Methodist Episcopal Church. That Wesley was well acquainted with New Testament teaching, and apostolic practice, is a fact made evident in his *Explanatory Notes upon the New Testament*, in his *Doctrinal Tracts*, and in his letters of instructions to the churches. Indeed, so vigorously did he advocate baptism for remission of sins in his *Doctrinal Tracts*, that a good deal of what he said upon that subject has been expunged in the latest editions, if the work itself has not been entirely suppressed. In his letter "to Dr. Coke, Mr. Asbury, and our brethren in North America," which we reproduced in a previous article, he "advises the elders to administer the Supper of the Lord *on every Lord's Day*" (which sounds very apostolic), and leaves them "at full liberty simply to *follow the Scriptures* and the *Primitive Church*" (which also sounds very apostolic). And it looks very apostolic when we quote and read the following words from the Preface of his "New Testament Notes:" "*Would to God that all the party names, and unscriptural phrases and forms, which have divided the Christian world, were forgot; and that we might all sit down together, as humble, loving disciples, at the feet of our common Master, to hear his word, to imbibe his spirit, and to transcribe his life into our own.*"

The case of John Wesley is but another illustration of the fact that a man may, as a scholar and as an honest interpreter of historical facts, acknowledge and advocate the truth, while at the same time his judgment is swayed by ecclesiastical associations, and by a love of some particular form of theology, or by self-interest, which not unfrequently outweighs all considerations for the unity and peace of the Church of Christ. When we open histories, and read the works of commentators, and examine the critical and exegetical authorities of educated men, we are made to rejoice at the unanimity with which they all speak of apostolic precedent and practice, and to rejoice in the hope that the restoration of apostolic Christianity will soon become an accomplished fact; but when we take a survey of the religious situation, and see the persistent efforts put forth by the various Protestant denominations to maintain ecclesiastical distinctions, and to support antagonistic creeds, and to apologize for divisions, we utterly despair of realizing the unity of Christians upon the basis of the Bible. Concerning the views of Wesley on church government, we here produce one who is competent to speak. Says Dr. Curry, of the *Christian Advocate* (New York, May 25, 1871):

No fact respecting the history of John Wesley is more clearly manifest than that he was always a strenuous supporter of the authority of the Established Church of England. He jealously regarded the exclusive ecclesiastical authority of that Church in all that he did as an evangelist, and seemed always determined that while he lived and ruled—and it was always understood that he *would rule as long as he lived*—nothing should be tolerated in his societies at all repugnant to the sole and exclusive ecclesiastical authority of the Established Church. This rule was applied to his societies in America before the Revolution just as strictly as to those in England. But the political separation of America from Great Britain, as it also ended the authority of the English Church in this country, made it lawful, according to his theory of the case, for the Methodist societies in America to become regularly organized churches.

The theological tenets and dogmas of Wesleyan Methodism, with perhaps two or three modifications, are the same as those which, by common consent, are at present deemed "evangelical" or "orthodox." The articles of religion drawn up by Wesley for his immediate followers, and substantially adopted by all Methodist bodies since, are but slightly modified from those of the Established Church of England. The sermons of John Wesley, and his notes on the New Testament, are recognized by his followers in Great Britain and America as the standard of Methodism, and as the basis of their theological creed. There are, according to McClintock and Strong's *Encyclopædia*, about nine subdivisions of the Methodist body in the old country, viz: the Wesleyan Methodists; the Calvinistic Methodists; the Wesleyan Methodist New Connection; the Band-Room Methodists; the Primitive Methodists; the Byranites, or Bible Christians; the Primitive Methodists of Ireland; the Protestant Methodists; the Wesleyan Methodist Association; the Reformers; the Wesleyan Reform Union. In the United States, we have the Methodist Episcopal Church; the Methodist Episcopal Church, South; the Wesleyan Methodist Church; the African Methodist Episcopal Church; the African Methodist Episcopal (Zion) Church; the United Brethren in Christ, sometimes called German Methodists; the Evangelical Association; the Free Methodist Church; the Colored Methodist Church, besides a few others of less significance. According to the apostle Paul, all this is "carnal," and not "spiritual." "The unity of the faith" is not found in all these divisions and subdivisions. The apostles of the Lamb never founded one of these. They have all originated within a little over a hundred years. As distinct organizations, they are all of the "earth, earthy." They are all founded upon the opinions and speculations and dreams of men, and the mark of the beast is impressed upon them all. At the Pan-Presbyterian Convocation, held in Glasgow, Scotland, in 1877, Dr. Bailie declared that there were "forty branches of the Presbyterian family" in existence, but he failed to tell that "the trail of the Serpent is over them all." In making these remarks, we speak not of good men and women, and of intelligent and philanthropic men and women, in them all; but we speak of the systems of theology and of the distinct ecclesiastical organizations, which these bodies represent, as wickedly sectarian, and as a burning disgrace to the Author of Christianity.

None of these sects originated under apostolic teaching, none of them can be dated beyond the sixteenth century; and hence, as *misrepresenting* the Church of Christ, which the apostles founded, we reject them all. The Methodist theology advocates "justification by faith alone," and the preachers of that distinctive theology tell us that it is a doctrine very "full of comfort," when at the same time, be it known, that there is no such doctrine in the word of God. What they call justification by faith alone, is justification by *sensuous feeling*—an ecstasy, an illusion, a dream, a vain imagination, the delights of animal magnetism—which they tell us is wrought directly by the mystic impulse of the Holy Spirit, without illumination and conviction by the testimonies of God's word. The Methodist Church make baptism a "non-essential" to salvation, thus directly insulting the Author of the Plan of Salvation, and substituting human expediency for divine law. The Methodist Episcopal system not only lodges legislative authority in a bench of Bishops—in a General Conference—where they make and unmake rules and regulations to suit the varying conditions of the captious and exacting world, and where they devise how to catch the tide of good fortune and ride out upon the wave of popular applause, but imitating the example of Romanism, it transgresses the laws of God, changes the ordinance, and breaks the everlasting covenant. (Isaiah xxiv. 5.) The Episcopal system, wherever found, whether in the Roman Catholic Missal, the Augsburg Confession of Faith, the Heidelberg Confession of Faith, the Westminster Confession, or in the Book of Prayer, or in the Methodist Discipline, recognizes infant church-membership as the corner-stone of every pedobaptist edifice. And, setting aside immersion, as practiced by the apostles, and which by the whole world of learning has been conceded to have been the exclusive practice of the Primitive Church, these innovators upon God's Plan of Salvation have substituted *rantism* and *affusion*; and they have the effrontery to tell the sinful world that sprinkling and pouring serve the same purpose as immersion, if "only the heart is right"—as if wicked men could have a heart right in the sight of God while rejecting the positive commands of the Son of God! And where did the "Mourning Bench" system of regeneration come from? Why, it is hardly fifty years of age. President Finney, of Oberlin College, in his book on "Revivals," issued within the last thirty years, was the first man who had the courage to proclaim from the house-tops that the "mourning bench" was intended to take the place of baptism! Viewed from the angle of apostolic teaching, we surely find no reformation in all this; on the other hand, we only see *de*-formation. We find that the Methodist Discipline is but a modification of the Episcopal Book of Prayer, and that the Book of Prayer is only a modification of the Roman Catholic Missal, which had its origin in the latter part of the fifth century. All these creed-formularies are but the product of the Dark Ages.

The Episcopalian form of church government, whether found in the Romish Church, or in the Church of England, or in the Methodist Episcopal Church, or, if you please, in the Mormon Church, is to all intents and purposes a spiritual despotism, possessing not the least semblance to the apostolic order of things. Luther attempted to reform the Romish Church by striking at the rottenness of the Romish priesthood, and failed; Zwingle also failed in the same direction; Calvin attempted to reform the Romish Church by denouncing the false theological dogmas of that Church, and failed; Knox, by herculean blows, undertook to reform the despotic government of the Church of Rome, and failed; Henry VIII. made a compromise between Romanism and Protestantism, and produced the Established Church of England; Wesley essayed to reform the Church of England, and produced—the Methodist Episcopal Church! It is utterly impossible to identify any of the so-called Protestant Churches with the Church of Christ as established by his apostles. Every one of them is defective, either in doctrine or in government; and, being defective in some part, and therefore antagonistic to the authority of Jesus Christ, we accept neither the one nor the other. Remove the Pope from the Romish Church, and the system falls to pieces, because the Papacy is the center of unity in that body. Remove Episcopacy from the Church of England, and that Church falls to pieces, because Episcopacy is its center of unity. Remove Episcopacy from the Methodist Episcopal Church, and that ecclesiastical edifice falls into detached fragments, because the power which is lodged in the Twelve Bishops, and which power is exerted through the General Conference, denotes the center of unity in that body. What we propose, is unity in Jesus Christ, the Head of the Church—the Head of the One Body. And this unity never can be effected, if we must carry with us the trumpery of creeds and confessions, the ecclesiastical lumber of the Dark Ages, the dogmas and traditions and speculations of fallible men. We must unload all these, and dump them into the mystic stream of

Babylon, and let them forever disappear beneath the waves of dark oblivion. The sects of Christendom are all adrift because they do not make Christ the center of unity—because they do not "keep the unity of the Spirit in the bond of peace," and because they do not strive to bring all men "into the unity of the faith, and of the knowledge of the Son of God, unto a *perfect man*, to the measure of the stature of the fullness of Christ:" which all lovers of the truth should do, "that we henceforth be no more children, tossed to and fro, and carried about by every wind of doctrine, by the slight of men, and cunning craftiness, whereby they lie in wait to deceive; but speaking the truth in love, may grow up into him in all things, which is the Head, even Christ: from whom the whole body, fitly joined together, and compacted by the service of every joint [Macknight], according to its energy, in the proportion of each particular part, effects the increase of the body, for the edification of itself in love." (Eph. iv.)

THE REFORMATION OF THE NINETEENTH CENTURY.

THOMAS CAMPBELL came from Scotland to the United States in May, 1807, and his son Alexander landed in New York, September 9, 1809. They both settled in Washington County, Pa. When Thomas Campbell landed in Philadelphia, he found the Seceder Synod in session, and, upon presenting his credentials, he was cordially received, and at once assigned by this Synod to the Presbytery of Chartiers in Western Pennsylvania. Both father and son were educated from childhood in the Westminster Confession of Faith.

When the Campbells landed on the shores of America, they found the various denominations in a deplorable condition, and the Presbyterian "branches" were, if anything, more powerless, as spiritual agencies, than any other "branch of the Church." All around, as they viewed the religious horizon, and as they gazed upon broken ranks of fiery zealots, they saw nothing but dissension and disunion. Bigotry, party intolerance, and sectarian selfishness, were everywhere phenomenal of divided churches, and of distracted members. Infidelity—gross infidelity—was fattening and waxing wanton on the spoils of an inglorious conquest. The aspect of religious affairs was dark and gloomy in the extreme. The great soul of Thomas Campbell was moved within him when he saw that the whole land was given over to the idolatrous worship of opinions, speculative theology, scholastic dogmas and men-made creeds, and to visions and dreams, and to mysticism and dreary superstition. He saw that where there is "no vision"—no divine revelation—the "people perish," for want of spiritual food. In the fearfully distracted condition of things, he saw the immediate necessity of providing an antidote, and that antidote was to be found in pleading for Christian union, in making an effort to remove all barriers, and in a determination to unite all hearts, if possible, upon the Word of God, as the only solvent of an intolerable evil. While yet in Scotland, the Campbells, and especially Thomas (for Alexander was not yet out of his teens), were impressed with the necessity and desirability of discussing Christian union by an appeal to the Word of God, and this necessity and desirability was impressed upon his mind by the "Haldanean reformation" in that country—inaugurated by Robert and J. A. Haldane —and by reading the discussions of such eminent Independents as Archibald McLean, Alexander Carson, William Jones, David Dale and Greville Ewing. Simultaneous with the movement of the Campbells in Washington County, Pa., there was a similar movement in Kentucky, led by a man of pronounced abilities, Barton W. Stone, whose movement for reform was subsequently absorbed in the stronger movement of the Campbells.

Thomas Campbell was witness to the severe contest, in the old country, between Presbyterianism and Prelacy, and was conversant with the history of the Covenanters, Seceders, Relief Church, Burghers, Anti-Burghers, Old and New Light Burghers and Anti-Burghers—all of which parties, in the right of private judgment and personal liberty, were trying to extricate themselves from the thralldom of Romanism, and from the clutches of a proud and imperious Prelacy. There was a pandemonium of sectism at the time the Campbells attempted a reformation of the Seceder Church, in the Presbytery of Chartiers; the Bible was a dead letter and inoperative among the people; the consciences of church communicants were fettered with Creeds and Confessions of Faith; the masses were ignorant of the Word of God; the clergy seemed to be absolutely ignorant of the rules of Bible interpretation; the various sects were quarreling and fighting over party shibboleths, and ungodly rivalry existed among the Protestant denominations; a line of distinction was clearly marked between the "clergy and the laity;" the denominations were all lost to the apostolic order of things.

The Seceder congregations in Washington County were much pleased with the accession of Thomas Campbell to their ministry, to whom they became strongly attached. His high order of talents rendered him very popular among the people. Soon, however, suspicions began to arise in the minds of his ministerial brethren that he was too much disposed to relax the rigidness of their ecclesiastical rules, and to cherish for sister denominations feelings of good will and fraternity in which they were unwilling to share. They watched his movements with jaundiced eyes, and avoided him with ill concealed feelings of envy, because he went among the destitute, who had for a long time been deprived of the ministrations of the gospel, and administered the Lord's Supper to other branches of the Presbyterian family. Mr. Wilson, a young minister, at the first meeting of the Presbytery, laid the case before it in the usual form of "libel," containing various formal and specified charges, the chief of which were that Mr. Campbell had failed to inculcate strict adherence to the church standard and usages, and that he had even expressed his disapproval of some things contained in said standard. Placed upon the defensive, he was somewhat guarded and conciliatory in his replies. His pleadings in behalf of Christian liberty and common fraternity were in vain, and his appeals to the Bible were wholly disregarded; and though he persisted that he had violated no precept of the Sacred Volume, the Presbytery finally found him deserving of censure for not adhering to the "Secession Testimony." Against this decision Thomas Campbell protested, and his case was, not long afterward, submitted to the first meeting of the Synod. In the meantime, he was apprised of the fact that many of his fellow-ministers had become inimical to him through the influence of those who conducted the prosecution; and knowing well that it was impossible for him, with his views of the Bible, and of the right of private judgment, he clearly perceived that if the Synod should sanction the decision of the Presbytery, he must at once cease to be a minister in the Seceder branch of the Presbyterian family. Anxious to avoid a collision which might prove detrimental to his usefulness, and which might excite discord and alienation, and still cherishing the desire to co-operate with those with whom he had been so long associated, he addressed an earnest appeal to the Synod, which was to be presented to that august body at its first meeting. The appeal was addressed, "To the Associate Synod of North America." That the reader may judge of the *animus* of this "appeal," and get an idea of the incipient stages of the great reformatory movement, which, in the course of time, was destined to shake the whole religious world, we make the following extract:

Is it, therefore, because I plead the cause of scriptural

and apostolic worship of the Church, in opposition to the various errors and schisms which have so awfully corrupted and divided it, that the brethren of the Union should feel it difficult to admit me as their fellow-laborer in that blessed work? I sincerely rejoice with them in what they have done in that way; but still, all is not yet done; and surely they can have no objections to go further. Nor do I presume to dictate to them or to others as to how they should proceed for the glorious purpose of promoting the unity and purity of the Church; but only beg leave, for my own part, to walk upon such pure and peaceable ground that I may have nothing to do with human controversy, about the right or wrong side of any opinion whatsoever, by simply acquiescing in what is written, as quite sufficient for every purpose of faith and duty; and thereby to influence as many as possible to depart from human controversy, to betake themselves to the Scriptures, and, in so doing, to the study and practice of faith, holiness and love. And all this without any intention on my part to judge or despise my Christian brethren who may not see with my eyes in those things which, to me, appear indispensably necessary to promote and secure the unity, peace and purity of the Church. Say, brethren, what is my offense, that I should be thrust out from the heritage of the Lord, or from serving him in that good work to which he has been graciously pleased to call me? For what error or immorality ought I to be rejected, except it be that I refuse to acknowledge as obligatory upon myself, or to impose upon others, anything as of Divine obligation for which I can not produce a *"Thus saith the Lord?"* This, I am sure, I can do, while I keep by his own word; but not quite so sure when I substitute my own meaning or opinion, or that of others, instead thereof.

In the same "appeal," he says: "And I hope it is no presumption to believe that saying and doing the very same things that are said and done before our eyes on the sacred page, is infallibly right, as well as all-sufficient for the edification of the Church, whose duty and perfection is to be in all things conformed to the original standard." After the reading of this protest, and the hearing of the case before the Synod, it was decided that "there were such informalities in the proceedings of the Presbytery in the trial of the case as to afford sufficient reason to the Synod to set aside their judgment and decision, and to release the protester from the censure inflicted by the Presbytery"—which they accordingly did. After this, the charges which had been before the Presbytery, with all the papers pertaining to the trial, were referred to a committee, who finally reported as follows:

"Upon the whole, the committee are of opinion that Mr. Campbell's answers to the two first articles of charge are so evasive and unsatisfactory, and highly equivocal upon great and important articles of revealed religion, as to give ground to conclude that he has expressed sentiments very different upon these articles, and from the sentiments held and professed by this Church, and are sufficient grounds to infer censure."

"From this extreme reluctance to separate from the Seceders, for many of whom, both preachers and people, he continued to cherish sentiments of Christian regard, Mr. Campbell was induced to submit to this decision, handing in at the same time a declaration 'that his submission should be understood to mean no more, on his part, than an act of deference to the judgment of the court, that, by so doing, he might not give offense to his brethren by manifesting a refractory spirit.' After this concession, Mr. Campbell fondly hoped that the amicable relations formerly existing between him and the Presbytery of Chartiers would be restored, and that he would be permitted to prosecute his labors in peace. In this, however, he soon found himself mistaken, and discovered, with much regret, that the hostility of his opponents had been only intensified by the issue of the trial, and was more undisguised than ever. Misrepresentations and calumny were employed to detract from his influence; a constant watch was placed over his proceedings, and he discovered that even spies were employed to attend his meetings, in order, if possible, to obtain fresh grounds of accusation against him." (*Memoirs of A. Campbell, Vol. I. pp.* 229-30).

Forbearance, under such circumstances, finally ceased to be a Christian virtue, and, having a thousand times more reverence for the word of God than for the selfish sectarian decrees of Synods and Presbyteries, his self-respect compelled him to secede from the Seceders, and accordingly he presented to the Synod a formal renunciation of its authority, announcing that he now abandoned "all ministerial connection" with it, and would hold himself thenceforth "utterly unaffected by its decisions." His withdrawal from the persecuting Seceders produced no interruption in his ministerial labors. Continuing to advocate toleration of private judgment and Christian union upon the basis of the Bible, the people in large numbers continued to follow him up, and to eagerly listen to his powerful pleas, wherever it was in his power to hold meetings—in school-houses, in maple groves, or in private houses. In view of the unsettled condition of religious affairs, and with a sincere desire to form a union upon the Bible alone, he proposed to the honest and conscientious persons of the Presbyterian congregations that a special meeting should be held in order to an interchange of sentiments upon the existing state of things, and to give, if possible, more distinctness to the movement in which they had thus far been co operating without any determinate arrangement. Up to this time, no separation from the religious denominations had been contemplated—no separate bond of union had been suggested; nor was there the remotest allusion to the formation of a new religious party. On the contrary, Thomas Campbell only desired to abolish sectism, and he labored to induce the different religious denominations to unite upon the Bible as the only authorized rule of faith and practice. His heart sickened at the sight of partyism, and he urged, with all the energy of his great intellect, that all religious parties should desist from shameful controversies about matters of mere opinion and expediency. Having separated himself from the Seceder branch, Mr. Campbell was soon surrounded by a large number of godly and intelligent persons, who, like himself, were disheartened with the evils growing out of sectarian envy and rivalry, and who were willing to unite with him in an effort to make the word of God the final appeal.

ATTEMPTS AT REFORMATION.

In our last article we made reference to a meeting called by Thomas Campbell, the specific object of which was to determine the course to be pursued by those who had separated themselves from the trammels of ecclesiasticism and from the domination of a persecuting Presbyterian priesthood, and from the deliberations of which meeting we date the origin of the plea for a return to apostolic teaching and practice. It is our purpose to acquaint our readers with the facts which gave rise to the reformatory movement of the nineteenth century, and to furnish the reasons of separation from all the ecclesiastical establishments of modern times. We have already traced out the origin of the Protestant sects, the origin of Protestant creedism, and have connectedly shown how one sect has grown out of another sect, and how one creed has succeeded another creed. When Thomas Campbell began his reformation, or when he first made his attempt to reform the Seceder Church, in which he held membership, he found the religious world in universal chaos. He saw no way out of this chaos, and discovered no basis of Christian union, except in the abandonment of all creedism, and in a complete restoration of the apostolic order of things.

The time for solemn consultation had arrived. There was a large assembly of interested people, all of whom seemed to feel the importance of the occasion, and to realize the responsibilities of their new religious attitude. A deep feeling of solemnity pervaded the assembly. The divine guidance was invoked, every heart seemed to be filled with prayerful solicitude, and all seemed to seek for that wisdom which comes from above. Thomas Campbell rehearsed the great question from the beginning. With unusual force he deplored the shameful existence of religious divisions, and mourned the desolations of Zion, and deprecated the ungodly rivalries of fighting sects. He called attention to the word of God as the infallible standard of spiritual truth, and as an all-sufficient guide in the Christian life, and as furnishing the only basis of Christian union and co-operation. He alluded to the departures that had been taken from the Sacred Volume, and how evil-minded men had substituted theories, speculations, opinions and human dogmas for the simplicity of the gospel of Christ, and how the Bible was set aside to make room for philosophical abstractions, and for all sorts of fancies and conceits. As the only means of removing all these evils, he insisted with great earnestness upon a radical return to the simple teachings of the holy Scriptures, and for an entire rejection of everything in the Christian world for which there could not be produced a Divine warrant. Finally, after thoroughly reviewing the premises which he and his friends occupied in the proposed reformation, he proceeded to announce, in the most simple and emphatic terms, the great regulating principle or rule which was intended to be the accepted guide of their future actions. "That rule, my highly respected hearers," said he in conclusion, "is this, that WHERE THE SCRIPTURES SPEAK, WE SPEAK; AND WHERE THE SCRIPTURES ARE SILENT, WE ARE SILENT."

13

Upon the enunciation of this supreme rule of action, a solemn silence pervaded the assembly, and thrilled with strange emotions every heart. They saw at a glance the vexatious problem solved, and in a manner so simple and rudimental, that it appeared to them like a new revelation. Here, now, at length, was an end put to all their doubts. The path of duty was now made clear. Here was the solvent of all religious strife. Encouragement seized every heart, and joy lighted up every eye, because, from henceforth, they were to take God at his word, and from this time forth they were to rely exclusively upon apostolic precept and example. All religious teaching, which consisted in remote inferences, fanciful interpretations, speculative theories, and in false rules of interpretation, was forever to be discarded—a consummation never attempted either by Luther, Zwingle, Calvin, Wesley, or by any other Protestant reformer. Whatever private opinions men might entertain in regard to matters not clearly revealed, must be reserved as private property, and must not be imposed on any one as a test of loyalty and Christian fraternity. The *silence* of the Bible must be respected equally with its positive and unquestioned revelations, which, by divine authority, were declared to be able to "make the man of God perfect, and thoroughly furnished unto every good work."

After Mr. Campbell finished his remarkable address, he called upon those present for a free and candid expression of their views. After an interval of some considerable time, the dead silence was broken by a shrewd Scotch Seceder, Andrew Munro, a bookseller and postmaster at Canonsburg, who arose and said: "Mr. Campbell, if we adopt *that* as a basis, then there is an end of infant baptism." This remark produced a profound sensation. "Of course," remarked Mr. Campbell, "if infant baptism be not found in Scripture, we can have nothing to do with it." Upon this, Thomas Acheson, of Washington, arose, greatly excited, and, advancing a short distance, exclaimed, laying his hand upon his heart: "I hope I may never see the day when my heart will renounce that blessed saying of the Scripture, 'Suffer little children to come unto me, and forbid them not; for of such is the kingdom of heaven.'" Upon saying this he was so much affected that he burst into tears, and while a deep sympathetic feeling pervaded the entire assembly, he was about to retire to an adjoining room, when James Foster, not willing that this misapplication of Scripture should pass unchallenged, cried out: "Mr. Acheson, I would remark that in the portion of Scripture you have quoted, *there is no reference whatever to infant baptism.*" Without offering a reply, Mr. Acheson passed out to weep alone; "but this incident," says Prof. Richardson, in his *Memoirs of A. Campbell*, "while it foreshadowed some of the trials which the future had in store, failed to abate, in the least, the confidence which the majority of those present placed in the principles to which they were committed. The rule, which Mr. Campbell had announced, seemed to cover the whole ground, and to be so obviously just and proper, that after further discussion and conference, it was adopted with apparent unanimity, no valid objections being urged against it."

THE WORD OF GOD THE SOLE RULE OF ACTION.

The rule of action adopted in that humble and obscure meeting was destined to revolutionize the religious world. "*Where the Scriptures speak, we speak; where these are silent, we are silent,*" is a sentiment that not only reaches back to the days of the apostles, but one which reaches into the far future with consequences of good to the world that are beyond all human estimate. For the purpose of promoting Christian union and producing peace in the religious world, and in order to carry out this purpose more effectively, it was resolved, at a meeting held on the headwaters of Buffalo Creek, August 17, 1809, that this little party of reformers would form themselves into a regular association, to be known as "The Christian Association of Washington." They then appointed twenty-one of their number to meet and confer together, and, with the counsel of Thomas Campbell, to determine the proper method by which to consummate the object of the Association. Mr. Campbell prepared his *Declaration and Address*, the object of which was not to formulate a new creed, but to set forth in a perspicuous and forcible manner the object of the movement in which he and those associated with him were enlisted. At a called and special meeting, he read the document in the presence of his brethren, that it might be approved and adopted by them. Having been unanimously adopted as an exponent of their pronounced principles, it was at once ordered to be printed, which was done September 7, 1809. We quote as follows from this "*Declaration;*" of the far reaching consequences of the principles which the document contained, neither Thomas Campbell nor his associates had a full conception:

"Our desire, therefore, for ourselves and our brethren would be, that, rejecting human opinions and the inventions of men, as of any authority, or as having any place in the Church of God, we might forever cease from further contentions about such things, returning to and holding fast by the original standard, taking the Divine Word alone for our rule, the Holy Spirit for our teacher and guide to lead us into all truth, and Christ alone as exhibited in the Word for our salvation; and that by so doing we may be at peace among ourselves, follow peace with all men, and holiness, without which no man shall see the Lord. Impressed with these sentiments, we have resolved as follows:"

I. That we form ourselves into a religious association, under the denomination of the Christian Association of Washington, for the sole purpose of promoting simple, evangelical Christianity, free from all mixture of human opinions and inventions of men.

II. That each member, according to his ability, cheerfully and liberally subscribe a specified sum, to be paid half-yearly, for the purpose of raising a fund to support a pure gospel ministry, that shall reduce to practice that whole form of doctrine, worship, discipline and government expressly revealed and enjoined in the Word of God; and also for supplying the poor with the Holy Scriptures.

III. That this society consider it a duty, and shall use all proper means within its power, to encourage the formation of similar associations; and shall, for this purpose, hold itself in readiness, upon application, to correspond with and render all possible assistance to such as may desire to associate for the same desirable and important purposes.

IV. That this society by no means considers itself a Church, nor does at all assume to itself the powers peculiar to such a society; nor do the members, as such, consider themselves as standing connected in that relation; nor as at all associated for the peculiar purposes of Church association, but merely as voluntary advocates for Church reformation, and as possessing the powers common to all individuals who may please to associate, in a peaceful and orderly manner, for any lawful purpose—namely, the disposal of their time, counsel and property, as they may see cause.

V. That this society, formed for the sole purpose of promoting simple, evangelical Christianity, shall to the utmost of its power, countenance and support such ministers, and such only, as exhibit a manifest conformity to the original standard, in conversation and doctrine, in zeal and diligence; only such as reduce to practice that simple, original form of Christianity expressly exhibited upon the sacred page, without attempting to inculcate anything of human authority, of private opinion, or inventions of men, as having place in the constitution, faith or worship of the Christian Church, or anything as matter of Christian faith or duty, for which there can not be expressly produced a "Thus saith the Lord!" either in express terms or by approved precedent.

By the wording of the foregoing statement of principles, it will be seen that the Association did not at all regard itself *as a Church*, or publish these statements as the articles of a creed, but simply to publish to the world their desire to urge "a pure evangelical reformation, by the simple preaching of the gospel, and the administration of its ordinances in exact conformity to the divine standard." Thomas Campbell wrote his *Declaration and Address* in the very midst of a paradise of religious partyism, and while sectarian rancor and hatred and jealously were consuming what little piety and spirituality were left in the country. "Each party strove for supremacy, and maintained its peculiarities with a zeal as ardent and persecuting as the laws of the land and the usages of society would permit. The distinguishing tenets of each party were constantly thundered from every pulpit, and any departure from the 'traditions of the elders,' was visited at once with the severest ecclesiastical censure. Covenanting, church politics, church psalmody, hyper-Calvinistic questions, were the great topics of the day; and such was the rigid, uncompromising spirit prevailing, that the most trivial things would produce a schism, so that old members were known to break off from their congregations simply because the clerk presumed to give out before singing *two* lines of a psalm instead of *one*, as had been the usual custom. Against this slavish subjection to custom, and to opinions and regulations that were merely of human origin, Mr. Campbell had long felt it his duty to protest; and knowing no remedy for the sad condition of things existing, except in a simple return to the plain teachings of the Bible, as alone authoritative and binding upon the conscience, he and those associated with him felt it incumbent upon them to urge this upon religious society. This they endeavored to do in the spirit of moderation and Christian love, hoping that the overture would be accepted by the religious communities around, especially by those of the Presbyterian order, whose differences were, in themselves, so trivial." (*Memoirs of A. Campbell*, Vol. I., p. 245.)

This, in brief, was the religious complexion of things when Alexander Campbell appeared upon the stage of action, who in the providence of God was destined to become the chosen and distinguished promulgator of the reformatory principles enunciated by his illustrious father. Up to the period when Alexander Campbell comes to the front, Thomas Campbell is still a Presbyterian in faith, but a free and independent thinker. While advocating Christian union upon the basis of the Bible, he still continues to baptize infants. He still continues to be trammeled by the dogmas of Calvinism, and to struggle in the meshes of ecclesiasticism, but, having placed himself upon the solid ground of honest Bible exegesis, and having adopted an infallible rule of Scripture interpretation, we shall soon see how his principle drove him, and his Presbyterian son, Alexander, back upon apostolic ground, and how the God of truth guided their feet in a way they knew not.

ATTEMPTS AT CHRISTIAN UNION.

WHILE Alexander Campbell was reading the proof-sheets of the "Declaration," in 1809, soon after his arrival in Washington from Scotland, he observed to his father: "Then, sir, you must abandon and give up infant baptism, and some other practices for which it seems to me you can not produce an express precept or an example in any book of the Christian Scriptures." To which, after some hesitancy, the father responded: "'To the law and to the testimony,' we make our appeal. If not found therein, we, of course, must abandon it." Then, as showing the perplexed condition of his mind, he added: "We could not unchurch ourselves now, and go out into the world, and then turn back again and enter the Church merely for the sake of form and decorum." When, in an accidental conversation with Rev. Mr. Riddle, of the Presbyterian Church Union, the principles of the "Declaration and Address" were introduced as matters of discussion, and when Alexander referred to the proposition that "nothing should be required as a matter of faith or duty for which a 'Thus saith the Lord' could not be produced, either in express terms or by approved precedent," "Sir," said Mr. Riddle, "these words, however plausible in appearance, are not sound. For if you follow these out, you must become a Baptist." "Why, sir," said the young Alexander, "is there in the Scriptures no express precept nor precedent for infant baptism?" The youthful enquirer was startled and chagrined that he could not produce one; and forthwith he appeals to Andrew Munro, the principal bookseller in Canonsburg, to furnish him all the treatises at his command in favor of infant baptism. He inquired for no works on the other side of the question, for at this time he had little or no acquaintance with the Baptists, and regarded them as a people comparatively ignorant and uneducated. He was thrown into a state of doubt and perplexity by pondering this law of scriptural exegesis as previously announced by his father: "We make our appeal to the law and to the testimony. Whatever is not found therein, we, of course, must abandon." He read the pedobaptist authorities in ardent hopes of fortifying his mind in favor of infant baptism. The more he investigated, the more his prejudices and predilections gave way, and the conviction gradually grew upon him that infant baptism was a human device. Thoroughly disgusted with the bald assumptions and fallacious reasonings of the pedobaptist authorities, he threw them all aside, and fled hopefully to the Greek New Testament in the fond expectation of finding convincing proof of the validity of infant baptism in the fountain head. But the plainness of the Greek text only served to strengthen his doubts. And when again he entered into a conversation with his father on this vexed question, he found him entirely willing to admit that there were neither "express terms" nor "precedent" to authorize the practice. "But," said he, "as for those who are already members of the Church and participants of the Lord's Supper, I can see no propriety, even if the scriptural evidence for infant baptism be found deficient, in their unchurching or paganizing themselves, or in putting off Christ, merely for the sake of making a new profession; and thus going out of the Church merely for the sake of coming in again."

By these continued discussions it will be perceived that a serious conflict was going on in the minds of these two men, and especially in the mind of the son, as to the question whether it were better, all things considered, to adhere to Presbyterian usages and to the "traditions of the fathers," or, enlightened by the Word of God, carry out the logic of their own rules of Bible interpretation. Being thoroughly honest men, and seeking only to know the truth, and, above all, desiring to effect Christian union exclusively upon the basis of the Bible, they determined to take the Word of God as their sole and infallible guide. The "Declaration and Address" contains the following sentiments, as illustrative of the religious condition of things then existing:

What dreary effects of those accursed divisions are to be seen, even in this highly favored country, where the sword of the civil magistrate has not yet learned to serve at the altar! Have we not seen congregations broken to pieces, neighborhoods of professing Christians first thrown into confusion by party contentions, and, in the end, entirely deprived of gospel ordinances; while, in the meanwhile, large settlements and tracts of country remain to this day destitute of a gospel ministry, many of them in little better than a state of heathenism, the churches being either so weakened by divisions that they can not send them ministers, or the people so divided among themselves that they will not receive them? Several, at the same time, who live at the door of a preached gospel, dare not in conscience go to hear it, and, of course, enjoy little more advantage in that respect than living in the midst of heathens.

Not discouraged by the small progress made toward

Christian union, and not dismayed by the powerful opposition he encountered from his former Presbyterian brethren, he thus, from time to time, addresses his little band:

"Dearly beloved brethren, why should *we* deem it a thing incredible that the Church of Christ, in this highly favored country, should resume that original unity, peace and purity, which belong to its constitution and constitute its glory? Or is there anything that can be justly deemed necessary for this desirable purpose but to conform to the model and adopt the practice of the primitive Church, expressly exhibited in the New Testament? Whatever alterations this might produce in any or in all of the churches, should, we think, neither be deemed inadmissible nor ineligible. Surely such alteration would be every way for the better and not for the worse, unless we should suppose the divinely-inspired rule to be faulty or defective. Were we, then, in our church constitution and managements to exhibit a complete conformity to the apostolic Church, would we not be in that respect as perfect as Christ intended us to be? And should not this suffice us?"

FUNDAMENTAL PRINCIPLES.

JUST before submitting his thirteen propositions to his brethren and to the religious world, with a view of drawing the people away from strife and contention, and in order to fix their minds upon the liberty of the gospel with which Christ makes all willing men free, he says: "Let us not imagine that the subjoined propositions are at all intended as an overture toward a new creed or standard for the Church, or as in any way designed to be made a term of communion; nothing can be further from our intention. They are merely designed to open up the way, that we may come fairly and firmly to original ground upon clear and certain premises, and take up things just as the apostles left them; and thus, disentangled from the accruing embarrassments of intervening ages, we may stand with evidence upon the same ground on which the Church stood at the beginning."

Here indeed was the beginning of radical work. Here was a proposition to pass back over all human authorities, over all the traditions and false dogmas of "intervening ages," and begin a thorough *restoration* of the ancient order of things. Neither Luther nor any one else since his day ever attempted such a revolution. Thomas Campbell proposed to set aside the decrees of Popes, Councils, Synods, Conferences and General Assemblies, and to ignore all the traditions and corrupt practices of an apostate Church, and to build upon Christ alone. Here was an invitation to come directly to the primitive model—to return to pristine purity and perfection—and, consentaneous with that act, the rejection of all human innovations, and the repudiation of all human authority. It seems as though God guided and guarded the hand that penned such grand and startling propositions.

What a mighty revolution have these propositions wrought within the last half century. The thoughts contained in these propositions have changed and modified the theology of the entire religious world, have influenced every pulpit, have changed the tone of every religious journal, and still continue to challenge investigation. As the propositions referred to are not accessible to many of our readers, we think we are rendering valuable service by reproducing several, if not all, of them in this connection.

PROPOSITION 1. That the Church of Christ upon earth is essentially, intentionally and constitutionally one; consisting of all those in every place that profess their faith in Christ and obedience to him in all things according to the Scriptures, and that manifest the same by their tempers and conduct; and none else, as none else can be truly and properly called Christians.

2. That, although the Church of Christ upon earth must necessarily exist in particular and distinct societies, locally separate one from the other, yet there ought to be no schisms, no uncharitable divisions among them. They ought to receive each other, as Jesus Christ hath also received them, to the glory of God. And, for this purpose, they ought all to *walk by the same rule; to mind and speak the same things,* and to be perfectly joined together in the same mind and in the same judgment.

3. That, in order to this, nothing ought to be inculcated upon Christians as articles of faith, nor required of them as terms of communion, but what is *expressly taught and enjoined upon them in the Word of God.* Nor

ought anything to be admitted as of divine obligation in their Church constitution and managements, but what is *expressly enjoined by the authority of our Lord Jesus Christ* and his apostles upon the New Testament Church, either *in express terms or by approved precedent.*

4. That, although the Old and New Testaments are inseparably connected, making together but one perfect and entire revelation of the divine will for the edification and salvation of the Church, and, therefore, in that respect can not be separated; yet, as to what directly and properly belongs to their immediate object, *the New Testament is as perfect a constitution for the worship, discipline and government of the New Testament Church, and as perfect a rule* for the particular duties of its members, as the Old Testament was for the worship, discipline and government of the Old Testament Church and the particular duties of its members.

5. That with respect to commands and ordinances of our Lord Jesus Christ, where the Scriptures are silent as to the express time or manner of performance, if any such there be, *no human authority has power to interfere in order to supply the supposed deficiency by making laws for the Church,* nor can anything be more required of Christians in such cases but only that they *so* observe these commands and ordinances as will evidently answer the declared and obvious ends of their institution. Much less has any human authority power to impose new commands or ordinances upon the Church, which our Lord Jesus Christ *has not enjoined.* Nothing ought to be received into the faith or worship of the Church, or be made a term of communion among Christians, that is not *as old as the New Testament.*

6. That although inferences and deductions from Scripture premises, when fairly inferred, may be truly called the doctrine of God's holy word, yet are they not formally binding upon the consciences of Christians further than they perceive the connection, and evidently see they are so, for their faith must not stand in the wisdom of men, but in the power and veracity of God. Therefore no such deductions can be made terms of

communion, but do properly belong to the after and progressive edification of the Church. Hence, it is evident that *no such deductions or infcrential truths* ought to have any place in the Church's Confession.

Proposition 12 reads as follows:

That all that is necessary to the highest state of perfection and purity of the Church upon earth is, first, that none be received as members but such as, having that due measure of scriptural self-knowledge described above, do profess their faith in Christ and obedience to him in all things according to the Scriptures; nor, secondly, that any be retained in her communion longer than they continue to manifest the reality of their profession by temper and conduct. Thirdly, that her ministers, duly and scripturally qualified, inculcate none other things than those very articles of faith and holiness expressly revealed and enjoined in the Word of God. Lastly, that in all their administrations they keep close by the observance of all divine ordinances, *after the example of the primitive Church, exhibited in the New Testament, without any additions whatsoever of human opinions or inventions of men.*

We have *italicized* certain phrases in these propositions, in order to enlist the special attention of our readers. The sentiments contained in these propositions are the sentiments strenuously advocated by the friends of the *Review*, and the same that we have persistently urged in the past. These sublime statements constitute no creed, but they simply indicate the fixed purpose of the author, which is also our fixed purpose, viz: the complete restoration of the primitive order of things, in commands, precepts, ordinances, worship and discipline.

THE RESTORATION.

In defending his thirteen propositions against the heated assaults of his Presbyterian ministerial brethren, who tried in every possible way to inveigle him in self-contradictions and inconsistencies, Thomas Campbell sought to draw a distinction between faith and opinion, between an express scriptural declaration and inferences which may be deduced from it. By the latter were meant such conclusions as were not *necessarily involved* in the Scripture premises, and which were to be regarded as private opinions, and not to be made a rule of faith or duty to any one. In order to obtain the true meaning of Scripture, "the whole revelation was to be taken together, or in its due connection upon every article, and not on any detached sentence." If, in consequence of thus allowing full freedom of opinion, any should bring forward the charge of latitudinarianism, they are requested to consider whether this charge does not lie against those who add their opinions to the Word of God, rather than against those who insist upon returning to the profession and practice of the primitive Church. A return to the Bible, he insisted, was the only way to get rid of existing sectarian evils. He goes on to say that "a manifest attachment to our Lord Jesus Christ in faith, holiness and charity, was the original criterion of Christian character; the distinguishing badge of our holy profession; the foundation and cement of Christian unity. But now, alas! and long since, an external name, a mere educational formality of sameness in the profession of a certain standard or formula of human fabric, with a very moderate degree of what is called morality, forms the bond and foundation, the root and reason of ecclesiastical unity. Thomas Campbell speaks like an oracle, as he continues his arraignment of the hypocritical clergy of his day, of whom we find a counterpart in the present day. What was then true of the clerical profession is still true. "Can an Ethiopian change his skin, or a leopard his spots?" Referring to those who love the creed above the Bible, and who prefer leadership in sectarian division to the unity of hearts in Christ, he says:

Take from such the technicalities of their profession, the shibboleth of party, and what have they more? What have they left to distinguish and hold them together? As to the Bible, they are little beholden to it; they have learned little from it, they know little about it, and therefore depend as little upon it. Nay, they will even tell you it would be of little use to them without their formula; they could not know a Papist from a Protestant by *it*; that merely by *it* they could neither keep the Church nor themselves right for a single week. You might preach to them what you please, they could not distinguish truth from error. Poor people! it is no wonder they are so fond of their formula. Therefore they that exercise authority upon them, and tell them what they are to believe and what they are to do, are called benefactors. These are the reverend and right reverend authors, upon whom they *can* and *do* place a more implicit confidence than upon the holy apostles and prophets. These plain, honest, unassuming men, who would never venture to say or do anything in the name of the Lord without an express revelation from heaven, and, therefore, were never distinguished by the venerable title of "Rabbi" or "Reverend," but just simply Paul, John, Thomas, etc.—*these* were but servants. They did not assume to legislate, and, therefore, neither assumed nor received any honorary titles among men, but merely such as were descriptive of their office. And how, we beseech you, shall this gross and prevalent corruption be purged out of the visible professing Church but by a radical reform, but by a returning to the original simplicity, the primitive purity of the Christian institution, and, of course, taking up things just as we find them upon the sacred page? And who is there that knows anything of the present state of the Church, who does not perceive that it is generally overrun with the aforesaid evils? Or who, that reads his Bible, and receives the impressions it must necessarily produce upon the receptive mind by the statements it exhibits, does not perceive that such a state of things is as distinct from genuine Christianity as oil is from water?

In opposition to the claim made that a creed secures uniformity of belief and purity of doctrine, history attests that Arians, Socinians, Arminians, Calvinists and Antinomians, have existed under the Westminster Confession, and under the Athanasian Creed or the Articles of the Church of England.

"Will any one say," it is asked, "that a person might not with equal ease, honesty and consistency, be an Arian or a Socinian in his heart while subscribing to the Westminster Confession or the Athanasian Creed, as while making his unqualified profession to believe everything that the Scriptures declare concerning Christ? —to put all that confidence in him, and to ascribe all that glory, honor and thanksgiving and praise to him professed and ascribed to him in the divine word? If you say not, it follows, of undeniable consequence, that the wisdom of men, in those compilations, has effected what the divine wisdom either could not, would not, or did not do in that all perfect and glorious revelation of his will contained in the Holy Scriptures. Happy emendation! Blessed expedient! Happy, indeed, for the Church that Athanasius arose in the fourth century to perfect what the apostles had left in such a crude and unfinished state? But if, after all, the divine wisdom did not think proper to do anything more, or anything else, than is already done in the sacred oracles, to settle and determine those important points, who can say that he determined such a thing as should be done afterward? Or has he anywhere given us any intimation of such an intention?"

In regard to the charge of an intention to make a new party, Thomas Campbell said, in further defense of his Thirteen Propositions: "If the divine word be not the standard of a party, then are we not a party, for we have adopted no other. If to maintain its alone-sufficiency be not a party principle, then we are not a party. If to justify this principle by our practice in making a rule of it, and of it *alone*, and not of our own opinions, nor those of others, be not a party principle, then we are not a party. If to propose and practice neither more nor less than it expressly reveals and enjoins be not a partial business, then we are not a party. These are the very sentiments we have approved and recommended, as a society formed for the express purpose of promoting Christian unity in opposition to a party spirit."

We have thus quoted copiously from the writings of Thomas Campbell, while he was yet a Presbyterian in name, if not in faith, to give our readers a clear conception of the origin of the so-called "Reformation" of the nineteenth century, and to show also that the plea we are now making in favor of a complete *restoration* of primitive Christianity is based upon the principles contained in that remarkable document styled the "Declaration and Address." Says Dr. Richardson, in his *Memoirs of A. Campbell:* "So fully and so kindly was every possible objection considered and refuted, that *no attempt was ever made by the opposers of the proposed movement to controvert directly a single position which it contained.*" Says the same biographer: "To all the propositions and reasonings of this Address, Alexander Campbell gave at once his hearty approbation, as they expressed most clearly the convictions to which he had himself been brought by his experience and observation in Scotland, and his reflections upon the state of religious society at large. Captivated by its clear and decisive presentations of duty, and the noble Christian enterprise to which it invited, he at once, though unprovided with worldly property, and aware that the proposed reformation would, in all probability, provoke the hostility of the religious parties, resolved to consecrate his life to the advocacy of the principles which it presented. Accordingly, when, soon afterward, his father took occasion to inquire as to his arrangements for the future, he at once informed him that he had determined to devote himself to the dissemination and support of the principles and views presented in the "Declaration and Address."

Thomas Campbell, having been solicited both by private members and by some of the ministers of the Presbyterian Church, to form an ecclesiastical union with them; and having been assured by certain Presbyterian ministers that the Presbytery generally would willingly receive him and the members of the Christian Association upon the principles they advocated, made overtures looking to that end, in the fond hope that by operating through the Presbyterian Church and its various agencies he might be enabled to advance more effectively the cause of Christian union. Alexander had little confidence that his father would succeed in propitiating the excited spirit of the Presbyterians, who stood more upon their ecclesiastical dignity than upon their love of Christian union. The "Synod of Pittsburg" assembled at Washington, Pa., on the second day of October, 1810. This august body refused to receive the reformer into their body. The grounds of their objection, it appears, were the fears they entertained in regard to the influence of the Christian Association, which, as before stated, was organized with the sole view of promoting Christian union. And it is a noteworthy fact that the Presbyterians have not, since that day, cultivated the least disposition for Christian union, upon the basis of the Bible or upon any other basis. In his address before the Synod, Mr. Campbell was careful to define clearly the position which the society occupied, and to state that it was in no sense a Church, but simply a society organized for the promotion of Christian unity. He earnestly and affectionately proposed to the Synod to be obedient to it in all things that the gospel and the law of Christ inculcated, only desiring to be permitted to advocate that sacred unity which Christ and his apostles expressly enjoined; or, in other words, that the Synod would consent to "Christian union upon Christian principles." The Synod rejected his overtures because he would not unite with them on *Presbyterian* principles.

THE BIBLE THE ONLY CREED.

WHEN Thomas Campbell, from a sense of duty, made his second appeal to the same Synod, which had in the first instance replied to him in very ambiguous terms, and asked for an explanation of the clause "many other important reasons," by which the Synod attempted to justify its action, this grave body of ecclesiastics finds one of them in the childish and frivolous pretext that Alexander had been allowed to exercise his gift of public speaking, as it alleges, "without any regular authority," or before ordination—a liberty taken both by Knox and Calvin, and one frequently granted to theological students. The unrighteousness of the rejection of the application of Thomas Campbell is made manifest by the fact that the Confession of Faith, under which the Synod acted, declares the Bible to be the only rule of faith and practice; and yet when a respectable body of Christian people ask for admission, they are ruled out —cashiered—because they will come under no other rule than the Bible! For adhering to the "only rule," admitted to be inspired and infallible, and for presuming to doubt the infallibility of the Westminster Confession —the production of uninspired men—they are rejected: rejected, not for any violation of the "only rule," but because they can not admit that a human creed or confession is in reality the "only rule." Says Dr. Richardson, in his *Memoirs of A. Campbell:* "How completely this verified the remark made by Mr. Campbell in his *Declaration and Address*, 'That a book adopted by any party as its standard for all matters of doctrine, worship, discipline and government, must be considered as the Bible of that party!' And how evident it is that, in the sectarian world, there are just as many different Bibles as there are different and authoritative explanations of the Bible, called creeds and confessions! In the case of Thomas Campbell, it was the 'Confession,' and not the Bible, that was made the standard by which one of the best men was denied religious fellowship." Is it possible for sectarian bigotry to go beyond this?

Alexander Campbell, at the age of twenty-two, now comes forward, enters the arena of public conflict, reviews the action of this Synod, and not only justifies the course pursued by his father, but takes more advanced ground than that occupied by his father. The Christian Association of Washington held its semi-annual meeting at Washington on Thursday, the first of November, 1810. Alexander, the young polemic, was not made of such stuff as to tamely submit to the proceedings of the Synod in relation to his father and the Christian Association, and he therefore resolved to avail himself of the first opportunity to examine them publicly. We have not space for the reproduction of this masterly review. As to the views entertained at this time by Alexander Campbell and his father, it appears from the contents of the address delivered on the occasion referred to, (1) that they regarded the religious parties around them as possessing the *substance* of Christianity, but as having failed to preserve "the form of sound words," in which it was proclaimed in apostolic days; and that the chief object in the proposed reformation was an effort to induce all good people to abandon every human system, and persuade them to the adoption of "this form of sound words," as the infallible basis of Christian union. (2) That they regarded each congregation as an independent organization, enjoying its own individuality, and maintaining its own internal government by elders and deacons, and yet not so absolutely independent of other congregations as not to be bound to them by fraternal and spiritual relations. (3) That they considered "lay preaching" as authorized, and denied the distinction between clergy and laity to be scriptural. (4) That they looked upon infant baptism as without direct scriptural authority, but that they were willing to let it rest as a matter of forbearance, and allow the continuance of the practice in the case of those who conscientiously approved it, as Paul and James permitted circumcision for a time in deference to Jewish prejudices. (5) That they clearly anticipated the probability of being compelled, on account of the refusal of the religious parties to accept their overture, to resolve the Christian Association into a distinct Church, in order to carry out for themselves the duties and obligations enjoined on them in the Scriptures. (6) That in receiving nothing but what was expressly revealed, they foresaw and admitted that many things deemed precious and important by the existing religious societies, must inevitably be excluded.

Where, among all the existing sects, do you find such sentiments uttered as were uttered by Thomas Campbell? Is there one prominent man among any of the denominations, at this time, who proposes such measures of reform as were instituted by Thomas Campbell? Do you hear any of our Protestant divines talk as he talked, and do you see any of them labor as he labored, to crush out sectarianism and to purify the Church of all tradition? Do you find one Protestant minister among ten thousand ministers making the least plea for Christian union upon the basis of the Bible? Not one. Intellectually and morally, in comparison with Thomas Campbell. they are all pigmies.

ALEXANDER CAMPBELL ABANDONS SECTARIANISM.

UP to March, 1812, when the first child of Alexander Campbell was born, the question of infant baptism had not given him much concern; it had not become to him a question of practical interest. Up to this period, the unity of the Church, and the overthrow of sectarianism, and the restoration of the Bible to its original position, had chiefly engaged his attention. In comparison with these objects, the question of baptism was one of small importance, and, hence, neither himself nor his father entertained any decided convictions upon this subject. About a year before the time we are speaking of, in a sermon founded on Mark xvi. 15, 16, he said: "As I am sure it is unsriptural to make this matter a term of communion, I let it *slip*. I wish to think and let others think on these matters." But the unqualified adoption of the principle, "*Where the Bible speaks, we speak; where the Bible is silent, we are silent,*" began to press upon him, and upon those who attended the Brush Run Church, where the question of baptism was beginning to be discussed as one of considerable importance. The reading and investigation of the great commission which Christ gave to his apostles, began to give him serious concern. Admitting that infant baptism was without divine warrant, the question began to assume quite a different aspect, and was now no longer, "May we safely reject infant baptism as a human invention?" but, "May we omit *believers'* baptism, which all admit to be divinely commanded?" He began to be troubled with the question, "If the baptism of infants be without divine warrant, it is invalid, and they who receive it are, in point of fact, still unbaptized. When they come to know this in after years, will God accept the credulity of the parent for the faith of the child? Men may be pleased to omit *faith* on the part of the person baptized, but will God sanction the omission of *baptism* on the part of the believer, on the ground that in his infancy he had been the subject of a ceremony which had not been enjoined? On the other hand, if the practice of infant baptism can be justified by inferential reasoning or any sufficient evidence, why should it not be adopted or continued by common consent, without further discussion?"

Such were some of the reasonings which, at this time, pressed heavily upon the clear mind and honest heart of the youthful Alexander Campbell. Having finally abandoned all uninspired authorities, he began a critical examination of the words rendered *baptism* and *baptize* in the original Greek, and, as a result of his research, he became thoroughly satisfied that they could mean only *immersion* and *immerse.* Further investigation led him to the clear and indisputable conviction that believers, and believers only, are proper scriptural subjects of baptism. The searching investigations he instituted, led him to perceive that the rite of sprinkling, to which he had been subjected in infancy, was wholly unauthorized, and that consequently he was, in point of fact, an unbaptized person, and hence could not, consistently, preach a baptism to others of which he himself had never been a subject. Concerning the immersion of A.

Campbell and others, we quote the following interesting narrative from the *Memoirs of A. Campbell:*

As he was not one who could remain long without carrying out his convictions of duty, he resolved at once to obey what he now, in the light of the Scriptures, found to be a postive divine command. Having formed some acquaintance with a Matthias Luce, a Baptist preacher, who lived above Washington, he concluded to make application to him to perform the rite, and, on his way to visit him, called to see his father and the family, who were then living on a little farm between Washington and Mt. Pleasant. Soon after arriving, his sister Dorothea took him aside, and told him that she had been in great trouble for some time about her baptism. She could find, she said, no authority whatever for infant baptism, and could not resist the conviction that she never had been scripturally baptized. She wished him, therefore, to represent the case on her behalf, to her father. At this unexpected announcement, Alexander smiled, and told her that he was now on his way to request the services of Mr. Luce, as he had himself determined to be immersed, and would lay the whole case before their father. He took the first opportunity, accordingly, of presenting the matter, stating the course he had pursued and the conclusions he had reached. His father, somewhat to his surprise, had but little to say, and offered no particular objection. He spoke of the position they had heretofore occupied in regard to this question, but forbore to urge it in opposition to Alexander's conscientious convictions. He finally remarked, "I have no more to add. You must please yourself." It was suggested, however, that in view of the public position they occupied as religious teachers and advocates of reformation, it would be proper that the matter should be publicly announced and attended to amongst the people to whom they had been accustomed to preach; and he requested Alexander to get Mr. Luce to call with him on his way down, at whatever time might be appointed.

Wednesday, the 12th day of June, 1812, having been

selected, Elder Luce, in company with Elder Henry Spears, called at Thomas Campbell's on their way to the place chosen for the immersion, which was the deep pool in Buffalo Creek, where three members of the Association had formerly been baptized. Next morning, as they were setting out, Thomas Campbell simply remarked that Mrs. Campbell had put up a change of raiment for herself and him, which was the first intimation given that they intended also to be immersed. Upon arriving at the place, as the greater part of the members of the Brush Run Church, with a large concourse of others, attracted by the novelty of the occasion, were assembled at David Bryant's house, near the place, Thomas Campbell thought it proper to present, in full, the reasons which had determined his course. In a very long address he accordingly reviewed the entire ground which he had occupied, and the struggles that he had undergone in reference to the particular subject of baptism, which he had earnestly desired to dispose of, in such a manner, that it might be no hindrance in the attainment of Christian unity which he had labored to establish upon the Bible alone. In endeavoring to do this, he admitted that he had been led to overlook its importance, and the very many plain and obvious teachings of the Scriptures on the subject; but having at length attained a clearer view of duty, he felt it incumbent upon him to submit to what he now plainly saw was an important Divine institution. Alexander afterward followed in an extended defense of their proceedings, urging the necessity of submitting implicitly to all God's commands, and showing that the baptism of believers only was authorized by the Word of God.

Seven persons were immersed—Alexander Campbell and his wife; his father and mother, and his sister; with James Hanen and his wife, the latter being a very intelligent and courageous woman. Alexander had stipulated with Elder Luce that the ceremony should be performed precisely according to the apostolic pattern, and that, as there was no account given to show that converts in primitive times were called upon to give what is termed a "Christian experience," *before* they had entered upon a Christian life, this modern custom should be omitted, and that the candidates should be admitted on the simple confession that "Jesus Christ is the Son of the living God." Elder Luce at first objected, as being contrary to Baptist usage, but finally yielded, believing that the demand was right, and that he would run the risk of censure. All were, therefore, admitted to immersion upon making the simple but comprehensive confession of Christ, the same as that which was required in apostolic times. This meeting, it is related, continued about *seven hours*. From what has been related in the foregoing chapters, one can readily perceive that the results of honest investigation thus practically brought to an issue, had been reached only through a series of severe mental struggles. Thomas Campbell had been a pedobaptist minister for twenty-five years. It never entered his mind, when he first began to advocate Christian union among Presbyterians, that his principles would actually lead to the abandonment of infant baptism. Having accomplished his special mission in propounding and developing the true basis of Christian union, which, in a general way, was enunciated in his "Declaration and Address," and beyond which general principle of union he did not seem disposed to advance, his illustrious son Alexander now changed positions with him, and advanced to the front as the master-spirit of the new revolution, deeply impressed with the conviction that the hand of God was guiding him in a path of duty and responsibility not contemplated by his father.

The Brush Run congregation continued to grow, by

frequent accessions of immersed believers; and as it had been with the church organized by the Haldanes at Edinburgh, so to this church, immersion became an apt emblem of separation from the world—a separation from the traditions of an apostate Church, a separation from mystic Babylon. They adopted immersion as the only scriptural mode; they rejected infant baptism as a human invention, and the simple confession that "Jesus is the Christ, the Son of God," made to Christ by the first converts, was acknowledged as the only requirement which could be scripturally demanded of those who desired to become members of the one body. All these matters were determined by the plain and unequivocal authority of the Holy Scriptures, as, from that time to this, they have continued to be prominent features in our plea for a restoration of the apostolic order of things. They had now, indeed, become *learners* in the school of Christ; and in this respect they differed widely from all preceding reformers, in the fact that, instead of *making* creeds, *re-*forming creeds, and *re-*adjusting creeds, to suit the changing times, and to please the changeable moods of men, they sought after and adopted the Bible as their only creed, and found the basis of Christian unity alone in the word of God. They proposed no patchwork of the divine order of things, but, finally, so far as Alexander Campbell is concerned, a radical reformation was determined upon. Abandoning all creeds, as the outgrowth of human weakness, and as the groundwork of selfish sectarian rivals, he proposed a reformation *de novo*—a reformation that would eventually result in a complete *restoration*. And, hence, he instituted at once a thorough research of the entire grounds of Christianity; and, by his voluminous writings, and public debates, and by his matchless sermons, repeated and published, he rescued the Bible from the hands of priests and hireling clergy, and, in defiance of the combined assaults of the infidel world, placed Christianity upon the basis of authenticity, credibility and inspiration. He found the plan of salvation in the Scriptures, and not in a set of cold, abstract propositions; he found a Savior in the person of Jesus the Christ, and not within the pale of some sectarian church; he discovered that the Church of Christ was established in Jerusalem, and not in Rome, or at Augsburg, or at Heidelberg, or at Oxford, or at Westminster.

A. CAMPBELL UNITES WITH THE BAPTISTS.

In 1813, as in 1883, baptism, as taught by Baptists, was not a command of Jesus Christ, made essential to the salvation of a sinner, as one of the conditions of pardon and acceptance, but it was simply made a door into the "visible Church"—a door into the Baptist Church. The regenerated sinner—enlightened, saved and sanctified by the direct, irresistible energy of the Holy Spirit, without faith in testimony and without obedience to the gospel—first became a member of the "invisible Church" (whatever that is), and afterward, by a vote of a local Baptist Church, he was allowed to be baptized in order that he might have the inestimable privilege of communing with Baptists in a visible Baptist Church! On the contrary, A. Campbell and those who worshiped with him in the Brush Run congregation, made the discovery, by honest and candid investigation, that no one, under apostolic teaching, was ever received into the one body—into a state of salvation and justification—without immersion into the name of the Father, and of the Son, and of the Holy Spirit. They discovered that it was by "the *obedience* of the faith," as well as by faith in Jesus Christ as the Son of God, that the sinner came into covenant relation with God, and that by this transition act he was conveyed from "the power of darkness into the kingdom of God's dear Son." In the *Harbinger* for 1848, page 344, A. Campbell tells how he came to unite with the Baptists, and the circumstances which led to a conditional union with the Redstone Baptist Association. And here is the narrative:

"After my baptism, and the consequent new constitution of our church of Brush Run, it became my duty to set forth the causes of this change in our position to the professing world, and also to justify them by an appeal to the Oracles of God. But this was not all; the position of baptism itself to the other institutions of Christ became a new subject of examination, and a very absorbing one. A change of one's views on any radical matter, in all its practical bearings and effects upon all his views, not only in reference to that simple result, but also in reference to all its connections with the whole system of which it is a part, is not to be computed, *a priori*, by himself or by any one else. The whole Christian doctrine is exhibited in three symbols—baptism, the Lord's Supper, and the Lord's Day institution. Some, nay, very many, change their views in regard to some one of these, without ever allowing themselves to trace its connections with the whole institution of which it is either a part or a symbol. My mind, neither by nature nor by education, was one of that order. I must know now two things about everything—its *cause* and its *relations*. Hence my mind was, for a time, set loose from all its former moorings. It was not a simple change of views on baptism, which happens a thousand times without anything more, but a new commencement. I was placed on a new eminence—a new peak of the mountain of God, from which the whole landscape of Christianity presented itself to my mind in a new attitude and position.

"I had no idea of uniting with the Baptists, more

than with the Moravians or the mere Independents. I had unfortunately formed a very unfavorable opinion of the Baptist preachers as then introduced to my acquaintance, as narrow, contracted, illiberal and uneducated men. This, indeed, I am sorry to say, is still my opinion of the ministry of that Association at that day; and whether they are yet much improved I am without satisfactory evidence.

"The people, however, called Baptists, were much more highly appreciated by me than their ministry. Indeed, the ministry of some sects is generally in the aggregate the worse portion of them. It was certainly so in the Redstone Association, thirty years ago. They were little men in a big office. The office did not fit them. They had a wrong idea, too, of what was wanting. They seemed to think that a change of apparel—a black coat instead of a drab—a broad rim on their hat instead of a narrow one—a prolongation of the face and a fictitious gravity—a longer and more emphatic pronunciation of certain words, rather than Scriptural knowledge, humility, spirituality, zeal and Christian affection, with great devotion and great philanthropy, were the grand desiderata.

"Along with these drawbacks, they had as few means of acquiring Christian knowledge as they had either taste or leisure for it. They had but one, two, or, at the most, three sermons, and these were either delivered in one uniform style and order, or minced down into one medley by way of variety. Of course, then, unless they had an exuberant zeal for the truth as they understood it, they were not of the calibre, temper or attainments to relish or seek after mental enlargement or independence. I could not, therefore, esteem them, nor court their favor by offering any incense at their shrine.

I resolved to have nothing especially to do with them more than with other preachers and teachers. The clergy of my acquaintance in other parties of that day were, as they believed, educated men, and called the Baptists illiterate and uncouth men, without either learning or academic accomplishments or polish. They trusted to a moderate portion of Latin, Greek and metaphysics, together with a synopsis of divinity, ready-made in suits for every man's stature, at a reasonable price. They were as proud of their classic lore and the marrow of modern divinity, as the Baptist was of his 'mode of baptism,' and his 'proper subject' with sovereign grace, total depravity, and final perseverance.

"I confess, however, that I was better pleased with the Baptist people than with any other community. They read the Bible, and seemed to care for little else in religion than 'conversion' and 'Bible doctrine.' They often sent for us and pressed us to preach for them. We visited some of their churches, and, on acquaintance, liked the people more and the preachers less. Still I feared that I might be unreasonable, and by education prejudiced against them, and thought that I must visit their Association at Uniontown, Pa., in the autumn of 1812. I went there as an auditor and spectator, and returned more disgusted than when I went. They invited me 'to preach,' but I declined it altogether, except one evening in a private family, to some dozen preachers and twice as many laymen. I returned home, not intending ever to visit another Association.

"On my return home, however, I learned that the Baptists themselves did not appreciate the preaching of the preachers of that meeting. They regarded the speakers as worse than usual, and their discourses as not edifying—as too much after the style of John Gill and Tucker's theory of predestination. They pressed me from every quarter to visit their churches, and, though not a member, to preach for them. I often spoke to the Baptist congregations for sixty miles around. They all pressed us to join their Redstone Association. We laid the matter before the Church in the fall of 1813. We discussed the propriety of the measure. After much discussion and earnest desire to be directed by the wisdom which cometh from above, we finally concluded to make an overture to that effect, and to write out a full view of our sentiments, wishes and determinations on that subject. We did so in some eight or ten pages of large dimensions, exhibiting our remonstrance against all human creeds as bonds of communion or union amongst Christian churches, and expressing a willingness, upon certain conditions, to cooperate or unite with that Association, provided always that we should be allowed to teach and preach whatever we learned from the Holy Scriptures, regardless of any creed or formula in Christendom. A copy of this document, we regret to say, was not preserved, and, when solicited from the clerk of the Association, was refused.

"The proposition was discussed at the Association, and, after much debate, was decided by a considerable majority in favor of our being received. Thus a union was formed. But the party opposed, though small, began early to work, and continued with a perseverance worthy of a better cause. There was an Elder Pritchard, of Cross Creek, Virginia; an Elder Brownfield, of Uniontown, Penn.; an Elder Stone, of Ohio, and his son Elder Stone, of the Monongahela region, that seemed to have confederated to oppose our influence. But they, for three years, could do nothing. We boldly argued for the Bible, for the New Testament

Christianity, vex, harass, discompose whom it might. We felt the strength of our cause of reform on every indication of opposition, and constantly grew in favor with the people. Things passed along without any prominent interest for some two or three years."

The next Redstone Association convened at Cross Creek, August 30, 1816. A. Campbell was nominated, with others, as one of the speakers for the occasion. Some of the jealous-minded ministers of the Association opposed the nomination, but the opposition was overruled by other members of that body. When it came Campbell's turn to preach, he selected for his topic the following words, as quoted from Rom. viii. 3: "For what the law could not do, in that it was weak through the flesh, God sending his own Son in the likeness of sinful flesh, and for sin, condemned sin in the flesh." This was the young polemic's famous "*Sermon on the Law*," which subsequently created such wonderful excitement in the Baptist community. It was the sudden explosion, in the Baptist camp, of an apostolic bombshell. Even during its delivery, as soon as Elder Pritchard and other opposing preachers perceived its drift, they used every means openly to manifest their disapprobation A lady in the congregation having fainted, Elder Pritchard rushed into the stand, called out some of the preachers, and created great disturbance in the large assembly, apparently with a design of distracting the attention of the eager listeners. As might be expected, much misrepresentation followed the delivery of this discourse. It was on account of these misrepresentations that Mr. Campbell thought it best, soon afterward, to publish this revolutionary sermon in pamphlet form, as the most effectual means of refutation. The sermon is published in full in the

Millennial Harbinger for 1846. It is certainly a remarkable production, which is too lengthy to reproduce upon these pages. His method of analysis was as follows:

1. Ascertain what ideas we are to attach to the phrase "the law" in this and similar portions of the sacred Scriptures. 2. Point out those things which *the law* could not accomplish. 3. Demonstrate the reason why *the law* failed to accomplish these objects. 4. Illustrate how God has remedied these relative defects of *the law*. 5. In the last place, deduce such conclusions from these premises as must obviously and necessarily present themselves to every unbiased and reflecting mind.

Measured by the Philadelphia Confession of Faith, this sermon, in the estimation of those bigoted Baptists, was most unorthodox and mischievously heterodox. And these clergy were the more incensed because they found themselves incapable of answering the points taken in the sermon. The object of the sermon was, by contrasting the law of Moses with the gospel of Christ, by contrasting the Old Covenant with the New Covenant—by showing the difference between "the letter that kills" and "the law of the Spirit" that gives life—to convince his hearers that they could not be saved and justified by any system of things not authorized by Jesus Christ, the Head of the Church, and not proclaimed by his apostles. This sermon invoked the wrath of some of the Baptist clergy, and stirred up vengeful and uncompromising opposition. Subsequent to the presentation of this unanswerable address, this Baptist Association, for several consecutive years, by means of a self-constituted ecclesiastical court, brought charges of heretical teachings against Thomas and Alexander Campbell. Whenever their persecutors failed to sustain the charge of heresy, they would attempt to tamper with the ignorance and prejudices of members under their influence, and by pursuing this unchristian course lessen the unanimity of the churches in favor of the defendants in the case, and increase the chances of success in their ultimate excommunication from the Baptist communion. The two Campbells, foreseeing that it was the fixed intention of their mischievous persecutors to gain a majority of votes in favor of their excommunication, severed their connection and withdrew from the Redstone Baptist Association, and united themselves with the Mahoning Baptist Association, in Eastern Ohio, and by this step frustrated the preconcerted schemes of their malignant opponents. This Association, being much more enlightened and liberal in their views of the truth, received the two reformers, with other delegates from the feeble churches, with much cordiality and Christian affection. This Association received them upon the New Testament platform alone, to the exclusion of all human creeds and "church standards."

A SIMILAR REFORMATION IN KENTUCKY.

At the time the Campbells were urging reformation in the Presbyterian churches in Western Pennsylvania, there was a movement, similar in character, going forward in Kentucky, led by Barton W. Stone, a man of great intellectual force and possessed of rare zeal and devotion. Both Alexander Campbell and B. W. Stone sought to accomplish the same ends by the same means. Both, almost simultaneously, having discarded all human creeds, sought Christian union exclusively upon the basis of the Bible. By comparing notes, it was discovered that both were opposed to creeds as terms of communion; that both desired to propagate only the primitive gospel; that both were alike persecuted and maligned by those who, glorying in orthodoxy of opinion, failed to recognize a scriptural unity of faith; and that both, after they came to understand the sentiments of each other, repudiating the despotism of *opinionism*, accepted only of faith that was founded upon indisputable testimony. In Kentucky, the adherents of Campbell were called "Reformers," while at the same time the adherents of Stone were known as "Christians," or "*Christ*-ians." The followers of Stone had been charged with holding the doctrine of Arianism, but by intercourse with Stone and others, Campbell discovered that the charges were unjust and untrue. Campbell advocated fellowship with all who received the teachings of the Scriptures in their simple and obvious meaning, and whose conduct corresponded with these teachings. He held that there was no need of strained interpretations, no need of specious glosses or textual perversions where no theological theory was to be sustained, but where all could learn the truth by taking the Bible in its proper connections, and construing it in harmony with the established laws of language and rules of interpretation. He held that the simple truths of the gospel could be received by babes in Christ, and that upon these common truths all could be united in one body. In short, the guiding principles of Campbell were substantially the same as those which guided the actions of Stone. Both were alike devoted to the great end of uniting the true followers of Christ into one communion upon the Bible alone, but, at first, each regarded the method of its accomplishment from his own angle of vision; and since Campbell contemplated the distinct congregations, with their proper functionaries, as the highest religious executive authority on earth, he was in doubt as to how a *formal* union could be attained, whether by a general convention of messengers or by a general assembly of the people. Suffice it to say, that the coalescing of the two peoples was brought about through the spirit of Christ and of brotherly love.

Some notable men fell into the wake of the reformatory movement of B. W. Stone, such as Samuel and John Rogers, Thomas M. Allen, F. R. Palmer and John Allen Gano—all grand characters—and all of whom, in subsequent years, distinguished themselves as advocates for a restoration of the apostolic order of things. A union of the "Christians" and "Reformers," or between the "Christian Church" and the Church of the "Reformers," was directly secured through the agency of

John T. Johnson, a man of rare self-denial, a man of noble Christian integrity, as well as a natural orator. Johnson was originally a Baptist, but after examining in the light of the Bible what was vulgarly denominated "Campbellism," he separated from the Baptists, and, in 1831, he formed the nucleus of a congregation of six on the basis of the Bible. Soon after abandoning the lucrative practice of law, he began the public advocacy of the primitive gospel. Becoming intimately acquainted with B. W. Stone, who lived near Georgetown, he was urged by the latter to become co-editor of the *Christian Messenger*, to which he agreed at the close of 1831. This paper was conducted in the interests of Christian union. Johnson found that a union in sentiment and religious aims already existed between the two peoples—the "Christians" and "Reformers"—to a large extent. The consummation of the union is thus described by Prof. Richardson in his *Memoirs of A. Campbell:*

This editorial union of B. W. Stone and John T. Johnson was soon followed by a fraternal union between the "Christian" Church and that of the "Reformers" meeting in Georgetown. Agreeing to worship together, they found so much agreement in all essential matters, and so happy an effect produced in the increased number of conversions, that they were induced near the close of 1831 to appoint a general meeting at Georgetown to continue four days, for the purpose of considering the subject of a complete union between the two people. This meeting included Christmas Day, and a similar one was appointed for the following week, including New Year's Day, at Lexington. Many of the leading preachers on both sides attended and took part in these meetings, and so much evidence was afforded of mutual Christian love and confidence, and such undoubted assurances were given of a firm determination on the part of all to have nothing to do with doctrinal speculations, but to accept as conclusive upon all subjects the simple teachings of the Bible, that there seemed to be no longer anything in the way of the most earnest and hearty co-operation. After the meeting at Lexington, some further friendly conferences were held by means of committees, and, by arrangement, the members of both churches communed together on the 19th of February, agreeing to consummate the formal and public union of the two churches on the following Lord's Day, the 26th. During the week, however, some began to fear a difficulty in relation to the choice of elders and the practical adoption of weekly communion, which they thought would require the constant presence of an ordained administrator. The person who generally ministered to the Christian Church at Lexington at this time was Thomas Smith, a man of more than ordinary abilities and attainments, and long associated with the movement of B. W. Stone. He was an excellent preacher, and was considered a skillful debater. He possessed withal a very amiable disposition, and was highly esteemed by Mr. Campbell, whom he often accompanied during his visits in Kentucky. He was at first, like others, apprehensive that the proposed union was premature, and that disagreement might arise in regard to questions of church order. The union was therefore postponed, and matters remained for a short time stationary; but it soon became generally apparent that there were no exclusive privileges belonging to *preachers* as it concerned the administration of ordinances, and Thomas M. Allen coming to Lexington, induced them to complete the union and to transfer to the new congregation, thus formed under the title of "the Church of Christ," the comfortable meeting-house which they had previously held under the designation of "the Christian Church." This wise measure secured entire unanimity, and was especially gratifying to the "Reformers," who had been meeting in a rented building. At Paris, also, Mr. Allen succeeded in effecting a union between the two churches, for one of which he had himself been preaching, while James Challen at this time ministered to the other. He proposed that both he and Mr. Challen should retire, and that the united churches should engage permanently the services of Aylette Raines. This was accordingly done, and Mr. Raines, leaving his field in Ohio, from this time continued to preach for the church at Paris, as well as for other churches in Kentucky, for more than twenty years, aiding besides in numerous protracted meetings, and by his steady, unremitting labors and able advocacy of the Reformation principles greatly extending their influence."—*Memoirs of A. Campbell*, pp. 383-85.

There were present at the Lexington Conference: B. W. Stone, John F. Johnson, John (Raccoon) Smith, John Rogers, G. W. Elley and Jacob Creath, Jr.—all notable men. The adherents of Stone did not all follow him, and some of his brethren censured him for the course he had pursued. However, in the course of time, the great majority were absorbed in the common plea for Christian union. B. W. Stone had been raised a Presbyterian. He began his plea for Christian union upon the basis of the Bible in 1804, eight years before Alexander Campbell was immersed.

It is a noteworthy fact that at the very time when these events were transpiring in Kentucky, the same spirit of union was prevailing over sectarianism and bigotry and prejudice in other States also. John Longley, of Rush County, Indiana, under date of the 24th of December, 1831, says:

The Reforming Baptists and we are all one here. We hope that the dispute between you and Bro. Campbell, about names and priority, will forever cease, and that you will go on, united, to reform the world.

Griffith Cathey, of Tennessee, on the 4th of January, 1832, writes substantially as follows:

The members of the Church of Christ, and the members known by the name of Disciples, or Reformed Baptists, regardless of all charges about Trinitarianism,

Arianism and Socinianism, and of the questions whether it is possible for any person to get to heaven without immersion, or whether immersion is for the remission of sins, have come forward, given the right hand of fellowship, and united upon the plain and simple gospel.

Alexander Campbell, by his commanding talents, by his great force of character and by his invincible courage, overshadowed all other reformers, and at once, by common consent of all parties, became the acknowledged champion—the admired leader—of the great onslaught upon the sectarian world. B. W. Stone died at the age of eighty-four, after having spent his life in laboring incessantly for the union of God's people. He was a grand character, a man of noble instincts, of superior intelligence, and greatly loved and admired for his unselfish and philanthropic devotion to the cause of Christ. He lives in history as one of the most distinguished factors in the greatest religious revolution of modern times.

THE CHURCH OF CHRIST IDENTIFIED.

By degrees the Baptist Mahoning Association lost its legislative and ecclesiastical character, under the reformatory movements of the Campbells and their coadjutors, and the ministers of a free people, heretofore living under the influence of this Association, gradually lost their affection for human tradition and theological speculations, which had been made tests of Christian fellowship; so that, in due course of time, by learning how to use the rules of Bible interpretation—how to quote and apply Scriptures—how to distinguish the law from the gospel —how to distinguish the Jewish from the Christian dispensation, and the Patriarchal from the Jewish—this Association entirely lost its distinctive ecclesiastical features, and was finally absorbed by the "Big Meetings" of the "Western Reserve."

It never was in the mind of either Thomas or Alexander Campbell to start a new sect; indeed, as we have already shown, they disclaimed and abhorred the very idea; they simply sought reformation within their own ranks, as did the reformers of the three preceding centuries. But now, under the guidance of a gracious Providence, having broken away from all traditional trammels—the principles of the "Declaration and Address" pushing them to the front by logical necessity— having escaped the clerical yoke of spiritual bondage— and having accepted the Bible as their only safe and infallible guide, and acknowledging Jesus the Christ as their only infallible lawmaker and legislator, these illustrious reformers, with other mighty men of influence and eloquence, from the Protestant denominations, from this time forward began to advocate, not simply church reformation—which was all that the earlier reformers sought to accomplish—*but an entire restoration of the apostolic order of things.* They now resolved to go back beyond Philadelphia, beyond Oxford, beyond Westminster, beyond Geneva, beyond Augsburg, beyond Heidelberg, beyond Rome, and back to Jerusalem, and there begin a new survey of the great domain of apostolic Christianity. Accordingly, it was not long until the *Christian Baptist,* and other contemporaneous periodicals, were started to advocate this plea; a Bible college was organized in the interest of this plea; a host of eloquent preachers entered body and soul into the work, and, as a consequence, converts from the world and from sectariandom were made by thousands.

If Martin Luther wrested the Bible out of the hands of the Roman priesthood, and gave it to the people—which had been a sealed book to the masses—Alexander Campbell did a mightier work by wresting from the hands of the Papal and Protestant clergy false keys of Bible interpretation, while at the same time he restored to the people the only correct and approved rules of interpretation, which, without the aid of the private and mystic explanations of especially "called and sent preachers," would enable them to understand the Word of God for themselves. He taught the people how to read the Scriptures intelligently, and how to "accurately divide the word of truth." He showed how necessary it is to know *where* a thing was done, *when* it was done, *how* it was done, and *by whom* it was done; whether the person speaking was a Jew or a Christian; whether the persons addressed were saints or sinners;

whether under the Old Covenant, or under the New Covenant; whether the speakers were discussing the law, or the gospel; whether those who wrote had reference to the Church of Christ, or to the "church that was set up in the wilderness" by Moses; or whether the gospel *in fact* was first preached by Abraham, or by the apostles of Jesus Christ; or whether the law of pardon, in relation to the sinner, emanated from Moses, a fallible man, or from Jesus of Nazareth, the divine Son of God.

Following the motto that "*where the Bible speaks, we speak; where the Bible is silent, we are silent,*" Alexander Campbell, both in preaching and writing, showed the difference between facts and opinions—between personal knowledge—the knowledge of the senses—and faith founded on testimony. He utterly repudiated the idea that the opinions of men should be made tests of Christian fellowship. These he regarded as only private property, and that, as such, they should be always held in abeyance, and never be intruded into the domain of fact and faith. He simplified the whole matter by showing that facts are to be *believed*, commands to be *obeyed*, and the promises of the gospel to be *enjoyed*. The commonest mind could apprehend these simple but grand divisions of the scheme of redemption.

He showed that the plan of salvation was a divine and sublime and glorious unity—that there is "one Lord, one faith, and one baptism," and that "*the* doctrine of Christ" is a proposition altogether different from the "doctrines of men," and from the "doctrines of demons." He contended—and his arguments remain unassailable to the present day—that the Bible, and the Bible only, can be made the basis of Christian unity, and that no unity, either in form or in spirit, can ever take place until all creeds, Confessions of Faith, "Church Standards," and denominational titles—such as Episcopal, Lutheran, Presbyterian, Baptist, Methodist and Roman Catholic—shall be removed out of the way. All these are divisive of the "one body," of which body Christ is the one living and all-animating Head.

Campbell insisted that Bible things should be inculcated in Bible words, that all theological terminologies should be abandoned, and that the nomenclature of scholastic schools should be rejected, as only serving to confuse and discourage "the common people who gladly hear the word," and who can not comprehend metaphysics, theological abstractions, and inferential deductions. He taught—as do the "Disciples of Christ" now uniformly—that "the gospel is *the* power of God unto salvation, and that God has revealed no power above and beyond the gospel, as essential to enlightenment and conviction of sin. He did not limit the power of the Spirit, but he maintained that we have no right to pry into mysteries which the Almighty Father has not revealed. "Secret things belong to God, but revealed things to us and our children."

He taught that the revealed promises of God are the only evidences of pardon in our possession, and while relying implicitly and unequivocally upon the Word of God, he rejected all sensuous evidence of pardon, such as psychological impressions, dreams, apparitions, supernatural visitations, ecstasies: all of which superstitious notions were prevailing at the time when— seventy years ago—the Campbells proposed to abandon the sectarian world and return to the Bible and apostolic teaching. Of course, as a consequence of the principles which they adopted, they could do no other than throw overboard, as lumber of the mystical and monkish ages, all speculative theories of conversion—the doctrine of direct supernatural agency—and show, by apostolic teaching, that it is the moral power of divine truth, as exerted through the gospel, that changes the moral nature of man.

By an appeal to the New Testament, they showed that the working of miracles, by the apostles, was designed as a "confirmation of the word," as revealed by the Holy Spirit, but that in no place is it recorded that a miracle ever changed the heart of a sinner. "Signs," says Paul, "are not for them that *believe*, but for them that *believe not*." The sinner is saved by faith in Jesus the Christ, and by obedience to the conditions of the gospel.

Giving up infant baptism, while they were yet Presbyterians in name, by a direct course, through Bible investigation, they came to that point, where, in the absence of all testimony, they were obliged to surrender both rantism and affusion, as being without the least authority in the Word of God.

While accepting all the measures of reform as accomplished by Luther, Zwingle, Calvin, Melancthon, John Wesley and Roger Williams, which were accomplished in harmony with the inspired Scriptures, Alexander Campbell, and those royal spirits co-operating with him, laid aside as impracticable all the theological speculations and false dogmas of those reformers, with all their contradictory deductions from human reason, unsupported by a "Thus saith the Lord."

Having fully committed himself to a "Restoration of the Ancient Order of Things," Alexander Campbell encountered, in the outset, three popular systems of denominational justification, all of which, while being essentially the same in principle, flatly contradict the Word of God. These were Calvinism, Arminianism and Universalism. The central idea of the first is this: That God had from all eternity decreed the salvation of his own elect few, whose number can neither be increased nor diminished, while condemning all the rest of mankind to eternal reprobation. And further, that man being totally depraved, and incapable of any volition toward good thoughts or good deeds, can only be renewed in life by the irresistible grace of God. The second theory embraces this idea: That, as it is impossible for man to repent of his sins, until he receives the gift of faith direct from heaven, he must remain in his sins until God, in his own good time, sends down the Holy Spirit to regenerate him. Man can do nothing. God must do all; man must wait, and if God chooses not to visit him, he is lost. The third theory is to this effect: That God has from all eternity decreed the salvation of all men, and that all men, without the loss of one soul, will be made finally holy and happy. Take either one of these systems, and it is clear to be seen that man has nothing at all to do in securing his own salvation—that his salvation or condemnation is wholly in the hands of a stern and implacable God; that salvation is entirely *unconditional;* that man is wholly and helplessly passive, and therefore irresponsible. Campbell held that if these systems are in harmony with the moral government of God, then is man not a free moral agent; that there is no virtue in preaching the gospel; that there is no need of a Mediator, and that a remedial scheme is a superfluity, if not an absolute myth.

The effects of the religious revolution inaugurated by the Campbells were not foreseen by them and their coadjutors. Their steps evidently were guided by the providence of God; and now there is not a pulpit or a religious journal in the land, that has not either directly or indirectly been influenced by the plea of those godly men, to reject many of the grosser forms of a perverted Christianity. On the question of Christian union—toward the consummation of which grand object Alexander Campbell gave the undivided energies of his eventful life—there is now a rapidly-growing sentiment among all good men in the various denominations. Campbell held that all denominations never could unite as one spiritual body—neither as Presbyterians, nor as Episcopalians, nor as Lutherans, nor as Methodists, nor as Baptists, nor upon any other sectarian name; but that they could unite as Christians, that being designated as the scriptural name of the followers of Christ, the Founder of the Church. He held that all these church titles were of purely human origin, that they tended continually toward carnality and the secularization of divine things, and that as central ideas of church polities—each polity antagonizing every other polity—they contradict the last intercessory prayer of our Savior, who prayed that all his disciples might be of one mind and heart; that as he and his Father are one, so his disciples might be one with them, that the world might believe that he is the Messiah—Christ himself representing the one true vine, and his disciples the branches, which fact forever excludes the idea that denominations constitute "branches" of the "one body." When Christ said, "Upon this rock I will build *my* Church," the conception of a Papal or Protestant Church, or a Gallican or Anglican Church, was not present in his mind. So many diverse bodies can not possibly possess the Spirit of Christ. The spirit of man is in them, and hence they can not be divine.

THE RESTORATION OF APOSTOLIC CHRISTIANITY.

In closing our series of articles on Reformatory Movements, we propose to give the results of the religious revolution as inaugurated by Alexander Campbell.

It has been made evident by the numerous facts which we have heretofore narrated, that Campbell worked himself out of spiritual Babylon by a thorough investigation of the Scriptures, and that he abandoned all Protestant sects because he could not find the basis of Christian union in any one of them. He faithfully followed the logic of God's Word to the end. He discarded the deductions of human reason as a logical necessity, and settled all controversies by a direct appeal to the law and authority of Jesus the Christ. He established the proposition that Jesus Christ is the only begotten Son of God, by the most majestic and incontrovertible arguments that were ever penned by mortal man. His arguments on the divinity of Christ stand before the world without a parallel. His theses on the Person of Christ, as Prophet, Priest and King, and as the only Savior of men, and as the only hope of the world, have never been excelled. He showed that salvation from sin is not in subscription to creeds or dogmas; not in joining some orthodox Church; not in indorsing the opinions of men, however hoary with age;

but in a person, in the Person of Christ: that "all the promises of God are in him yea, and in him amen."

The ground of assurance we occupy may now be briefly stated:

I. Our creed is the Inspired Word of God; no more, no less.

II. We believe with all the heart that the Word of God—the Plan of Salvation—was miraculously revealed by the Holy Spirit, and that the revealed word was confirmed by miraculous attestations of divine power.

III. We believe that the gospel—which consists of the death, burial and resurrection of Christ—is the power of God unto salvation to every one who believes it and obeys it.

IV. Accepting of no theory of regeneration, and discarding alike all mystical influences and all scholastic vagaries, we believe that sinners who are brought under the power of the truth, are *begotten* of the Word of God —are *begotten* through the gospel—are *made alive* by the truth, and *born* of water.

V. We believe that immersion, preceded by genuine faith in Jesus Christ as the Savior of men, and preceded by genuine repentance toward God, is, if done in the name of the Father, and of the Son, and of the Holy Spirit, for the remission of past sins, and that it is the consummating act in the divine process of salvation.

VI. Taking the Scriptures as our infallible guide in all spiritual things, we believe that the heart of the sinner is changed by the truth contained in the Scriptures, and that it is the moral power of God found in the divine testimonies, which, when brought to bear upon the sinner's heart, changes his moral nature, and makes him a "new creature" in Christ Jesus. We believe that the truth, as revealed by the Holy Spirit, was intended by the heavenly Father to "convince the world of sin, of righteousness, and of judgment to come;" that in conversion, the Holy Spirit is the *agent*, and the word revealed by the Spirit the *instrument*. We believe that it is the Word of God, wielded by the Spirit, that does the execution, and that it is the Word of God, as the sword of the Spirit, that slays the sinner and destroys his love of sin. As we do not believe in the efficacy of the word *without the presence of the Spirit*, neither do we believe in a direct mystical operation of the Spirit *without the presence of the word* in the sinner's heart.

VII. We believe that the act of pardon takes place in the mind of God, and not in the sinner's heart; and we know this to be so, because the conditions of pardon are found recorded in the revealed will of God. We do not believe that a sinner—by the mere testimony of his *feelings*—has a personal consciousness of the pardon of his sins. Remission of sins is purely a matter of faith in the promises of God, and not a mere matter of *conscious feeling*, as produced by a psychological state of heart or affections. It is the love of God that changes the sinner's heart, and it is the truth that convicts the sinner of sin; and it is God who remits sin through obedience to the gospel. Of course, we here only propose to give statements, not arguments.

VIII. We do not pretend to limit the power of the Holy Spirit, but, in the absence of testimony, we can not believe that there is a superadded power, beyond and apart from the gospel, necessary to the conviction of the sinner. Such a speculation was never even hinted at by Christ and his apostles. In all doctrinal matters, and in all questions of commands and personal obedience, "where the Bible speaks, we speak; and where the Bible is silent, we are silent." We are, therefore, as much bound to respect the silence of the Bible, as we are bound to honor its utterances.

IX. We believe that God only acknowledges one body of believers, and that all converted men, in order to become members of the one body of Christ, must, by the teachings of the Holy Spirit, be "immersed into the one body." We designate the one body, of which Christ is the one all-animating Head, the Church of Christ, because the body is constituted of those who believe in Christ, obey Christ, and walk in Christ. We call ourselves Christians, because Christ is our only King and lawgiver, and him only do we propose to follow. We call ourselves the Disciples of Christ, because we learn only from Christ and his apostles.

X. In church edification, in worship, in disciplinary matters, and in the weekly communion, we take the New Testament as our only rule of faith and practice.

There are some things we do not believe, because not authorized and sustained by the Word of God.

1. We do not believe in sectarian churches, nor in Protestant denominationalism, nor in the Roman Catholic Church, or any other Church that has an existence without the sanction of God's Word.

2. We do not believe in human creeds, in speculative dogmas, in theories of regeneration, in the mourning-bench business, in dreams and apparitions, in phantasies and ecstasies, nor in sensuous feelings, as guides in the way of obedience and of a divine life.

3. We do not believe in a direct, special, irresistible theory of regeneration.

4. We do not believe in infant baptism, nor in affusion, nor rantism. We have good reason to believe that they originated in an apostate Church.

5. We do not believe in a Roman Church, nor in an

Episcopal Church, nor in a Lutheran Church, nor in a Presbyterian Church, nor in a Baptist Church, nor in a Methodist Church, nor in any other Church, not known in the apostolic age. We do not believe in any human organization as a substitute for the Church of the living God.

6. We do not believe that persons who have never been immersed into Jesus Christ—into the death of Christ—into the one body—are members of the one body.

7. We do not believe that morality, no matter how high its character or how highly prized by men, will save a soul from eternal death, without the righteousness of Christ, and without the righteousness of God.

8. We do not believe that God will save men by faith alone, or by repentance alone, or by baptism alone, or by grace alone, or by works alone. We believe that God will save men who sustain the relation of a Christian, and who have the character of a Christian. This is inclusive of all possible good.

9. We do not believe in a Papal form of church government, nor in an Episcopal form of church government, nor in a Presbyterial form of church government; but we do believe in the independency of every congregation, as regards church government, and in the sovereign right of every congregation to choose its own officers, such as elders and deacons. We also believe that while the congregations maintain a separate governmental independency, they are at the same time spiritually and sympathetically united in Christ as one harmonious body, and that they are mutually bound to co-operate in the accomplishment of the same grand objects, especially in proclaiming the glad tidings of

salvation and establishing congregations according to the apostolic model.

What we have now mapped out as the ground we occupy, we are thoroughly convinced is truly the apostolic ground, and a ground of unity about which there can be no intelligent controversy. The ground we occupy excludes all sectarianism. All the people of God may occupy this ground. We invite all men to receive the same Bible we receive; to accept the same creed we accept; to honor the same Lord we honor; to obey the same gospel we obey; to bear the same scriptural titles we bear; to "walk by the same rules," to "mind the same things," to "speak the same things," to be "joined together in the same judgment," to contend earnestly for the same faith.

HISTORY OF CHURCH COUNCILS.

MANY writers, Protestant as well as Romanist, have regarded the assembly of the apostles and elders of Jerusalem, of which we read in Acts xv., as the first ecclesiastical council, and the model on which others were formed, in accordance, as they suppose, with a divine command or apostolic institution. But this view of the subject is unsupported by the testimony of the apostolic times, and is at variance with the opinions of the earliest writers, who refer to the councils of the Church. Tertullian speaks of the ecclesiastical assemblies of the Asiatic and European Greeks as a human institution; and in a letter written by Firmilian, Bishop of Cæsarea, to Cyprian, about the middle of the third century, the same custom is referred to merely as a convenient arrangement existing at that time among the churches of Asia Minor for common deliberation on matters of extraordinary importance. Besides this, it will be discovered, upon examination, that the councils of the Church were assemblages of altogether a different nature from that of the apostles; the only point in which the alleged model was really imitated being, perhaps, the form of the preface to the decree, " It has seemed good to the Holy Spirit and to us." (*Studien u. Kritiken*, 1842, i. 102 sq.)

A council is an assembly of bishops or pastors called together for the discussion and regulation of ecclesiastical affairs. The beginning of the system of church councils is traced to the meeting of the apostles and elders at Jerusalem, as recorded in Acts xv. This, as mentioned above, is generally considered to be the first council; but it differed from all others in this circumstance, that it was under the special guidance of the Holy Spirit. Roman Catholic writers speak of four Apostolical Councils, viz: Acts i. 13, for the election of an apostle; Acts vi., to choose deacons; Acts xv., the one named above; Acts xxi. 18 sq. But none of these had a public and general character, except the one in Acts xv. (Schaff *History of Christian Church* ii. sec. 65). Although the gospel was soon after propagated in many parts of Europe, Asia and Africa, there is not a particle of evidence to show that any public meeting of Christians was held for the purpose of discussing any contested point until the middle of the second century. From that time councils became frequent; but as they consisted only of those who belonged to particular districts or countries, they are usually termed *diocesan, provincial, patriarchal* or national councils, in contradistinction to *œcumenical* or *general* councils, *i. e.*, supposed to comprise delegates or commissioners from all the churches in the Christian world, and consequently supposed to represent the Church universal.

According to Dr. Schaff, the word *œcumenical* occurs first in the sixth canon of Constantinople, A. D. 381. But no such assembly was held, or could be held, before the establishment of the Christian religion over the ruins of paganism in the Roman Empire. Their title to represent the whole Christian world is not valid. After the fourth century the "lower clergy and the laity" were entirely excluded from the councils, and bishops only admitted. The number of bishops gathered at the greatest of the councils, constituted but a small portion of the number who claimed to be bishops. The œcumenical councils which are generally admitted to bear that title most justly were rather Greek than general councils. In the strict and proper sense of the term, therefore, no œcumenical council has ever been held. There are seven councils admitted by both the Greek and Latin churches as œcumenical, to which number the Roman Catholics add twelve, making nineteen in all, which we now shall notice in their regular historical order.

I. APOSTOLICAL COUNCIL.

This council convened in Jerusalem, A. D. 47, and, according to the meaning of the term, is the only council mentioned in the New Testament. The conversion of Cornelius having thrown open the Church of Christ to the Gentiles, many uncircumcised persons were soon gathered into the congregation formed at Antioch under the labors of Paul and Barnabas; but, on the visit of certain Jewish Christians from Jerusalem, a dispute arose as to the admission of such Gentiles as had not even been proselytes to Judaism, but were brought in directly from paganism. To settle this question, the brethren at Antioch deputed Paul and Barnabas, with several others, to lay the matter before a general meeting of the apostles and elders in the Jerusalem congregation, which was the first congregation formed under the apostles, and obtain their formal and final decision on a point of so vital importance to the progress of the gospel in all heathen lands. On their arrival and presentation of the subject, a similar opposition (and of a heated character, as we find from the notices in Gal. ii.) was made by Christians formerly of the Pharisaic party at the metropolis; so that it was only when, after considerable dispute, Peter had rehearsed his experience with reference to Cornelius, and the signal results of the labors of Paul and Barnabas among the Gentiles had been recounted, that James, as president of the council, pronounced in favor of releasing those received into the church from the Gentiles, without requiring circumcision or the observance of the Mosaic ceremonial law. This conclusion was generally assented to, and promulgated in a regular authoritative form, and was sent back to Antioch by Paul and Barnabas by letter message, to be thence circulated in all the churches in pagan countries. By the decision of this council, the faithful were commanded to abstain (1) from meats which had been offered to idols (so as not even to appear to countenance the worship of the heathen), (2) from blood and strangled things, and (3) from fornication—the prevailing vice of the Gentiles.

II. COUNCIL OF NICE.

Two Church councils have been held at Nicæa, but only the first of these was properly œcumenical, and it is regarded as the most important of such assemblies. It was convened by the Emperor Constantine in A. D. 325. Along with the imperial summoning of the council, the different bishops were proffered the service of public conveyances for themselves and two presbyters and three servants; and when the 318 bishops who had complied with the Emperor's request gathered at Nice, the Emperor himself opened the council, June 19, in his own palace, and its use for future sessions was afforded to this august body of ecclesiastics, as it appears from the records that the sessions continuing for two months, were held sometimes at the palace, and sometimes at a Church or some public building. The Empire, at the time of the call of the council, contained in all about 1800 bishops (1000 for the Greek provinces, 800 for the Latin), and of these, if 318 attended as reported by Athanasius (*Ad. Apos.* c. 2. et al), Socrates (*Hist. Eccles.* bk. viii.) and Theodoret (*Hist. Eccles.* i. 7), there were one-sixth of the "episcopal sees" represented at Nice—a large number, indeed, if we take into consideration the vastness of the imperial realm, and the difficulty of travel in those times. Including the presbyters and deacons and other attendants, the number may have amounted in all to between 1500 and 2000. Most of the Eastern provinces were strongly represented. Besides a great number of obscure mediocrities, there were several venerable and distinguished men, as e. g., Eusebius of Cæsarea, who was most eminent for learning; the "young archdeacon Athanasius," who accompanied the bishop Alexander of Alexandria, and who was noted for zeal, intellect and eloquence.

"Some, as confessors, still bore in their bodies the marks of Christ from the times of persecution; Paphantias of the Upper Thebaid, Potamon of Heraklea, whose right eye had been put out, and Paul of Neo-Cæsarea, who had been tortured with red-hot iron under Licinius, and was crippled in both his hands. Others were distinguished for extraordinary ascetic holiness, and even for miraculous works; like Jacob of Nisibis, who spent years as a hermit in forests and caves, and lived like a wild beast on roots and leaves, and Spyridion (or St. Spiro), of Cyprus, the patron of the Ionian Isles, who even after his ordination remained a simple shepherd. The Latin Church, on the contrary, had only seven delegates: from Spain Hosius or Osius, of Cordova, the ablest and most influential of the Western representatives; from France, Nicasius of Dijon; from North Africa, Cæcelian of Carthage; from Pannonia, Domnus of Strido; from Italy, Eustorgias of Milan, and Marcus of Calabria; from Rome, the two presbyters Victor, or Vitus, and Vincentius, as delegates of the aged Pope Sylvester I. who found it impossible to attend in person. A Persian bishop, John, also, and a Gothic bishop, Theophilus, the forerunner and teacher of the Gothic Bible translator Ulfilas, were present." (*McClintock and Strong's Encyc.* vol. vii. p. 44.)

Various theories have been propounded to explain Constantine's aim in calling this council. By some it is represented as serving a political purpose (based on Eusebius *Vita. Constant* iii. 4); by others it is regarded as intended to restore quiet to the Church and unite all its parties in the great Trinitarian question on which the Church was at that time greatly divided—there existing three parties: one, which may be called the *orthodox* party, held firmly to the doctrine of the deity of Christ; the second was the Arian party, who regarded Christ as only a man; and the third, which was in the majority, taking conciliatory or middle ground, and consenting to the use of such christological expressions as all parties could consistently agree upon; they acknowledged the divine nature of Christ in general biblical terms, but avoided the use of the term *homoousian* (which means *like substance* with the Father), which the Arians decried as unscriptural, Sabellian, and materialistic. According to Pusey, "Constantine did not understand the doctrine, and attached as much or more importance to uniformity in keeping Easter as to unity of faith. Indeed, he himself at this time believed in no doctrine but that of Providence, and spared no terms of contempt as to the pettiness of the dispute between Alexander and Arius" (*Councils of the Church* p. 102); yet it would seem that Constantine only called a council when he believed it impossible to restore peace between the contending parties, led respectively by Arius and Alexander, and now turned over the case for settlement to the bishops, who appeared to him to be the representatives of God and Christ, the organs of the divine Spirit "that enlightened and guided the Church," and he appears to have hoped that when in council assembled, analogous to the established custom of deciding controversies in the single provinces by assemblies composed of all the provincial bishops, they would be able to dispose of the present controversy.

No complete collection of the transactions of this Nicæan œcumenical council have come down to us. Some account of the bishops who composed this assembly is given by Socrates, Sozomen and Theodoret. It is uncertain who presided, but it is generally supposed that the president was Hosius, bishop of Cordova in Spain. From the reports of two of its attendants, Athanasius and Eusebius of Cæsarea, we learn that it busied itself mainly with the settlement of the different christological views. The opening sessions were principally devoted, according to these writers, to a consideration of Arian views, and resulted finally in the examination of Arius himself. He did not hesitate to maintain that the Son of God was a creature, made from nothing; that there was a time when he had no existence; that he was capable of his own free will of right and wrong. Athanasius, although at the time but a deacon, drew the attention of the whole council by his marvelous penetration in unraveling and laying open the artifices of the heretical views of Arius and his followers. He resisted Eusebius, Theognis, and Maris, the chief supporters of Arius, and evinced such zeal in defense of the truth that he attracted both the admiration of all the anti-Arian party and the bitter hatred of the Arian party. We are told that so great and far-reaching was the influence of the criticism of Athanasius that many of the Arians became doubtful of their own standpoint, and eighteen of them abandoned the cause of Arius. The orthodox party themselves became enthusiastic in behalf of their cause, and when Eusebius of Cæsarea proposed a confession of faith—an ancient Palestinian confession, which was very similar to the Nicene, and acknowledged the divine nature of Christ in general biblical terms, but avoided the term in question (*homoousios, of the same essence*), they rejected it, though the emperor had seen and approved this confession, and even the Arian minority were ready to accept it. They wished a creed which no Arian could honestly subscribe, and especially insisted on inserting the expression *homo-usios*, which the Arians so much objected to. The fathers finally presented through Hosius of Cordova another confession, which became the *substance* of what is now known and owned by the orthodox churches as the well-known Nicene Creed. Here is the Nicene Creed, as translated from the Greek, and which was adopted at the council of Nice in 325:

THE NICENE CREED.

We believe in one God, the Father Almighty, Maker of all things visible and invisible; and in one Lord Jesus Christ, the Son of God begotten of the Father: only-begotten, that is of the substance of the Father; God of God; Light of Light; very God of very God; begotten, not made; of the same substance with the Father; by whom all things were made, both things in heaven and things in earth; who for us men and our salvation descended and became flesh, was made man, suffered, and rose again the third day. He ascended into heaven; he cometh to judge the quick and dead. And in the Holy Spirit. But those who say *there was a time when* he was not; or that he was not before he was begotten; or that he was made from that which had no being; or who affirm the Son of God to be of any other substance or essence, or *created,* or variable, or mutable, such persons doth the Catholic and Apostolic Church anathematize.

This creed was enlarged at the Second Council of Constantinople, in 381, by which the faith of the Church with regard to the person of Christ was set forth in opposition to certain errors, notably Arianism. Moreover, not only the Semi-Arians, but even many of the Niceni- ans (followers of the Nicene Creed), held, with the Arians, and especially the Macedonians, that the Holy Spirit was created by the Father (Gieseler i. c.). After ineffectual attempts, at several synods, to agree upon a formula, the Nicene Symbol, with certain additions, was adopted in 381, as already stated, at the second œcumenical Council of Constantinople. The parts added at Constantinople are put in brackets. We append it below as enlarged:

(1) I believe in one God, the Father Almighty, Maker [of heaven and earth], and of all things visible and invisible. (2) And in one Lord Jesus Christ, the only-begotten Son of God, begotten of his Father [before all worlds]; [God of God]; Light of Light; very God of very God; begotten, not made; being of one substance with the Father, by whom all things were made. (3) Who for us men and our salvation came down from heaven, and was incarnate [by the Holy Spirit of the Virgin Mary], and was made man [and was crucified, also, for us under Pontius Pilate]; he suffered and was buried; and the third day he rose again, according to

the Scriptures; and ascended into heaven [and sitteth on the right hand of the Father]. And he shall come again with glory to judge both the quick and the dead [whose kingdom shall have no end]. And I believe in the Holy Spirit [the Lord and Giver of Life], who proceedeth from the Father [and the Son], who, with the Father and the Son together is worshiped and glorified; who spake by the prophets. And I believe in one catholic and apostolic Church. I acknowledge one baptism for the remission of sins, and I look for the resurrection of the dead, and the life of the world to come. Amen.

The decision of the council having been laid before Constantine, he saw clearly that the Eusebian formula would not pass; and as he had at heart, for the sake of peace, the most nearly unanimous decision which was possible, he gave his voice for the disputed word, and declared that he recognized in the unanimous consent of the bishops the work of God, and received it with reverence, declaring that all those persons should be banished who refused to submit to it. Upon this the Arians, through fear, also anathematized the dogmas condemned, and subscribed the faith laid down by the council; that they did so only outwardly was shown by their subsequent conduct. It was declared by its advocates that it was presented after mature deliberation, and after diligent consultation of all that the holy evangelists and apostles have taught upon the subject; and it proceeded to set forth the true doctrine of the Church in a creed, in which, in order to defy all the subtleties of the Arians (says a modern "orthodox" historian), the council thought good to express by the term "consubstantial"—*homoousios*—the divine essence or substance which is common to the Father and the Son. According to Athanasius, this creed was in a great measure composed by Hosius, of Cordova. It was written out by Hermogenes, bishop of Cæsarea, in Cappadocia, and subscribed, together with the condemnation of the dogmas and expressions of Arius, by all the bishops present with the exception of a few of the Arians. Socrates (*lib. i., ch.* 5) says that all the bishops except five; Baronius, that all except Eusebius, of Nicomedia, and Theognis, of Nicæa, assented to the use of the word ὁμοούσιος—*homoousios*. According to Cave, Secundus, of Ptolemais, and Theognis, of Marmorica, alone refused. Arius himself was banished, by Constantine's order, to Illyria, where he remained until his recall, which took place five years after.

We have now transcribed the chief acts of the Nicene Council; but that our readers may have, if possible, the full benefit of the minor proceedings of "the great and holy council," which "holds the highest place among all the councils," we proceed to show what other grave matters were disposed of by these famous bishops.

First. They considered the subject of the Meletian schism, which for some time past had divided Egypt, and they decreed that Meletius should keep the title and rank of bishop in his see of Lycopolis, in Egypt, forbidding him, however, to perform any episcopal functions; also, that they whom he had elevated to any ecclesiastical dignities should be admitted to communion, upon condition that they should take rank after those who were enrolled in any *parish* (the district under a bishop's jurisdiction, which is now called a "diocese," was so styled in the Church at that time), and who had been ordained by Alexander. Second. They decreed that throughout the Church, the festival of Easter should be celebrated on the Sunday after the full moon which happens next after March 21. Third. They published twenty canons or rules; and here they are:

1. Excludes from the exercise of their functions those persons in holy orders who have made themselves eunuchs.

2. Forbids to raise neophytes to the priesthood or episcopate.

3. Forbids any bishop, priest or deacon to have women in their houses, except their mothers, sisters, aunts, or such women as shall be beyond the reach of slander.

4. Declares that a bishop ought, if possible, to be constituted by all the bishops of the province, but allows of his consecration by three, at least, with the consent of the absent bishops signified in writing; the consecration to be finally confirmed by the metropolitan.

5. Orders that they who have been separated from the communion of the Church by their own bishop shall not be received into communion elsewhere. Also, that a provincial synod shall be held twice a year in every province to examine into sentences of excommunication; one synod to be held before Lent, and the second in autumn.

6. Insists upon the preservation of the rights and privileges of the bishops of Alexandria, Antioch, and other provinces.

7. Grants to the bishop of Ælia (Ælia Capitolina, the new city built by Ælius Hadrianus upon the site of Jerusalem, or near it), according to ancient tradition, the second place of honor.

8. Permits those who had been ministers among the Cathari, and who returned into the bosom of the Catholic and Apostolic Church, having received imposition of hands, to remain in the ranks of the clergy. Directs, however, that they shall, in writing, make profession to follow the decrees of the Church; and that they shall communicate with those who have married twice, and with those who have performed penance for relapsing in time of persecution. Directs, further, that in places where there is a Catholic bishop and a converted bishop of the Cathari (those pretending to peculiar purity of life), the former shall retain his rank and office, and the latter be considered only as a priest; or the bishop may assign him the place of chorepiscopus.

9. Declares to be null and void the ordination of priests made without due inquiry, and of those who have, before ordination, confessed sins committed.

10. Declares the same of persons ordained priests in ignorance, or whose sin has appeared after ordination.

11. Enacts that those who have fallen away in time of persecution without strong temptation shall be three years among the hearers, seven years among the prostrators, and for two years shall communicate with the people without offering ("communicate with the people in prayer, without being admitted to the oblation;" *i. e.*, to the holy eucharist, according to Johnson's way of understanding it).

12. Imposes ten years' penance upon any one of the military, who, having been deprived of a post on account of the faith, shall, after all, give a bribe, and deny the faith, in order to receive it back again.

13. Forbids to deny the holy communion to any one likely to die.

14. Orders that catechumens who have relapsed shall be three years among the hearers.

15. Forbids bishops, priests or deacons to remove from one city to another; or any one offending against this canon to be compelled to return to his own church, and his translation to be void.

16. Priests or deacons removing from their own church not to be received into any other; those who persist, to be separated from communion. If any bishop dare to ordain a man belonging to another church, the ordination to be void.

17. Directs that all clerks guilty of usury shall be deposed.

18. Forbids deacons to give the eucharist to priests, and to receive it themselves before the priests, and to sit among the priests; offenders to be deposed.

19. Directs that Paulianists coming over to the Church shall be baptized again. Permits those among their clergy who are without reproach, after baptism, to be ordained by the Catholic bishops; orders the same thing of deaconesses.

20. Orders that all persons shall offer up their prayers on Sundays and Pentecost, *standing*.

It was also proposed to add another canon, enjoining continence upon the married clergy; Paphnutius warmly opposed the imposition of such a yoke, and prevailed, so that the proposal fell to the ground. The creed and the canons were written in a book, and signed by the bishops. The council issued a letter to the Egyptian and Libyan bishops as to the decision of the three main points; the emperor also sent several edicts to the churches, in which he ascribed the decrees to divine inspiration, and sent them forth as laws of the realm. On July 29, the twentieth anniversary of his accession, the emperor gave the members of the council a splendid banquet in his palace, which Eusebius (quite too susceptible of worldly splendor) describes as a figure of the reign of Christ on earth. Constantine remunerated the bishops lavishly, and dismissed them with a suitable valedictory, and with letters of commendation to the authorities of all the provinces on their homeward way.

COUNCILS OF CONSTANTINOPLE.

The first œcumenical Council of Constantinople was convoked in this eastern city in 381 by Theodosius the Great. There were present 150 "orthodox bishops" (mostly eastern) and 36 followers of Macedonius, who left Constantinople when his doctrine was rejected by the majority. The council condemned, besides the Macedonians, the Arians, Unomians and Eudoxians, and confirmed the resolutions of the Council of Nice. It assigned to the bishop of Constantinople the second rank in the Church, next to the bishop of Rome, and in controversies between the two reserved the decision to the emperor.

The Second Council of Constantinople.—This council (the fifth in the list of œcumenical councils) was held in 553 on account of the Three Chapters' controversy, by 165, mostly Oriental bishops. This council excommunicated the defenders of the Three Chapters—Theodore of Mopsuestia, Ibas, and others, and the Roman bishop Vigilius, who refused to condemn the Three Chapters unconditionally.

Third Council of Constantinople.—This is the sixth in the list of œcumenical councils, and was held from 680 to 681 in the Trullan palace, and was attended by 289 bishops, among whom were three Oriental patriarchs, and four legates of the Roman bishop Agathon. The opinions of the Monothelites were condemned, especially through the influence of the Roman legates, as heretical. The General Council convoked in 691 by the Emperor Justinian II., was also held in the Trullan palace. As it was regarded as supplementing the fifth and sixth œcumenical councils, *which had given no Church laws*, it was called *Quinisexta* (*Synodus*) or *Quinisextum* (*Concilium*). It enacted 102 stringent canons on the morals of clergymen and ecclesiastical discipline. It is recognized as an œcumenical council by the Greeks only.

Fifth Council of Constantinople.—This assembled in 754, and was attended by 383 bishops. It passed resolutions against the veneration of images, which were repealed by the second œcumenical council of Nice. It is not recognized by the Latin Church, but only by the Greek Church.

Sixth Council of Constantinople.—This was held in 869, and by the Church of Rome is regarded as the fourth œcumenical council of Constantinople, or the eighth in the list of œcumenical councils. It deposed the patriarch Photius, restored the patriarch Ignatius, and enacted laws on Church discipline. It is, of course, not recognized by the Greek or Eastern Church. In 879 another General Synod was held at Constantinople, attended by 380 bishops, among whom were the legates of Pope John VIII. Photius was recalled, the resolutions of the preceding council against him repealed, and the position of the patriarch of Constantinople to the Pope defined. The Greeks number this as the eighth œcumenical council. The ninth œcumenical council of the Greek Church was held in Constantinople, under the Emperor Adronicus the Younger, in 1341. It condemned the opinions of Barlaam as heretical.

PARTICULAR SYNODS.—The most important of the particular synods are: 1 and 2. In 336 and 339, two Arian synods, under the leadership of Eusebius, of Nicomedia. The former deposed and excommunicated Marcellus, of Ancyra; the latter deposed and expelled Bishop Paulus, of Constantinople, and appointed Eusebius his successor. 3. A semi-Arian Synod against Ætius, who was banished. 4. In 426, a synod held against the Messalians; in 418, 449 and 450, synods against the Eutychians. 5. In 495 and 496, Eutychian synods, condemning their opponents, and recognizing the *Henoticon*, of Geno. 6. A synod, in 516, condemned the resolutions of the council of Chalcedon. 7. In 536, against Severus, Anthimus, and other chiefs of the Acephali. 8. In 541 (543?) against some views of Origen. 9. In 815, two synods on the question of veneration of images; the one, attended by 270 bishops, in favor, and the second against the images. 10. In 861, introducing the patriarch Photius, and approving the veneration of images. 11. In 1170 (according to others, 1168), a synod, attended by many Eastern and Western bishops, on the reunion of the Eastern and Latin churches. Similar synods were held in 1277, 1280, 1285, all without effect. 12. In 1450, a council convoked by the Emperor Constantine Palæologus deposed the patriarch Gregory, put in his place the patriarch Athanasius, and declined to accept the resolutions passed by the council of Florence in favor of the union of the Greek and the Latin churches. 13. In 1638 and 1642, two synods held against the crypto-Calvinism of the patriarch Cyril Lucaris.

GENERAL COUNCIL OF EPHESUS.

The third œcumenical council, convoked by the emperor Theodosius II., was held at Ephesus in 431, upon the controversy raised by Nestorius, bishop of Constantinople, who objected to the application of the title of θεοτοκος*[*] (theotokos) to the Virgin Mary. Celestine, the Pope, not seeing fit to attend in person, sent three legates, Arcadius and Projectus, bishops, and *Philip*, a priest. Among the first who arrived at the council was Nestorius, with a numerous body of followers, and accompanied by Irenæus, a nobleman, his friend and protector Cyril of Alexandria also, and Juvenal of Jerusalem came, accompanied by about fifty of the Egyptian bishops; Memnon of Ephesus had brought together about forty of the bishops within his jurisdiction; and altogether more than two hundred bishops were present. Candidianus, the commander of the forces of Ephesus attended, by order of the emperor, to keep peace and order; but by his conduct he greatly favored the party of Nestorius. The day appointed for the opening of the council was June 7th; but John of Antioch, and the other bishops from Syria and the East not having arrived, it was delayed till the 22d of the same month. At the first session of the council (June

---
* The offspring of God.

22), before the Greek and Syrian bishops had arrived; Cyril and the bishops present condemned the doctrines of Nestorius, and deposed and excommunicated him. This sentence was signed by 198 bishops, according to Tillemont, and by more than 200 according to Fleury; it was immediately made known to Nestorius, and published in the public places. At the same time, notice of the act was sent to the clergy and to the people of Constantinople, with a recommendation to them to secure the property of the Church for the successor of the deprived Nestorius. As soon, however, as Nestorius had received notice of this sentence, he protested against it, and all that had passed at the council, and forwarded to the Emperor an account of what had been done, setting forth that Cyril and Memnon, refusing to wait for John and the other bishops, had hurried matters on in a tumultuous and irregular way. On the 27th of June, twenty-seven Syrian bishops arrived, chose John of Antioch for their president, and deposed Cyril in their turn. In August, Count John, who had been sent by Theodosius, arrived at Ephesus, and directed the bishops of both synods to meet him on the following day. Accordingly, John of Antioch and Nestorius attended with their party, and Cyril with the orthodox; but immediately a dispute arose between them; the latter contending that Nestorius should not be present, while the former wished to exclude Cyril. Upon this, the Count, to quiet the dispute, gave both Cyril and Nestorius into custody, and then endeavored, but in vain, to reconcile the two parties. And thus matters seemed as far from settlement as ever. The emperor at last permitted the fathers of the council to send to him eight deputies, while Orientals or Syrians, on their part, sent as many. The place of meeting was at Chalcedon, whither the emperor proceeded, and spent five days in listening to the arguments on both sides; and here the Council of Ephesus may, in fact, be said to have terminated. Nothing is known of what passed at Chalcedon, but the event shows that Theodosius sided with the Catholics, since upon his return to Constantinople he ordered, by a letter, the Catholic deputies to come there, and to proceed to consecrate a bishop in the place of Nestorius, whom he had already ordered to leave Ephesus, and to confine himself to his monastery near Antioch. Afterwards he directed that all the bishops at the council, including Cyril and Memnon, should return to their respective dioceses. The judgment of this council was at once approved by the whole Western Church, and by far the greater part of the East, and was subsequently confirmed by the Œcumenical Council of Chalcedon, consisting of 630 bishops. Even John of Antioch and the Eastern bishops very soon acknowledged it. But Nestorius protested to the last that he did not hold the heretical opinions anathematized by the council.

Of the other Councils of Ephesus, the following are all that need to be mentioned: 1. In 245 (?) against the Patropassian Nœtus; 2. In 400, under Chrysostom, where Heraclidus was consecrated bishop of Ephesus, and six simoniacal bishops deposed; and the "*Robber Council*," the details of which it is unnecessary to give.

COUNCIL OF CHALCEDON.

This (the fourth œcumenical council) was held in 451, and was convoked by the emperor Marcianus, at the request of the bishops (especially of Leo I.) to put down the Eutychian and Nestorian heresies. The emperor had first summoned the bishops to meet at Nicæa, but when the time approached he was prevented by political troubles from going so far from the imperial city, and therefore changed the place of meeting to Chalcedon, in Bithynia, on the Bosphorus, opposite Constantinople. The council was attended by 630 bishops and deputies, all Eastern except four legates sent by Leo I. from Rome. The sessions began October 8, 451, and ended October 21. As the two parties in the council were roused to the highest pitch of passion, the proceedings, especially during the early sessions, were very tumultuous, until the lay commissioners and senators had to urge the bishops to keep order, saying that such ἐκβοήσεις δημοτικαί (vulgar outcries) were disgraceful. (Mansi, as quoted by Stanley, *Eastern Church* lect. ii p. 165.)

At the *first* session (October 8, 451) the council assembled in the church of St. Euphemia; in the center sat the officers of the emperor; at their left, or on the epistle side, sat the bishops of Constantinople, Antioch, Cæsarea in Cappadocia, and of the other Eastern dioceses, and Pontus, Asia and Thrace, together with the four legates; on the other side were Dioscurus, Juvenal, Thalassius of Cæsarea, and the other bishops of Egypt, Palestine and Illyria, most of whom had been present in the pseudo-council of Ephesus. In the midst were the holy gospels, placed upon a raised seat. When they had taken their seats, the legates of the Pope demanded that Dioscurus should withdraw from the assembly, accusing him of his scandalous conduct at Ephesus, and declaring that otherwise they would depart. Then the imperial officers ordered him to withdraw from the council, and to take his seat among the accused. The acts of the so-called "Robber Council" of Ephesus were discussed and condemned, and Dioscurus was left with only twelve bishops to stand by him. The Eutychian heresy, that in our Lord were two natures before his incarnation, and but one afterwards, was anathematized. The majority of the assembled bishops then proceeded to anathematize Dioscurus himself, and demanded that he, together with Juvenal of Jerusalem, Thalassius of Cæsarea, Eusebius of Ancyra, Eustachius of Berytus, and Basil of Seleucia, who had presided at the council, should be deposed from the episcopate.

At the *second* session (October 10) the following exposition of faith, substantially taken from a letter of Leo to Flavianus, was approved, and its opponents anathematized: "The divine nature and the human nature, each remaining perfect, have been united in one person, to the intent that the same Mediator might die, being yet immortal and impossible. . . . Neither nature is altered by the other; he who is truly God is also truly man. . . . The Word and the flesh preserve each its proper functions. Holy Scripture proves equally the verity of the two natures. He is *God*, since it is written, 'In the beginning was the Word, and the Word was God.' He is also *man*, since it is written, 'The Word was made flesh, and dwelt among us.' As *man*, he was tempted by the devil; as God, he is ministered unto by angels. As man, he wept over the tomb of Lazarus; as God, he raised him from the dead. As man, he is nailed to the cross; as God, he makes all nature tremble at his death. It is by reason of the unity of the person that we say that the Son of man came down from heaven, and that the Son of God was crucified and buried, although he was so only as to his human nature."

At the *third* session the deposition of Dioscurus was pronounced irrevocable, and, soon after, he was banished to Gangra, in Paphlagonia, where, in the course of three years, he died.

In the *fifth* session, the following formula of faith, on the question at issue, was adopted: "We confess, and with one accord teach, one and the same Son, our Lord Jesus Christ; perfect in the divinity, perfect in the humanity, truly God and truly man, consisting of a reasonable soul and body; consubstantial with the Father according to the Godhead, and consubstantial with us according to the manhood; in all things like unto us, sin only excepted; who was begotten of the Father before all ages, according to the Godhead; and in the last days, the same was born according to the manhood, of Mary the Virgin, mother of God, for us and for our salvation; who is to be acknowledged one and the same Christ, the Son, the Lord, the only begotten in two natures, without mixture, change, division or separation; the difference of natures not being removed by their union, but rather the propriety of each nature being preserved, and concurring in one person and in one ὑπόστασις, so that he is not divided or separated into *two persons*, but the only Son, God, the Word, our Lord Jesus Christ, and one and the same person." At the later sessions (ix.–xv.), a number of questions of order, supremacy, discipline, etc., were settled. But, by far, the most important was the twenty-eighth canon, session xv., by which the patriarch of Constantinople was placed on equality of authority with the bishop of Rome, saving only to the latter priority of honor. The Roman delegates protested against this, and, after its adoption, Leo constantly opposed it, upon the plea that it contradicted the sixth of Nicæa, which assigned the second place in dignity to Alexandria; however, in spite of his opposition and that of his successors, the canon remained and was executed. The acts of this council in Greek, with the exception of the anathemas, are lost.

THE SECOND COUNCIL OF NICE.

This is called the seventh œcumenical council, though falsely so, as some assert. It assembled August 17, 786, by order of the Empress Irene and her son Constantine. Owing to the tumults raised by the Iconoclastic party, it was dissolved and reconvened on September 24, 787. (Theophanes, who was present, says that the opening of the council was made on October 11.) There were present 375 bishops from Greece, Thrace, Natolia, the Isles of the Archipelago, Sicily and Italy. Pope Hadrian and all the Oriental patriarchs sent legates to represent them in the synod, those of Rome taking the first place; two commissioners from the emperor and empress also assisted at it. The causes which led to the assembling of this council were briefly as follows: The Emperor Leo (and afterwards his son Constantine Copronymus), offended at the excess of veneration often offered to the images of Christ and the saints, made a decree against the use of images in any way, and caused them everywhere to be removed and destroyed. These severe and summary proceedings raised an opposition almost as violent, and both the patriarch of Constantinople (Germanus) and the Pope (Hadrian) defended the use of images, declaring them to have been always in use in the churches, and showing, or attempting to show, the difference between *absolute* and *relative* worship. However, in a council assembled at Constantinople in 754, composed of 338 bishops, a decree was published against the use of images. But at this time Constantine Copronymus died, and Tarasius, patriarch of Constantinople, induced the Empress Irene and her son Constantine to convoke this council, in which the decrees of the council of 754 at Constantinople were set aside.

The first session was held in the church of St. Sophia. Tarasius, the patriarch, spoke first, and exhorted the bishops to reject all novelties, and to cling to the traditions of the Church. After this, ten bishops were brought before the council, accused of following the party of the Iconoclasts (image breakers)—three of whom, Basil of Ancyra, Theodore of Myra, and Theodosius of Amorium, recanted, and declared that they received with all honor the relics and sacred images of Jesus Christ, the blessed Virgin, and the saints; upon which they were permitted to take their seats; the others were remanded to the next session. The forty-second of the apostolic canons, and the eighth of the Nicæa, and other canons relating to the reception of converted heretics, were read.

In the second session, the letters of Pope Hadrian to the empress and to the patriarch Tarasius were read. The latter then declared his entire concurrence in the view taken of the question by the bishop of Rome, viz: that images are to be adored with a *"relative* worship," reserving to God alone faith and the worship of Latria. This opinion was warmly applauded by the whole council.

In the third session, the confession of Gregory of Neo-Cæsarea, the leader of the Iconoclast party, was received, and declared by the council to be satisfactory; whereupon he was, after some discussion, admitted to take his seat, and with him the bishops mentioned above. Then the letters of Tarasius to the patriarchs of Alexandria, Antioch and Jerusalem, and their replies, as well as the confession of Theodore of Jerusalem, were read and approved. The passages of Holy Scripture relating to the cherubim which overshadowed the ark of the covenant, and which ornamented the interior of the temple, were read, together with other passages taken from the fathers, showing that God had, in other days, worked miracles by means of images.

In the fifth session, the patriarch Tarasius endeavored to show that the innovators, in their attempts to destroy all images, were following in the steps of the Jews, pagans, Manichæans, and other heretics. The council then came to the conclusion that the images should be restored to their usual places, and be carried in processions as before.

In the sixth session, the refutation of the definition of faith, made in the council of Iconoclasts at Constantinople, was read. They had there declared that the eucharist was the only image allowed of our Lord Jesus Christ; but the fathers of the present synod, in their refutation, maintained that the eucharist is nowhere spoken of as the *image* of our Lord's body, but as the very body itself. After this, the fathers replied to the passages from Holy Scripture and from the fathers which the Iconoclasts had adduced in support of their views, and, in doing so, insisted chiefly upon perpetual tradition and the infallibility of the Church.

In the seventh session a definition of faith was read, which was to this effect: " We decide that the holy images, whether painted or graven, or of whatever kind they may be, ought to be exposed to view—whether in churches, upon sacred vessels and vestments, upon walls, or in private houses, or by the wayside; since the oftener Jesus Christ, his blessed mother, and the saints are seen in their images, the more will man be led to think of the originals, and to love them. Salutation and the adoration of honor ought to be paid to images, but not the worship of *Latria* (adoration due to God alone), which belongs to God alone; nevertheless, it is lawful to burn lights before them, and to incense them, as is usually done with the cross, the books of the gospels, and other sacred things, according to the pious use of the ancients; for honor so paid to the images is transmitted to the original, which it represents. Such is the doctrine of the holy fathers and the tradition of the Catholic Church; and we order that they who dare to think or teach otherwise, if bishops or other clerks, shall be deposed; if monks or laymen, shall be excommunicated." This decree was signed by the legates and all the bishops.

Another session (not recognized either by Greeks or Latins) was held at Constantinople, to which place the bishops had been cited by the Empress Irene, who was present, with her son Constantine, and addressed the assembly. The decree of the council and the passages from the fathers read at Nicæa were repeated, and the former was again subscribed. The council of Constantinople against image-worship was anathematized, and the memory of Germanus of Constantinople, John of Damascus, and George of Cyprus, held up to veneration. Twenty-two canons of discipline were published.

1. Insists upon the proper observation of the canons of the Church.
2. Forbids to consecrate those who do not know the psalter, and will not promise to observe the canons.
3. Forbids princes to elect bishops.
7. Forbids to consecrate any church or altar in which relics are not contained.
14. Forbids those who are not ordained to read in the synaxis from the Ambon.
15 and 16. Forbid plurality of beneficences, and luxury in dress among the clergy.
20. Forbids *double* monasteries, for men and women.

This council was not for a long period recognized in France. The grounds upon which the French bishops opposed it are contained in the celebrated Caroline Books, written by order of Charlemagne. Their chief objections were these: 1. That no Western bishops. except the Pope, by his legates, were present; 2. That the decision was contrary to their custom, which was to use images, but not in any way to worship them; 3. That the council was not assembled from all parts of the Church, nor was its decision in accordance with that of the Catholic Church. The Caroline Books were answered by Pope Adrian, but with little effect, so far as the Gallican Church was concerned, which continued long after this to reject this council *in toto*.

LATERAN COUNCILS.

Lateran Councils is a general name applied to the ecclesiastical councils that have been convened in the Lateran Church at Rome, but especially to the five great councils held there, and regarded by the Roman Catholics as œcumenical, viz: those which were held in the years 1123, 1139, 1179, 1215 and 1512-17. We have only room to notice the most important of all these councils, and that with reference to their principal enactments and historical connections.

I. The council of 649, under Martin I., condemned the Monothelitic doctrine, or that of *one* will in the person of Christ. This view was developed as a continuation of the Monophysite controversy. The council of Chalcedon, in 451, had affirmed the existence of *two natures* in Christ in *one person*, against the Antiochians. the Nestorians and Eutychians. This determination of the council did not obtain final supremacy in the Greek and Latin Churches till after the time of Justinian, and the conflict with it was continued under various forms. From the council of Chalcedon till that of Frankfort, in 793, the Church councils, especially, sought to maintain the *twofoldness* of the nature of Christ asserted at Chalcedon, with less regard to the *unity*, which was at the same time established. An early source for the rise of Monothelitism appeared in the writings of Pseudo-Dionysius the Areopagite, which, originating in the fourth century, probably obtained for many centuries thereafter great credit in the Church. A Neo-Platonic mysticism in these writings seeks to mediate between the prevalent Church doctrine and Monophysitism (or the doctrine of one nature in Christ). "The Areopagite is not an outspoken Monophysite, and yet with him the human in Christ is only a form of the divine, and there is in all the acts of Christ but one *mode of operation*, the theandric energy" (*mia theandrikee henergeia*). This expression became a favorite one with all the Monophysite opponents of the Chalcedonian decisions.

The Monothelitic controversy proper extends from 623 to 680, at which latter date the synod of Constantinople gave the most precise definition of *two wills* in the nature of Christ. "The earlier stage of the controversy, extending to the year 638, concerns rather the question of one or two energies or *modes of working* in the acts of Christ." The Emperor Heraclius, on the occasion of his reconquering the Eastern provinces from the Persians in the year 622, and there coming in contact with certain Monophysite bishops, conceived the idea of reconciling them to the Church, by authorizing the expression in reference to the acts of Christ which was used by Dionysius. Sergius, patriarch of Constantinople, being consulted, admitted the propriety of the expression as one sanctioned by the fathers, and recommended it to Cyrus, bishop of Phasis, who, being made soon after bishop of Alexandria, set up a compromise for the Monophysites with the council of Chalcedon on nine points. Sophronius, a monk of Alexandria, seriously objected to the course taken by Sergius, and, on being made bishop of Jerusalem, became so strong an opponent that Sergius called to his aid the influence of Honorius, bishop of Rome, who expressed himself in favor of the view, "rather one will than of one opera tion," but advised that controversy be avoided. "It is unquestionably the fact that the expressed views of Honorius, though a Pope, were subsequently condemned in council." By occasion of the more decided opposition of Sophronius, the Emperor Heraclius, under advice of Sergius, issued his edict, the *Ecthesis*, in 638, in which he forbade the use of either expression, "one mode of working," or "two modes of working," in a controversial way; but especially prohibited the latter, since it is evident that Christ can have but *one will*, the human being subordinate to the divine. This was distinct Monothelitism. A powerful opponent of this view was the monk Maximus, whose writings had a controlling influence with the Lateran Council. "He asserts that for the work of redemption a completeness in the two natures of Christ is necessary; there must be a complete human will. The *Logos*, indeed, works all through the human working and willing. There is a theandric energy in his own sense. It is rather as a *tropos antidoscos*, or what was subsequently called the *communicatio idiomatum*."

Maximus worked with great zeal against Monothelitism in Rome and in Africa, sending out thence tracts on the subject into the Eastern countries. Sophronius still carried on the controversy, as also, with him,

Stephen, bishop of Doria, his pupil. After the death of Honorius, in 638, the bishops of Rome were decidedly opposed to Monothelitism, and Martin I., who had zealously contended against the view while representative of the Roman Church at Constantinople, became, when made Pope in 649, the chief pillar of the contrary opinion. Advocates of the view enunciated in the *Ecthesis* of Heraclius were Theodore, bishop of Phasan, and Pyrrhus, of Constantinople. In 648, the Emperor Constans II., under the influence of the patriarch Paul, issued his *Type* (τύπος πίστεως), which, though not so decidedly Monothelitic as the *Ecthesis*, condemns, under threat of the severest penalties, any further controversy upon the subject. Without consulting the emperor, Martin I. now convoked this first Lateran Council, in which he presided over about 104 bishops from Italy, Sicily, Sardinia and Africa. The Pope sought to obtain generally recognition for the council, and it was finally everywhere received with the five œcumenical councils. Five sessions were held; the writings of the prominent Monothelites were examined and condemned; Pope Martin explained the proper meaning of Dionysius' term "theandric operation," stating that it was designed to signify *two* operations of one person; the *Ecthesis* of Heraclius and *Type* of Constans were condemned; and the judgment of the council pronounced in twenty canons, which "anathematize all who do not confess in our Lord Jesus Christ two wills and two operations."

II. The councils of 1105, 1112 and 1116, under Pascal II., concern the contest about *investitures* between the Pope and the emperor, which was brought to a close in the council of 1123, called and presided over by Calixtus II. This body consisted of 300 bishops and 600 abbots, all of the Latin Church. The investiture contest, which began as early as 1054, when, by mutual decrees of excommunication, the breach between the eastern and western churches was made final, arose from the claim made by the German emperors to an inheritance of rights, exercised by the Greek emperors, concerning the appointment of candidates to ecclesiastical offices, and their investiture with the right to hold church property as subjects of the empire. Under the new German empire, from Otho the Great to Henry IV., 936–1056, the popes themselves were confirmed in their seats by the emperor. Henry III. obtained from the Council of Sutry, which was held near Rome, in the midst of his own army, in 1046, the power of nominating the popes, without intervention of clergy or people. The influence of Hildebrand was now felt—an influence which he had begun to exert from the time of Leo IX., in 1048, and which secured from Nicolas II. (1063) a decree transferring the election of popes to a conclave of cardinals. Hildebrand, as Gregory VII., maintained a celebrated contest with Henry IV., to whom, in 1075, he forbade all power of investiture, excommunicating the emperor the next year, and causing him to do penance at Canossa. With his victorious campaign in Italy (1080–83) Henry drove the Pope into exile at Salerno, where he soon after died.

His immediate successors, however, were such as he had designated for the post, and were the inheritors of his doctrines and plans for the supremacy of the church. Urban II. sent forth an encyclical, declaring his adhesion to the principles of Gregory—the *Dictatus Gregorii*; and Pascal II. (1099–1118), who had been one of Gregory's cardinals, showed more zeal than firmness in the same course. In the Lateran Council under the Pope

(1105), an oath of obedience to the Pope was taken by the clergy, and a promise rendered to affirm whatever he and the church in council should affirm. The Count De Meulan and his confederates were excommunicated for having encouraged the King of England in his conduct concerning investitures. Henry V., who, in the rebellion against his father, was encouraged by Pascal, would nevertheless yield nothing on becoming emperor (1105), in the matter of investitures; his example being followed in this respect by France and England. Henry marched into Italy and imprisoned the Pope in the year 1111, forcing from him the concession of rendering back to the emperor the fiefs of the bishops, on condition that there should be no imperial interference with the elections. For his weakness in this and in other points, the Pope was bitterly reproached, and the council of 1112 revoked all these concessions and excommunicated the emperor. Notwithstanding the rebellion of his German subjects, Henry collected an army and invaded Italy anew in 1116. The council convoked the same year, thereupon renewed the revocation of the concessions which Pascal had formerly made, and anathematized the emperor. At last, the German people, weary of the conflict between Church and State, brought a peaceful compromise in the concordat at the imperial diet of Worms, in 1122. The principles of this concordat were adopted by the council of 1123. The terms of the compact are as follows:

"The emperor surrenders to God, to St. Peter and Paul, and to the Catholic Church, all right of investiture by king and staff. He grants that elections and ordinances in all churches shall take place freely in accordance with ecclesiastical laws. The Pope agrees that the election of German prelates shall be had in the presence of the emperor, provided it is without violence or simony. In case any election is disputed, the emperor shall render assistance to the legal party, with the advice of the archbishop and the bishops. The person elected is invested with the imperial fief by the royal scepter pledged for the execution of everything required by law. Whoever is consecrated shall also receive in like manner his investiture from other parts of the empire within six months." (Haso, *Church History*, p. 200; Gieseler, *Eccles. Hist.*, iii., 181 sq.) The Pope here made considerable concessions in form, but actually, through his influence, obtained all power at the elections. The council of 1123 also renewed the grant of indulgences promulgated by Urban II. in promotion of the first crusade in 1095, and decreed the celibacy of the clergy. Twenty-two canons of discipline were enacted.

III. The council of 1139, under Innocent II., condemned the anti-pope Anacletus II., with his adherents, and deposed all who had received office under him. On the same day with the installation of Innocent II., in 1130, Peter of Leon, a cardinal, and grandson of a rich Jewish banker, had been proclaimed Pope, as Anacletus II., by a majority of the cardinals. Innocent took refuge in France, where he was supported by the king. His cause was very warmly espoused by Bernard of Clairvaux, through whose influence chiefly Innocent recovered his position in Italy, and marched into Rome triumphantly with Lothaire II., in 1136. Anacletus died in 1138, and a successor was chosen by his party only with the purpose of making peace. Roger of Sicily had supported Anacletus, and was on this account condemned in the council of 1139, though the origin of the kingdom of the Two Sicilies belongs to the same year, Roger having taken Innocent prisoner, and having compelled the Pope to bestow upon him the investiture of this kingdom. At this council Arnold of Brescia was also condemned. This was a young clergyman of the city of Brescia, a disciple of Abelard, who, inspired by the free philosophical spirit of his master, devoted himself to the promotion of practical reform in Church and State. A marked spirit of political independence was manifesting itself about this time in Lombardy, as an inheritance from the old Roman municipalities established there. The popes, from the days of Leo IX., had themselves inspired movements of ecclesiastical reform. Pascal II. had admitted that the secular power of the bishops interfered with their spiritual duties. Bernard, though a zealous opponent of Arnold, yet writes as follows in his *Contemplations on the Papacy:* "Who can mention the place where one of the apostles ever held a trial, decided disputes about boundaries, or portioned out lands?" "I read that the apostles stood before judgment seats, not sat on them."

Arnold preached with great zeal against the political power and wealth of the clergy. "The church ought rather to rejoice," he said, "in an apostolic poverty." He was driven successively from Italy, France and Switzerland, but in 1139 was recalled to Rome by the populace, who sought to revive the sovereignty, the State, established a Senate, limited the Pope to the exercise of spiritual power, and the possession of voluntary offerings, and invited the German emperor to make Rome his capital. Arnold and his "politicians" at Rome thus gave Pope Innocent and his immediate successors—Lucius II., Eugenius III., and Adrian IV.—more trouble than any political movements elsewhere. This condemnation at the council did not effectually diminish his power. When, however, Adrian, in 1154, put the city of Rome under ban, and prohibited all public worship, Arnold was abandoned by the Senate, sacrificed by Frederick I., and hung at Rome in 1155, his body being burned and thrown into the river Tiber. Among the canons of the council, the twenty-third condemns the heresy of the Manichæans, as the followers of Peter de Brins were called. This heresy was attributed to the early Waldensians in France and elsewhere, arising partly from their ascetic mode of life. About 1,000 prelates were present at this council; thirty canons of discipline were published, and among them reaffirmations of former canons against simony, and concubinage in the clergy.

IV. The council of 1179, under Alexander III., numbering 280, mostly Latin bishops, was called to correct certain abuses which had arisen during the long schism just brought to a close by the peace of Venice, 1177. Until near the end of the twelfth century the popes were hard pressed by Hohenstauffen emperors. It is the contest of Ghibelline and Guelph. Frederick I. had taken umbrage at the use of the term "beneficium," in a letter addressed to him by Adrian IV., about the rudeness of German knights to pilgrims visiting Rome, as if the Pope meant to imply that the imperial authority had been conferred by him. The emperor marched into Italy, and other letters were interchanged between him and the Pope, when, upon the death of Adrian, in 1159, the two parties—the hierarchic and the moderate among the cardinals—chose two opposing popes, viz.: Alexander III. and Victor IV. The Emperor's Council, called at Pavia in 1160, recognized the latter. Pascal III. and Calixtus III. followed at the imperial dictation, with but little influence. Alexander, from his refuge in France, enjoyed great popularity. He had on his side the Lombard League. The cause of Frederick was defended by the lawyers of Bologna, who ascribed to him unlimited power, to the prejudice of the people. Defeated at Legnano, in 1176, the emperor subscribed, at the dictation of Alexander, the peace of Venice, the provisions of which were based on the concordat of Worms. The first and most important of the twenty-seven canons es tablished by this council, which were mostly disciplinary, provides that henceforth "the election of the popes shall be confined to the college of cardinals, and *two-thirds* of the votes shall be required to make a lawful election, instead of a majority only, as heretofore. It was by this council also that the "errors and impieties" of the Waldenses and Albigeuses were declared heretical. At the unimportant council of 1167 Pope Alexander excommunicated Frederick I.

V. The council of 1215, under Innocent III., was the most important of all the Lateran Councils. It is usually styled the Fourth Lateran. It continued in session from November 11 to November 30, there being present 71 archbishops, 412 bishops, 800 abbots, the patriarchs of Constantinople and Jerusalem, and the legates of other patriarchs and crowned heads. The Pope opened the convocation with a sermon on Luke xxii. 15, relating to the recovery of the Holy Land and the reformation of the church. The remarkable power of Innocent III. is displayed in his influence over this council, which was submissive to all his wishes, and received the seventy canons proposed by him. The papal prerogatives attained their greatest supremacy in Innocent, whose pontificate extended from 1198 to 1216. The bull, *Unam Sanctam*, of Boniface VIII., directed against Philip the Fair in 1302, marks the limit from which the power of the popes evidently began to decline. Innocent III., a man of great personal influence, of marked ability as a writer and orator, bold, crafty, and ever watchful of the affairs of Church and State, had his eye on all that transpired through his legates. The chief objects which his pontificate sought were, first, "the strengthening of the States of the Church; second, separation of the two Sicilies from all dependence on the German empire; third, the liberation of Italy from all foreign control; fourth, the exercise of guardianship over the confederacy of its States; fifth, the liberation of the Oriental Church; sixth, the extermination of heretics, and, seventh, the exercise of ecclesiastical discipline." (Hase, *Church Hist.*, p. 207.)

Hitherto England, Germany and France had constituted a balance of power against the Pope, but under Innocent the two former, as well as Italy, submitted to the claims of the pseudo-Isodorean decretals. France was early laid under interdict (1200), on account of Philip Agustus' repudiation of Ingeburge and the French bishop's approval of the act, while John of England was deprived of his realm, to receive it back (in 1213) only as a fief of Rome. Deciding at first for Otto IV., the Guelph, against the Hohenstauffen Philip, in Germany, Innocent subsequently secured from the council the recognition of Frederick II., vainly seeking in this his German policy to free Italy entirely from the power of the emperor. The famous seventy constitutions of Innocent, if not discussed in a conciliatory manner, by the bishops, or passed with every form of enactment, were nevertheless regarded as the canons of the council, so recognized by the Council of Trent, and by church authorities of the intervening age, and they have constituted a fundamental law for many well-known practices of the church. The *first* of these canons asserts the

Catholic faith in the unity of God against the Manichæan sects. It also, for the first time, makes the doctrine of substantiation, in the use of this express term, an article of faith. "The body and blood of Jesus Christ in the sacrament of the altar are truly contained under the species of bread and wine, the bread being, by the divine omnipotence, *transubstantiated* into his body, and the wine into his blood." The *second* canon condemns the treatise of Joachim, the prophet of Calabria, which he wrote against Peter Lombard on the subject of the Trinity.

The *third* canon is of great importance, furnishing the basis for the crusade against the Albigenses, and for all severities of a like character on the part of the Romish Church. It "anathematizes all heretics who hold anything in opposition to the preceding exposition of faith, and enjoins that, after condemnation, they shall be delivered over to the secular arm; also excommunicates all who receive, protect or maintain heretics, and threatens with deposition all bishops who do not use their utmost endeavors to clear their diocese of them." (Landon, *Manual of Councils,* p. 295.)

The *fourth* canon invites the Greeks to unite with and submit themselves to the Romish Church. The *fifth* canon regulates the order of precedence of the patriarchs: 1. Rome; 2. Constantinople; 3. Alexandria; 4. Antioch; 5. Jerusalem; and permits these several patriarchs to give the pall to the archbishops of their dependencies, exacting from themselves a profession of faith and of obedience to the Roman see, when they receive the pall from the Pope. The *sixth to the twentieth,* inclusive, are of minor importance to the Christian world. (Landon, p. 296). The *twenty-first* canon enjoins "all the faithful of both sexes, having arrived at years of discretion, to confess all their sins at least once a year to their proper priest, and to communicate at Easter." This is the first canon known which orders sacramental confession generally, and may have been occasioned by the teaching of the Waldenses, that neither confession nor satisfaction was necessary in order to obtain remission of sin. From the words with which it begins it is known as the canon "*Omnis utriusque sexûs*," and was solemnly reaffirmed by the Council of Trent. The canons (given completely by Landon, *Manual of Councils*, p. 293, sq.) in general constitute a body of full and severe disciplinary enactments. This council reaffirmed and extended the "Truce of God" on plenary indulgence which had been previously proclaimed in behalf of the eastern crusades, and fixed the time, June 1, and the place Sicily, as a rendezvous for another crusade.

This council confirmed Simon de Montfort in possession of lands which the crusaders had obtained by papal confiscation from the Waldenses, and decreed the entire extirpation of the heresy. The Waldenses or Albigenses in the south of France were the followers of Peter Waldo, a wealthy citizen of Lyons, who, from religious principle, adopted a life of poverty. His adherents were also called Leonistæ and "poor men of Lyons." They were allied in their sentiments to the Vaudois of the Piedmontese valleys, with whom they became united for mutual defense. They protested against these points in the doctrine of the Romish Church: First, transubstantiation; second, the sacraments of confirmation, confession and marriage; third, the invocation of saints; fourth, the worship of images; fifth, the temporal power of the clergy. A crusade had been instituted against them by the papal power in 1178. Innocent sought to win them over and make monks of them by establishing, in 1201, the order of "Poor Catholics." Unsuccessful in this, he confiscated their lands to the feudal lords, and established an inquisition among them under the direction of Dominic, which was formally sanctioned by the council under consideration. The warfare against them, incited and directed by the monks of Citeaux, was allowed by Philip Augustus. Count Raymond, of Toulouse, espoused the cause of his persecuted vassals. The papal legate, Peter of Castelman, sent to convert the Waldenses, was murdered by Raymond, whose dominions were thereupon assaulted, in 1209, by a fiercer crusade of so-called "Christian Pilgrims," led on by Simon de Montfort and Arnold, the Abbot of Citeaux. The Count of Toulouse submitted, but a bloody warfare was prosecuted against Raymond Roger, viscount of Beziers and Albi, and subsequently 200 towns and castles, within the boundaries of the two counts, were granted to the successful Simon de Montfort. A rebellion, however, against his power deprived him of all; but Raymond of Toulouse, who appeared at the council of 1215, obtained no favor, and his territory was declared to be alienated from him forever.

VI. The Lateran Council of 1512-1517, under Julius II. and Leo X., was convened for the "reformation of abuses," for the condemnation of the Council of Pisa, "and attained its most important result in the abolition of the Pragmatic Sanction." France, under Louis XII., had obtained great military successes in Italy by the League of Cambray, formed in 1509 against Venice. In the interests of France, and by the friendship of some of the cardinals, Louis XII. summoned a Church Council at Pisa, November, 1511, which in 1512 was moved to Milan, but was entirely fruitless of results, being dissolved by the presence of the Pope's army. Julius I, though at first jealous of Venice, had nevertheless, aroused by the successes of the French general, formed the Holy Alliance with Venice, Spain, England and Switzerland, and now, at the head of his army, drove the French beyond the Alps and himself summoned a council at the Lateran, May 10, 1512. This council extended over twelve sessions, until March, 1517. The Bishop of Guerk had actively promoted the summoning of the council, and attended as representative of the German emperor. All the acts of the Council of Pisa were at once annulled. Julius having died in February, 1513, Leo X. presided over the sixth session.

At the eighth session, in December, 1513, Louis XII., through his ambassador, declared his adhesion to this Council of the Lateran. At the eleventh session, in December, 1516, the bull was read which, in place of the Pragmatic Sanction of Bourges (1438), wherein France accepted the decisions of the Basle Council, in so far as they were consistent with the liberties of the Gallican Church, substituted the concordat agreed upon this year (1516) between Leo X. and Francis I. Through hope of increasing his power in Italy, Francis largely sacrificed the liberties of the church. Several of the articles of the Pragmatic, which had re-established the right of election, while the concordat declares that the chapters of the cathedrals in France shall no longer proceed to elect the bishop in case of vacancy, but that the king shall name a proper person, whom the Pope shall nominate to the vacant see. The concordat, on account especially of this provision, met with great opposition in the parliament, universities and the church at Paris. It was a great advance of the papacy against the liberties of France (Janus, *Pope and Council*, xxviii. and xxix.).

Neither this council, nor the other four, viz.: those of

1123, 1139, 1179 and 1215, styled æcumenical by the Romish Church, can be properly regarded as such. Some writers mention as the sixth Lateran the council convened by Pope Benedict XIII. on the bull *Unigenitus*, and for the purpose of general reform in the church.

THE COUNCILS OF LYONS.

Lyons is a city of France, and is situated 316 miles southeast of Paris, and is noted in ecclesiastical history as the seat of two œcumenical councils, the first of which was held in 1245, consisting of 140 bishops, and convened for the purpose of promoting the crusades, restoring ecclesiastical discipline, and dethroning Frederick II., emperor of Germany. It was also decreed at this council that cardinals should wear red hats.

At the second council, held in 1274, there were 500 bishops present, and about 1,000 "inferior clergy." Its principal object was the reunion of the Greek and Latin Churches. The first of these councils was held under the pontificate of Innocent IV., and the second under the pontificate of Gregory X.

COUNCILS OF VIENNE.

Vienne is a city of Dauphinè, France, where numerous Church councils were held.

I. The first of which mention is made was held in 474; of its transactions nothing is known beyond the fact that it sanctioned the solemn observance of the three days preceding Ascension-day, which Bishop Mamercus, of Vienne, had ordered.

II. The one held in 870 simply confirmed the privileges bestowed upon a monastery.

III. Held in 892, by order of Pope Formosus, whose two legates, Pascal and John, presided. Several bishops

were present, and the following canons were published:
1, 2. Excommunicate those who seize the property of the Church, or maltreat clerks.

4. Forbids laymen to present to churches without the consent of the bishop of the diocese; also forbids them to take any present from those whom they present. (Mansi, *Concil* ix, 433).

IV. Held in 907; was concocted by Archbishop Alexander, of Vienne, and adjusted a dispute between Abbots Aribert and Barnard respecting the income receipts of monasteries.

V. Held in 1112 by Archbishop Guido; excommunicated Emperor Henry V., because he claimed the right of episcopal investiture, and revoked the treaty of 1111 which conferred such right upon the crown.

VI. Held in 1119; was called by Pope Gelasius II., who had again excommunicated Henry V., on the occasion of his setting up an anti-pope in the person of Gregory VIII.; but nothing whatever concerning the transactions of this synod is known.

VII. Held in 1124; was incited by Pope Calixtus II., and called by Archbishop Peter, of Vienne; legislated with reference to the securing of ecclesiastical privileges and possessions.

VIII. Held in 1142; was chiefly concerned with the election of a new bishop.

IX. Held in 1164, at which Archbishop Reginald, of Cologne, vainly endeavored to secure a recognition of Paschal III., whom the Emperor Frederick had endorsed.

X. Held in 1199, by the Cardinal-legate Peter of Capua, for the purpose of promulgating the decree of Pope Innocent III., which punished the King Philip Augustus with excommunication on account of his renunciation of Inneburgis, his lawful consort; and his subsequent marriage with Agnes, of Meran. (Mansi *Concil* xi, 11).

XI. Held in 1289; is barely mentioned in the records, and some authorities deny that it was held.

XII. Held in 1311; known as the fifteenth œcumenical council, and the only one of the series to which attaches any considerable importance. It was originally ordered, by a papal bull of 1308, to meet Oct. 1, 1310, but was subsequently postponed for one year. The council finally convened under the presidency of Pope Clement V., October 16, 1311. The number of prelates present is fixed by some at 114, and by others at 300, including the patriarchs of the Latin Rite of Alexandria and Antioch. It discussed methods for preserving the purity of the faith, which was impaired by the heretical influence of John, of Olivia, and of the Fratricelli, Dolcinists, Beghards and Beguins; also the aid to be afforded the Holy Land; the reform of ecclesiastical discipline; and especially the disposition to be made of the Order of Knights Templars. The decision abrogated the Order of Templars; declared the legitimacy of the late Pope Boniface VIII., and his freedom from the crimes charged against him; conceded titles for six years to the kings of France, England and Navarre, in order that they might organize a crusade; and regulated the government of the begging friars and similar matters. Most of the decrees which have to do with matters of doctrine and discipline are contained in the so-called *Clementines*, and were first promulgated by Pope John XXII. (London *Manual of Councils*, 5 v.).

XIII. Held in 1557; it determined several questions of Church discipline; discussed the use of sermons as a means of instructing the people; forbade the admission of strangers to the pulpits; demanded the rendition of heretics; and prohibited merry-makings on feast-days and association with suspected persons; gave directions concerning the tonsure and garb of priests; denied to monks and nuns the privilege of leaving their convents, etc. (Martine *Thesaur. Novus Anecdot*—Lutet Par. 1717, iv, 446 sq.).

COUNCIL OF CONSTANCE.

This council was summoned at the dictation of Pope John XXIII., in accordance with the writ of the Emperor Sigismund, and continued its sessions from 1414 to 1418. One of its professed objects was to put an end to the schism which had lasted for thirty years, and which was caused by the several claimants for the pontificate. At this time, besides John (Balthasar Cossa), two others claimed the title of pope, viz., Pedro of Luna, a native of Catalonia, who styled himself Benedict XIII., and Angelo Corrario, a Venetian, who assumed the name of Gregory XII. Another object of the council was to take cognizance of the so-called heresies of Huss and Wickliffe. The council was called to meet at Constance on the festival of All-Saints, in 1414, and so great was the influx of people, that it was estimated that not less than 30,000 horses were brought to Constance, which may give some idea of the immense multitude of human beings. It is stated that during the session, the Emperor, the Pope, twenty princes, 140 counts, more than twenty cardinals, seven patriarchs, twenty archbishops, ninety-one bishops, 600 other clerical dignitaries, and about 4000 priests, were present at this celebrated convocation. The pretended heresies of Wickliffe and Huss were here condemned, and the latter, notwithstanding the assurances of safety given him by the Emperor, was burnt at the stake July 6, 1415, and his friend and companion, Jerome of Prague, met with the same fate, May 30, 1416. The three popes were formally deposed, and Martin V. was legally chosen to the chair of St. Peter; but instead of furthering the Emperor's wishes for a reformation in the affairs of the Church, he thwarted his plans, and nothing was accomplished till the council of Basle. At this council the question was very warmly agitated whether the authority of an œcumenical council is greater than that of the Pope or not? Gerson "proved (so it is asserted) that in certain cases the Church, or, which is the same thing, an œcumenical council, can assemble without the command or consent of the Pope, even supposing him to have been canonically elected, and to live respectably." These peculiar cases, he states to be, "1. If the Pope, being accused, and brought into a position requiring the opinion of the Church, refuses to convoke a council for the purpose. 2. When important matters, concerning the government of the Church, are in agitation, requiring to be set at rest by an œcumenical council, which, nevertheless, the Pope refuses to convoke." (Herzog, *Real Encykl.*, iii, 144, and many other authorities.)

THE COUNCIL AT BASLE.

This council was called by Pope Martin V., and continued by Eugenias IV. It was opened July 23, 1431, by Cardinal Julian, and closed May 16, 1443, forty-five sessions in all having been held, of which the first twenty-five were acknowledged by the Gallican Church. The Ultramontanes reject it altogether, but "on grounds utterly untenable," it is said. The council, in its thirtieth session, declared that "a general council is superior to a pope;" and, in 1437, Eugenius transferred its sessions to Ferrara. The council refused to obey, and continued its sessions at Basle, the capitol of a canton of the same name in Switzerland. The principal objects for which this council was called, were the reformation of the Church, and the reunion of the Greek with the Roman Church. "Many of its resolutions were admirable both in spirit and form; and had the council been allowed to continue its sessions, and had the Pope sanctioned its proceedings, there would have ensued a great and salutary change in the Roman Church." But the power of the papacy was at stake, and the reform was suppressed. Its most important acts were as follows:

In the first session, December 7, 1431, the decree of the council of Constance, concerning the celebration of a general council after five and after seven years, was read, together with the bull of Martin V. convoking the the council, in which he named Julian, president; also the letter of Eugene IV. to the latter upon the subject; afterward the six objects proposed in calling the council were enumerated: 1. The extirpation of heresy. 2. The reunion of all Christian persons with the Catholic Church. 3. To afford instruction in the true faith. 4. To appease the wars between Christian princes. 5. To reform the Church in its head and in its members. 6. To re-establish, as far as possible, the ancient discipline of the Church.

It soon appeared that Pope Eugene was determined to break up the council, which took vigorous measures of defense. In the *second* session (Feb. 15, 1432) it was "declared that the synod, being assembled in the name of the Holy Spirit, and representing the Church militant, derives its power directly from our Lord Jesus Christ, and that all persons, of whatever rank or dignity, not excepting the Roman pontiff himself, are bound to obey it; and that any person, of whatever rank or condition, not excepting the Pope, who shall refuse to obey the laws and decrees of this or any other general council, shall be put to penance and punished."

In the *third session* (April 29, 1432) Pope Eugene was summoned to appear before the council within three months. In August the Pope sent legates to vindicate his authority over the council; and in the eighth session (Dec. 18,) it was agreed that the Pope should be proceeded against canonically, in order to declare him contumacious, and to visit him with the canonical penalty; two months' delay, however, being granted him within which to revoke his bull for the dissolution of the council.

On the 16th of January, 1433, deputies arrived from the Bohemians, demanding (1) liberty to administer the Eucharist in both kinds; (2) that all mortal sin, and especially open sin, should be repressed, corrected, and published, according to God's law; (3) that the Word of God should be preached faithfully by the bishops, and by such deacons as were fit for it; (4) that the clergy should not possess authority in temporal matters. It was afterward agreed that the clergy in Bohemia and Moravia should be allowed to give the cup to the laity; but no reconciliation was effected. In April, 1433, Eugene signified his willingness to send legates to the council to preside in his name, but the council refused his conditions. In the twelfth *session* (July 14, 1433,) the Pope, by a decree, was required to renounce within sixty days his design of transferring the council from Basle, upon pain of being pronounced contumacious. In return, Eugene, irritated by these proceedings, issued a bull, annulling all the decrees of the council against himself. Later in autumn, the Pope, in fear of the council, supported as it was by the Emperor and by France, agreed to an accommodation. He chose four cardinals to preside with Julian at the council; he revoked all the bulls which he had issued for its dissolution, and published one according to the form sent him by the council. [Session XIV]. It was to the effect that, although he had broken up the council at Basle lawfully assembled, nevertheless, in order to appease the disorders which had arisen, he declared the council to have been lawfully continued from its commencement, and that it would be so to the end; that he approved of all that it had offered and decided, and that he declared the bull for its dissolution, which he had issued, to be null and void; thus, as Bossuet observes, setting the council above himself, since, in obedience to its order, he revoked his own decree, made with all the authority of his pontifical see. In spite of this forced yielding, Eugene never ceased plotting for the dissolution of the council. In subsequent sessions earnest steps were taken toward reform; the annates and taxes (the Pope's chief revenues) were abrogated; the papal authority over chapter elections were restricted; citations to Rome on minor grounds were forbidden, etc. These movements increased the hatred of the papal party, to which, at last, Cardinal Julian was won over. The proposed reunion of the Greek and Roman churches made it necessary to appoint a place of conference with the Greeks. The council proposed Basle or Avignon; the papal party demanded an Italian city. The latter, in the minority, left Basle, and Eugene called an opposition council to meet at Ferrara in 1437. After Julian's departure the Cardinal Archbishop of Arles presided.

In the thirty-first *session*, Jan. 24, 1438, the council declared the Pope Eugene contumacious, suspended him from the exercise of all jurisdiction, temporal or spiritual, and pronounced all that he should do to be null and void. In the twenty-fourth *session*, June 25, 1439, sentence of deposition was pronounced against Eugene, making use of the strongest possible terms. France, England and Germany disapproved of this sentence. On October 30, Amadeus, Duke of Savoy, was elected Pope, and took the name of Felix V. Alphonso, King of Aragon, the Queen of Hungary, and the Dukes of Bavaria and Austria, recognized Felix, as also did the Universities of Germany, Paris and Cracow; but France, England and Scotland, while they acknowledged the authority of the council of Basle, continued to recognize Eugene as the lawful Pope. Pope Eugene dying four years after, Nicholas V. was elected in his stead, and recognized by the whole Church, whereupon Felix V. renounced the pontificate in 1449, and thus the schism ended. (*Mansi*, vols. 29 to 31; London, *Manual of Councils*, 74; Palmer, *On the Church;* Moshiem; *Church History;* Ranke, *History of Papacy*, i, 36, 243.

COUNCIL OF TRENT.

This council is regarded by the Roman Catholic Church as the last in the order of assemblies known as æcumenical or general, and as the great repository of all the doctrinal judgments of that ecclesiastical body on the chief points at issue with the reformers of the sixteenth century. "Very early in this conflict with Leo X., Luther had appealed from the Pope to a general council; and after the failure of the first attempts at an adjustment of the controversies, a general desire grew up in the Church for the convocation of a general council, in which the true sense of the Church upon the controversies which had been raised, might be finally and decretorially settled. Another, and, to many, a still more pressing motive for desiring a council, was the wish to bring about a reform of the alleged abuses as well of the Court of Rome as of the domestic discipline and government of local churches, to which the movement of the reformers was in part at least ascribed. But the measures for convoking a council were long delayed, owing partly, it has been alleged, to the intrigues of the party who were interested in the maintenance of those profitable abuses, and especially of the officials of the Roman court, including the cardinals, and even the popes themselves; but partly also the jealousies, and even the actual conflicts, which took place between Charles V. and the King of France, whose joint action was absolutely indispensable to the success of any ecclesiastical assembly." (Chamber's *Encyclopædia*, vol. ix., p. 533.)

It was not till the pontificate of Paul III. (1534–1549) that the design assumed a practical character. One of the great difficulties was that in regard to a place of meeting. In these discussions much time was lost; and without entering into detail, it is sufficient to say that the assembly did not actually meet till December 13, 1545, at which time four archbishops, twenty-two bishops, five generals of orders, and the representatives of the Emperor and of the King of the Romans, assembled at Trent, a city of the Tyrol. The number of prelates afterwards increased. The Pope was represented by three legates, who presided in his name, viz., Cardinals del Monte, Cervino and Pole. The first three sessions were devoted to preliminaries. It was not till the fourth session (April, 1546) that the really important work of the council began. It was decided, after much disputation, that the doctrinal questions and the questions of reformation should both be proceeded with simultaneously. Accordingly, the discussions on both subjects were continued through the fourth, fifth, sixth and seventh sessions, in all of which "matters of great moment were decided;" when a division between the Pope and the Emperor, who, by the victory of Mühlberg, had become all-powerful in the empire, made the former desirous to transfer the council some place beyond the reach of Charles' arbitrary dictation. The appearance of the plague at Trent furnished a cause for removal, and in the eighth session a decree was passed (March 11, 1547) transferring the council to Bologna.

The change of place was opposed by the bishops who were in the imperial interest, and the division which ensued had the effect of suspending all practical action. In the meantime, Paul III. died. Julius III., who had, as Cardinal del Monte, presided as legate in the council, took measures for its resumption at Trent, where it again assembled, May 1, 1551. The sessions 9-12, held partly at Bologna, and partly at Trent, were spent in discussions regarding the suspension and removal; but in the thirteenth session the real work of the assembly was renewed, and was continued, slowly, but with great care, till the sixteenth session, when, on account of the apprehended insecurity of Trent, the passes of the Tyrol having fallen into the hands of Maurice, of Saxony, the sittings were again suspended for two years.

But the suspension was destined to continue for no less than nine years. Julius III. died in 1555, and was followed rapidly to the grave by his successor (who had also been his fellow-legate in the council as Cardinal Cervina) Marcellus II. The pontificate of Paul IV. (1555-1559) was a very troubled one, as well on account of internal dissensions as owing to the abdication of Charles V.; nor was it till the accession of Pius IV.

(1559–1565) that the bishops and legates were again brought together to the number of 102, under the presidency of Cardinal Gonzaga, reopening their deliberations with the seventeenth session. All the succeeding sessions were "devoted to matters of the highest importance," among which may be mentioned such doctrines and practices as (1) communion under one kind, (2) the sacrifice of the mass, (3) the sacrament of orders, (4) the nature and origin of the grades of the hierarchy, (5) marriage and the many questions relating to it. These grave discussions occupied the sessions 17–24, and lasted till November 11, 1563. . Much anxiety was expressed on the part of many bishops to draw the council to a conclusion, in order that they might be able to return to their sees in a time so critical; and accordingly, as the preliminary discussions regarding most of the remaining questions had already taken place, decrees were prepared in special congregations comprising almost all the remaining subjects of controversy, as (1) purgatory, (2) invocation of saints, (3) images, (4) relics, and (5) indulgences. Several other matters, rather of detail than of doctrinal principle, were referred to the Pope, to be by him examined and arranged; and on the 3d and 4th of December, 1563, these important decrees were finally read, approved and subscribed by the members of the assembly, consisting of four cardinal legates, two other cardinals, twenty-five archbishops, 168 bishops, seven abbots, seven generals of orders and thirty-nine proxies of bishops, comprising in all 252.

These decrees were confirmed January 10, 1564, by by Pius IV., who had drawn up, based upon them in conjunction with the creeds previously in use, a profession of faith known under his name. "The doctrinal decrees of the council were received at once throughout the Western Church, a fact which it is necessary to note, as the question as to the reception of the decrees of doctrine has sometimes been confounded with that regarding the decrees of reformation or discipline." As to the latter, delays and reservations took place. The first country to receive the decrees of the council as a whole, was the Republic of Venice. France accepted the disciplinary decrees only piece meal and at intervals.

The canons and decrees of the council of Trent were issued in Latin, and have been reprinted innumerable times. They have also been translated into almost every modern language. One of the supplementary works assigned to the Pope by the council at its breaking up, was the completion of a catechism for the use of parish priests and preachers. This work has not all the authority of the council, but it is of the very highest credit, and is extensively used, having, like the canons and decrees, been very generally translated. Another similar work was the publication of an authentic edition of the Vulgate version of the Bible, as well as of the Breviary and Missal. All these have been accomplished at intervals; and there is besides at Rome a permanent tribunal, a congregation of cardinals, styled "*Congregatio Interpres Concilii Tridentini,*" to which belongs the duty of dealing with all questions which arise as to the meaning, the authority, or the effect of the canons and decrees of this celebrated council. (Chamber's *Encyclopædia*, vol. ix., p. 534.)

It would occupy entirely too much space to give the dry and uninteresting details of this council. But we have given a faithful outline of its proceedings. Suffice to say that the Roman Catholic Church of the present day is but a counterpart, theologically and morally, of the council of Trent. During the various sittings of the sessions, such questions as these were discussed: the personal sin of Adam; original sin; the immaculate conception of the Virgin Mary; non-resident bishops; justification as opposed to Luther and other reformers; infant baptism; the validity of baptism; the conferring of grace by the sacraments; transubstantiation as opposed to consubstantiation; extreme unction; priestly vestments; a visible priesthood; whether the cup should be given to the laity at the communion; pictures and images; a general overhauling of the theology of Luther and Zwingle and Melancthon.

The importance of the so-called æcumenical councils has often been greatly over-estimated, not only by the Greeks and Roman Catholics, but also by many Protestants. John Jortin, D.D., an eminent preacher of the eighteenth century, and of the Church of England, tells us very forcibly that councils " were a collection of men who were frail and fallible. Some of these councils were not assemblies of pious and learned divines, but cabals, the majority of which were quarrelsome, fanatical, domineering, dishonest prelates, who wanted to compel men to approve all their opinions, of which they themselves had no clear conceptions, and to anathematize and oppose those who would not implicitly submit to their determinations." (*Works*, vol. iii., charge 2).

The Romanists hold that the Pope alone can convene and conduct æcumenical councils, which are supposed, on their theory, to represent the universal Church under the guidance of the Holy Spirit. In matters of faith, councils profess to be guided by the Holy Scriptures and the traditions of the Church, while in lighter matters human reason and expediency are consulted. In matters of faith, æcumenical councils are held to be infallible, and hence it is maintained that all such synods have agreed together; but in matters of discipline, etc., the authority of the latest council prevails. The Roman claim is not sanctioned by history. The emperors called the first seven councils, and either presided over them in person or by commissioners; and the final ratification of the decisions was also left to the Emperor. But the Greek Church agrees with the Latin in ascribing absolute *authority* to the decisions of truly œcumenical councils. Gregory of Nazianzus (who was president for a time of the second æcumenical council) speaks strongly of the evils to which such assemblies are liable. He says: "*I am inclined to avoid conventions of bishops; I never knew one that did not come to a bad end, and create more disorders than it attempted to rectify.*" A remarkable view of the authority of councils was that of Nicolas of Clamengis, viz., that they, in his opinion, could claim regard for their resolutions only if the members were really believers, and if they were more concerned for the salvation of souls than for secular interests. His views on general councils were fully set forth in a little work entitled: *Disputatio de concilio generali*, which consists of three letters, addressed in 1415 or 1416, to a professor at the Paris University (printed apparently at Vienna in 1482). He not only places the authority of general councils over the authority of the popes, but the authority of the Bible over the authority of the councils. He doubts whether at all the former œcumenical councils the Holy Spirit really presided, as the Holy Spirit would not assist men pursuing secular aims. He denies that a council composed of such men represents the Church, and asserts that God alone knows who are his people, and where the Holy Spirit dwells, and that there may be times when the Church can only be found in one single woman. After the lapse of over 300 years, the Pope in 1867 signified his purpose to summon another œcumenical (or universal) council; but of course none but Roman bishops attended it. (McClintock and Strong's *Encyclopædia*, vol. ii, p. 539.)

GOSPEL PRINCIPLES.

FAITH AND SIGHT.

IN this age of unbelief and gross skepticism, where every possible attempt is made to undermine the very foundation of Christianity, and, if possible, to dethrone Jesus Christ, and rob him of his glory and his divinity, and where scoffers take pleasure in reducing the word of God to a level with the words of uninspired men, it devolves upon the defenders of the faith to review and reconsider the ground of their hope, and to re-establish in the hearts of believers their confidence in a divine revelation. Christians walk by faith, not by sight. Their faith in a divine revelation is founded upon testimony. They depend upon the common rules of evidence. They apply the same rules of interpretation to a divine revelation that they apply to a human composition. Where there is no testimony there is no faith— upon any subject. Faith is made strong or weak according to the degree of testimony. In the absence of testimony there can be no faith. Every proposition must be established by its own kind of testimony. That is to say, a historical proposition must be proved by historical testimony; a proposition in mathematics must be demonstrated by mathematical principles; the science of geology (if there is such a science) must be established by the proofs of geology; a proposition in chemistry must be sustained by the laws of physics; a supernatural proposition can only be sustained by supernatural testimony, and can not be sustained by the laws of nature. The proof of spiritual things must be found, and can only be found, within the sphere of spiritual things, as the proof of mathematics, can only be found within the realm of that science. These are all self-evident propositions, which no reasonable man will deny.

Men testify to what they see and hear. But their own senses may deceive them, if there is not corroborative and cumulative evidence. Circumstantial evidence is stronger than the evidence of the natural senses, and is so held in all courts of law and judicature. The qualities of a reliable witness are, (1) good eye-sight, (2) good hearing, (3) an honest heart. These were the qualities of the witnesses chosen by Jesus of Nazareth. Living in the open air continually, as was the case of the witnesses chosen by Christ, their hearing would naturally become very acute, and their vision would become very sensitive to all external objects. Christ did not go among princes to select his witnesses, nor choose from among the wealthy and the educated classes, nor draw from the schools of philosophers and rhetoricians, but he chose honest-hearted men, who, divested of the fetters and cares of a commercial and trading life, and of the conventionalities of the polite world, enjoyed the full possession of all their natural powers. The apostles were the witnesses of Jesus the Christ, and they testified before the court of the world as to what they saw and heard in the life of Christ, and their accumulated evidence challenges the world. If the testimony—the accumulated testimony—of the apostles can not be relied upon, then no testimony in the world can be relied on, and all the testimony of the past ages, in all the domains of fact, is nothing but a shapeless heap of chaos.

It is not our purpose in this series of essays to investigate the supernatural claims of Christianity, nor to undertake to prove that which, in a thousand ways and a thousand times, has been placed beyond doubt. We simply appeal to common-sense principles. We meet the infidel upon his own ground and ask no favors of him. The infidel believes there were such persons as Washington, Lafayette, Napoleon Bonaparte, Byron, Bacon, Plato, Aristotle, Cæsar, Cicero, Demosthenes, Alexander the Great, Pliny, Plutarch, Herodotus, *et al.* *How* does he know there were such persons in existence at the times indicated by history? We answer by saying that by the same rules of evidence with which he proves the personalities of those historical characters, we prove the personality of Jesus of Nazareth. If once we prove the *personality* of Christ, it is easy to prove his supernatural origin, and hence his divinity; and this we propose to do by concessions which infidels themselves unwillingly make. Men who stand highest in the ranks of infidelity, concede that Jesus was absolutely a pure and good man, and absolutely a perfect man, without the least taint of sin, and without the least semblance of imperfection. A man absolutely good and absolutely perfect can not lie. This man, who is conceded to be absolutely perfect *as a man*, said: "I am the Son of God;" "I came down from heaven to seek and to save the lost;" "I am the Savior of men;" "I and my Father are one;" "I was in the bosom of my Father before the worlds began to be;" "I am the way, the truth and the life;" "Before Abraham was I am;" "I am the resurrection and the life;" "No man can come to me, except the Father who sent me draw him, and *I* will raise him up at the last day." What we want to know is this: Did Christ utter a falsehood when he uttered these sentiments? Not if he was, as conceded by the infidel, absolutely good and absolutely pure and perfect. As it was morally impossible for him to utter a falsehood, it is morally certain that he was Immanuel—God manifested in flesh.

We now propose to consider the following questions, as they relate to the subject of faith: (1) What is the definition of faith? (2) What is the foundation of faith? (3) How many kinds of faith are there? (4) How does faith come? (5) The objects of faith? (6) Illustrations of faith?

I. Paul defines faith as "the evidence of things hoped for, the conviction of things not seen." (Heb. xi. 1, Macknight's translation.) The best human definition of faith we ever heard of came from the lips of an Irish woman. When interrogated by her bishop as to the meaning of faith, she answered, after some hesitation, "Sir, faith means *taking God at his word*." Very simple, and yet how comprehensive. If all people were to "take God at his word," what a happy world this would be. If all men and all priests and pastors would put out of sight all theories and all speculations, and all dreams and figments of the fancy, and all psychological sensations, and all mysterious and mystical impressions, and simply "take God at his word," not only, as an effect, would God's children come to see eye to eye and stand upon the same basis of Christian union, but infidelity itself would be shorn of its greatest strength of opposition, and quail before the majesty of God's eternal truth.

We must distinguish between faith as an act of the mind, as influenced by testimony, and "the faith" as representing the system of salvation. To "contend earnestly for the faith," is to contend for that system of things which contains all the elements of the gospel. The apostles use the terms "the faith" and "the law of faith" interchangeably with "the doctrine" or the teaching. The apostles place "the faith" of the gospel in contrast with the "law of Moses."

II. The foundation of faith is found in the divine testimonies. Facts produce testimony. A fact is something *done*. An opinion is not something *done*. An opinion is what a man *thinks*, and his opinion may be right or it may be wrong. Opinions differ, but facts never. And yet many systems of religion, formulated in creeds, are but the systematized opinions of men, and, therefore, human, fallible and misleading, and also very sinful. Present knowledge does not produce faith. Whatever we are conscious of, by the sensation of hearing, seeing and tasting, does not constitute faith. We must always, to reason correctly and deduce logical conclusions, distinguish between *conscious knowledge, opinion* and *fact*. The knowledge of *sensation* never enters the domain of faith, and yet many religious teachers substitute sensations for facts, and make sensations the evidence of pardon, instead of God's word or the Holy Scriptures, which are revealed to us as facts. Paul tells us distinctly, in his grand culminating argument, as recorded in Hebrews xi., that "*without faith* it is impossible to please God," and that "they who come to God must believe that he is, and that he is the rewarder of them who diligently seek him." Under the Jewish law, and in the days of the prophet Jeremiah, there were false prophets who presumed to substitute dreams, and psychological sensations, and vain imaginations, for the statutes of the Almighty. Jeremiah compares these animal sensations and God's word, and, while he represents sensations as "chaff," he, at the same time, represents the word of God as "wheat." Please read the entire twenty-third chapter. The prophet of God says: "To the law and to the testimony; if any speak not according to this word, it is because there is no light in him."

The accumulative testimonies of Matthew, Mark, Luke and John, concerning the Messiahship of Christ, and as regards his life and miracles, and, also, as touching upon the doctrine of immortality, which he enunciated, stand before the world as irrefutable facts. Says the apostle John, "And many other signs [miracles] truly did Jesus in the presence of his disciples, which are not written in this book. But these *are written*, that you might believe that Jesus is the Christ, the Son of God; and that believing, you might have life through his name." (John xx. 30, 31.) Luke opens his narrative as follows: "Forasmuch as many have taken in hand to set forth in order a declaration of those things which *are most surely believed among us*, even as they delivered them to us, who, from the beginning, *were eye-witnesses* and ministers of the word: it seemed good to me also, having had *perfect understanding of all things* from the very first, to write to thee in order, most excellent Theophilus, that thou mightest *know the certainty* of those things wherein thou hast been instructed." In the preface of his second treatise—Acts of the Apostles—Luke thus writes: "The former treatise [the Gospel of Luke] have I made, O Theophilus, of all that Jesus began both to do and teach, until the day in which he was taken up, after that he through the Holy Spirit had given commandments to the apostles whom he had chosen: to whom, also, he showed himself alive after his passion [his sufferings and death], *by many infallible proofs*, being seen of them forty days, and speaking of the things pertaining to the kingdom of God: and, being assembled together with them, commanded them that they should not depart from Jerusalem, but wait for the promise of the Father, which, saith he, you have heard of me."

These treatises, with the corroborative testimonies of contemporaneous historians, furnish the facts of the foundation of our faith; to which also may be added the invaluable testimony of Paul as recorded in the fifteenth chapter of First Corinthians, the honest investigation of which has converted many an infidel.

Having in a previous number established the foundation of Christian faith, we next propose to ascertain how *many kinds of faith* there are to be found in the Bible. On examination, we discover that there is only *one kind* of faith, for we are so informed by the apostle Paul, who tells us in Eph. iv. 5 that there is "one Lord, *one faith* and one baptism."

III. God has endowed every rational man with intellectual power with which to examine testimony. The same faculties of the mind with which he investigates one proposition he investigates every proposition, whether human or divine. There is not one set of mental faculties fitted, in a peculiar manner, for the investigation of one proposition, and another set furnished for the examination of a different proposition, or a new set furnished as often as the character of the subject changes. We use the same faculties in examining the testimonies concerning Jesus Christ as the Son of God, and in investigating his claims upon the world, that we use in trying to discover whether such a man as Moses, or Cyrus, or Pompey, or Cato, or Aurelius, had a real existence. The same rules of evidence and of interpretation are applied in the exploration of all kinds of truth, just as the same eyes are used in viewing all objects, and just as the same ears are used in hearing all sounds, whether soft or harsh, whether harmonious or inharmonious. It does not follow that because we see different objects' we have different sets of eyes, or that because we hear varied sounds we have various sets of ears, or that we have as many palates as the objects we taste. Dr. Buck's "Theological Dictionary" contains different *kinds* of faith, such as "saving faith," "evangelical faith," "historical faith," "direct faith," "reflex faith," "dead faith," "living faith," the "faith of works," the "faith of devils," the "faith of miracles," etc. No such incongruities are found in the Bible. These are all fanciful and speculative distinctions, conjured up in the minds of mystics and ascetics, who, having retired from the world and having entered their closets and their cloisters, lost their wits and became fools. Says Pollock:

> "Faith was bewildered much by men who meant
> To make it clear, so simple in itself,
> A thought so rudimental and so plain,
> That none by comment could it plainer make.
> All faith was one. In object, not in kind,
> The difference lay. The faith that saved a soul,
> And that which in the common truth believed,
> In essence were the same. Hear then, what faith,
> True Christian faith, which brought salvation, was:
> Belief in all that God revealed to men :
> Observe in all that God revealed to men,
> In all he promised, threatened, commanded, said,
> Without exception and without a doubt."

IV. How does faith come? Paul informs us that "faith *comes by hearing the word of God.*" (Rom. x. 17.) Some hold, and especially the mystics of many of the orthodox churches, that faith is the direct gift of God, and that no one can believe until he receives this gift. John Wesley says that faith, or the power to believe, is the gift of God, just as seeing is the gift of God, or hearing the gift of God; but if we close our eyes, which are the gift of God, we can not see; or if we stop our ears, which are also the gift of God, we can not hear. In like manner, though the *power* to believe be the gift of God, if we close the eyes of our understanding we can not perceive the truth. The *power* to believe is one thing, to *exercise* that power is quite another thing. Just see how our Savior in his address to the multitude explains the method of perceiving and understanding the truth. He says:

"And in them is fulfilled the prophecy of Esaias, which says: By hearing you shall hear, and shall not understand; and seeing you shall see, and shall not perceive; for this people's *heart is waxed gross*, and *their ears are dull of hearing*, and their eyes they have closed; lest at any time they should *see with their eyes*, and *hear with their ears*, and should *understand with the heart*, and should turn [new version] and I should *heal them*. But blessed are your eyes, for they *see;* and your ears, for they *hear.* For truly I say unto you, that many prophets and righteous men have desired to see those things which *you see* and have not seen them; and to hear those things which *you hear*, and have not heard them." (Matt. xiii. 14-17.)

"*Faith comes by hearing the word of God*," and does not descend from heaven on a sunbeam or on a moonbeam; does not drop down from heaven in a napkin; does not flash from the golden tip of an angel's wing; does not appear upon the face of a cloud in the form of a cross; does not whisper salvation in a passing breeze; is not imparted to the soul of a sinner by a spark of electricity; is not conveyed upon the white wings of a descending evangel of the skies; does not come upon stealthy wing from some dark cavern or whip out of some dense jungle. "But the righteousness which is of faith speaks on this wise: Say not in thine heart, Who shall ascend into heaven (that is, to bring Christ down from above)? or who shall descend into the deep (that is, to bring up Christ again from the dead)? But what says it? *The word is nigh thee*, even in thy mouth and in thy heart; that is, the *word of faith*, which we *preach*. That if thou shalt confess with thy mouth the Lord Jesus, and shalt *believe in thy heart* that God hath raised him from the dead, thou shalt be saved. For *with the heart* man *believes* unto righteousness; and with the mouth confession is made unto salvation." (Rom. x. 6–10.)

Salvation is the gift of God, and this blessing is received *through* the medium of faith. See Eph. ii. 8. Facts produce testimony, testimony produces conviction —"convicts of sin, of righteousness, and of judgment to come;" conviction leads to repentance; repentance results in "the obedience of the faith," which is immersion into the name of the Father, and of the Son, and of the Holy Spirit. Faith is the medium of salvation from sin, just as eating and drinking are a medium through which physical life is sustained. It is not the *manner* of eating and drinking that sustains animal life, but it is the *thing eaten*. There is no virtue in faith as an act of the mind to save the soul, but it is the *thing* appropriated by faith or through faith that saves the soul. It is the *thing* believed that saves, and not the *manner* of believing.

V. What is the great object of Christian faith? On what object must faith terminate? Salvation is not in a *thing*, but in a *person*. The object of faith is not a creed, not a confession of faith, not a set of dogmas, not a "church standard," not a platform of principles, not a church, not the law of Moses, not the "Institutes" of Calvin, or the institutes of any other man; but Jesus Christ the Savior of the world. Salvation is in the person of Christ. "All the promises of God are *in him* yea, and in him Amen." The apostles preached "Christ and him crucified." They preached Christ as the "wisdom of God and the power of God." "But of him are you *in Christ Jesus*, who of God is made unto us wisdom, and righteousness, and sanctification, and redemption." (1 Cor. i. 30.) On the day of Pentecost Peter presented the Lord Jesus Christ as the great object of faith. "This is the stone which was set at naught of you builders, which is become the head of the corner. Neither is there salvation in any other; for there is none other name under heaven given among men whereby we must be saved." (Acts iv. 11, 12.) "Him hath God exalted with his right hand to be a prince and a Savior, for to give repentance to Israel and forgiveness of sins." (Acts v. 31.) "To him gave all the prophets witness, that through his name whosoever believes in him shall receive remission of sins." (Acts x. 43.) When Philip preached to the Ethiopian eunuch he "began at the same Scripture, and preached to him *Jesus.*" The apostles never preached the Holy Spirit as the object of faith, but, being endowed with the Holy Spirit, they always presented the risen and glorified Christ as the supreme object of faith. They presented him as Prophet, Priest and King. They presented him in his death, burial and resurrection. They presented him in all his commandments and ordinances. To "believe on the Lord Jesus Christ" is the same as to "*obey* the gospel of our Lord and Savior Jesus Christ." Christ says, "He that hath the Son hath eternal life, and he that *obeyeth* [new version] not the Son hath not eternal life, but the wrath of God abideth upon him." Ever since the introduction of sin, God has said, "The soul that sins, it shall surely die;" but Satan has persistently asserted from the beginning, in direct contradiction of the word of God, that the soul that sins shall *not* surely die.

And this conflict between truth and falsehood has been raging through all past ages. As in the days of the prophet Ezekiel, so is it now; the land is flooded with lies and impostures. Many who profess to be leaders of the people "prophesy out of their own heart," and will not obey the word of the Lord; "they have seen vanity and lying divination," and the pulpits of the present day are filled with "vanity and lying divination." These modern deceivers "follow their own spirit;" they "divine lies," and they seduce the people with "visions of peace" when "there is no peace, saith the Lord God;" and "with lies" they make "the hearts of the righteous sad and strengthen the hands of the wicked, that he should not turn from his wicked way by *promising him life.*" (Ezek. xiii.)

VI. The Bible is replete with illustrations of faith. Paul, in Heb. xi., furnishes a whole chapter of noted examples. These illustrious characters shall live on in history to the final consummation. Men of faith, and only men of faith in all dispensations, have made the desert wastes of the world to bloom and blossom as the rose. Faith in God and confidence in his word hold the moral universe together—hold the moral government of God in equipoise. Infidelity would precipitate a universal crash. Remove such men of faith from the calendar of the first four thousand years of the world, as Abel, Enoch, Noah, Abraham, Isaac, Jacob, Moses,

Joseph, Joshua, David, Samuel, Samson, Jeremiah, Ezekiel, Isaiah, Nehemiah and Daniel, and there would be nothing left worthy of contemplation and admiration. Where men of faith have never lived and have never "walked with God;" where they have never lived in the "fear" of God; and where they never have "endured as seeing him who is invisible;" and where men and women, as "strangers and pilgrims on the earth," have not obeyed God, seeing the "promises" of God "afar off"—there you will find fields of desolation, unrest, spiritual darkness, human misery, starving hearts and thirsty souls, business stagnation, undeveloped powers, the dead doctrine of fatalism, gloomy superstition, groveling idolatry, selfishness, sordidness, hopelessness, and the glamour of eternal forgetfulness. Blot out of history the name of Jesus Christ, and the names of his apostles, and the names of the martyrs of God, and the names of all philanthropists, and the names of all reformers, and the names of all who have "walked with God," and you have nothing left to contemplate but a base world of blank desolation. It is a paradise lost. But thanks be to God that he has confirmed his oath by two immutable things, in which it is impossible for him to lie, that "we might have a strong consolation, who have fled for refuge to lay hold upon the hope set before us; which hope we have as an anchor to the soul, both sure and steadfast, and which enters into that within the vail; whither the forerunner is entered for us, even Jesus." (Heb. vi. 18, 19.)

REFORMATION OF LIFE.

If belief in testimony produces the conviction that Jesus Christ is the Son of God and the hope of the sinner, it is the "goodness of God that leads men to repentance." (Rom. ii. 4.) Convicted sinners are very apt to repent of their sins. Without conviction of sin there is no genuine reformation of life. Belief in testimony does not necessarily result in conviction of sin. It is said concerning Jesus of Nazareth, that "among the chief rulers also many believed on him; but because of the Pharisees they did not confess him, lest they should be put out of the synagogue: for they loved the praise of men more than the praise of God." (John xii. 42.) The testimonies of God were not only intended to illuminate the mind, but also, through conviction of sin, to change the character of the believer. When, like the prodigal son, a sinner comes to himself, he will change his course of life and return to God. Conscious of his helplessness and utter unworthiness; conscious of guilt with a sense of shame, and also realizing the infinite mercy and goodness of God, the sinner will seek to know the will of the Lord, and, having ascertained his will, he will hasten to carry out, in overt acts of obedience, the conditions of that will. God has commanded all men everywhere to repent—reform; but all men do not reform, though satisfied of the truth of the gospel. Christ told the apostles that when the Spirit came, the "Spirit of truth," or the truth revealed by the Spirit, whether spoken by the apostles or by "faithful men," would "convict the world of sin, of righteousness, and of judgment." Men thus convicted are ready to cry out, "Men and brethren, what must we do to be saved?" To convince men of the truth of Christianity is one thing; to convict them of sin is another thing. Men who love sin more than they love God, will not reform as long as they remain in that condition of heart.

John's preaching convicted of sin; Christ's preaching convicted his hearers of sin. The preaching of the apostles had the same effect. Little of that kind of preaching is done at the present day, hence the failure in producing reformation of life in thousands who hear the truth and assent to it. The sensational preachers of this age induce thousands to subscribe to the fact that Jesus Christ is the Son of God and the Savior of men; but in less than six months from the time they gave assent to the proposition, they lapse back into the world, for the reason, first, that their "converts," were not grounded in the truth; and, second, because they were not thoroughly convicted of the guilt and shame of sin. It is a "godly sorrow" that leads to a reformation of life, but "the sorrow of the world" "works death." (1 Cor. vii. 10.)

Paul, before the Athenians, announces the broad proposition that God "now commands all men everywhere to repent"—to reform; "because he has appointed a day in the which he will judge the whole world in righteousness by that man whom he has ordained; whereof he has given assurance to all men in that he has raised him from the dead." (Acts xvii. 30, 31.)

The law of reformation is the same in all ages, whether under the law of Moses or under the gospel of Christ. God, by Jeremiah, thus spoke to the house of Israel: "At what instant I shall speak concerning a nation, and concerning a kingdom, to pluck up and to pull down, and to destroy it; if that nation against whom I have pronounced, turn from their evil way, I will repent of the evil that I thought [or purposed] to do unto them. And at what instant I shall speak concerning a nation, and concerning a kingdom, to build and plant it; if it do evil in my sight, that it obey not my voice, then I will repent of the good wherewith I said I would benefit it." (Jer. xviii. 7–10.) Says Isaiah: "Seek ye the Lord while he may be found, call ye upon him while he is near: let the wicked forsake his way, and the unrighteous man his thoughts: and let him return unto the Lord, and he will have mercy upon him; and to our God, for he will abundantly pardon." (Isa. lv. 6, 7.) This principle of reformation under the Jewish economy, shows that when the violators of God's law "cut off their sins by righteousness"—by obeying the voice of the Lord—he will turn from his purpose of punishing them and pardon them. Under John's reformatory movement, while the old Jewish covenant was still alive and in force, and while he was "preaching the baptism of repentance for the remission of sins," as a work under the law, preparatory to the actual setting up of the kingdom of Christ, "the people asked him, saying, What shall we do then? He answers and says to them, He that has two coats, let him impart to him who has none; and he that has meat [food], let him do likewise. Then came also publicans to be baptized, and said to him, Master, what shall we do? And he said to them, Exact no more [or extort no more taxes from the people] than that which is appointed you. And the soldiers likewise demanded of him, saying, And what shall we do? And he said to them, Do violence to no man, neither accuse any falsely, and be content with your wages"—as those in the Roman Government. (Luke iii. 10-14.) John was unwilling to immerse any one who did not "bring forth fruits worthy of repentance." John laid the axe of reform "unto the root of the trees," and when he saw many of the Pharisees and Sadducees come to his baptism, he said to them: "O brood of vipers, who has warned you to flee from the wrath to come? Bring forth, therefore, fruits worthy of repentance." John, as a Jewish prophet and teacher, was addressing God's people under the law—addressing those who had apostatized from the faith of their fathers. John came to prepare a people for the Lord—to "prepare the way of the Lord"—but after the Lord came and established his church or kingdom by his apostles, the preparatory work of John ceased. A more thorough reformatory work was inaugurated by the apostles of Jesus Christ; a work which was not to be confined to the single race of the Jews, but which was intended to extend to all the nations of the earth, "beginning at Jerusalem."

Before Christ ascended on high, he said to his apostles: "Thus it is written, and thus it behooved Christ to suffer, and to rise from the dead the first day: and that repentance and remission of sins should be preached *in his name* among all nations, beginning at Jerusalem." (Luke xxiv. 46, 47.) The new dispensation, under Jesus Christ, was inaugurated on the memorable day of Pentecost. Here reformation of life and remission of sins, for the first time, was preached *in the name* of the risen, coronated and glorified King. The gospel *in fact* never was preached until the apostle Peter preached it—"Out of Zion shall go forth the law [of "the Spirit of life"], and the word of the Lord from Jerusalem." (Isa. ii. 3.) Peter, on the day of Pentecost, thus concluded his great sermon, as addressed to the Jews:

This Jesus hath God raised up, whereof we are all witnesses. Therefore, being by the right hand of God exalted, and having received of the Father the promise of the Holy Spirit, he has shed forth this, which you now see and hear. For David is not ascended into the heavens: but he says himself, The Lord said unto my Lord, Sit thou on my right hand, until I make thy foes thy footstool. Therefore let all the house of Israel know assuredly, that God has made that same Jesus, whom you have crucified, both Lord and Christ. Now when they heard this, they were pierced in their heart, and said to Peter and to the rest of the apostles, Men and brethren, what shall we do? Then Peter said to them, Repent [*reform* your lives], and be immersed every one of you in the name of [or *by the authority* of] Jesus Christ for the remission of sins, and you shall receive the gift of the Holy Spirit. For the promise is to you and your children [your descendants], and to all who are afar off, even as many as the Lord our God shall call [by the gospel. See Rom. x. 14, 15]. And with many *other words* did he testify and exhort, saying, *Save yourselves* from this untoward generation. (Acts ii. 32–40.)

Here were three thousand sinners—the "murderers and betrayers of Jesus Christ"—who were willing to reform their lives; and, as a proof of genuine reformation, which was also a test of their faith in the glorified Christ, they were willing to submit to the positive ordinance of immersion, which, in other portions of apostolic teaching, is called "the *obedience* to the faith," or "that *form* of doctrine which was delivered," and which they had "*obeyed* from the heart." (Rom. i. 5, and vi. 17.)

At the conclusion of the second sermon, delivered to the same people, Peter said: "Repent [*reform*] ye, therefore, and *turn* [new version], that your sins may be blotted out, when the times of refreshing shall come from the presence of the Lord." (Acts iii. 19.) The word "*turn*" here corresponds with immersion in the first sermon; "blotted out" corresponds with "remission of sins;" and "the times of refreshing" corresponds with "the gift of the Holy Spirit," in the first sermon. In the first sermon, the order stands thus: (1) Reform, (2) be immersed, (3) remission of sins, (4) the gift of the Holy Spirit. As Peter would not contradict himself, being infallibly directed by the Holy Spirit, the order of the second sermon stands thus: (1) Reform, (2) turn (the overt act of immersion), (3) remission or (figuratively) the blotting out of sins, (4) the gift of the Spirit, or times of refreshing. If repentance is not mentioned in every case of conversion, it is implied; just as immersion is implied where it is not mentioned. Genuine repentance for sin leads to a salvation not to be repented of.

Paul makes a clear distinction between a godly sorrow and a worldly sorrow, which conditions of the heart are represented in the original Greek by two different words. He thus addresses his Corinthian brethren:

For though I made you sorry with a letter, I do not repent, though I did repent: for I perceive that the same epistle has made you sorry, though it were but for a season. Now I rejoice, not that you were made sorry, but that you *sorrowed to repentance;* for you were made sorry after a *godly manner,* that you might receive damage by us in nothing. For *godly sorrow works repentance to salvation* not to be repented of; but the *sorrow of the world works death.* (2 Cor. vii. 8-10.)

When the "goodness of God" leads men "to repentance," being deeply convicted of sin, and they reform their lives from principle, they manifest a godly sorrow. But when men are suddenly taken down sick and think they are going to die, they become alarmed and begin to cry for help; but it is not genuine repentance, because they do not repent through love for God; for, though they make promises of reformation upon their beds of sickness, when they recover they become worse sinners than they were before their sickness. As the captured thief is not sorry because he has *stolen goods,* but sorry because he has *been caught,* and goes to stealing again as soon as he is liberated, so the sinner, whose sorrow is only a worldly sorrow, is not sorry because he has *sinned against God,* but sorry because *God has captured him* and laid him low upon a bed of sickness; for when restored to health, though in his extremity he lustily called upon God for help, he goes off and sins worse than ever. This is what Paul means by the "sorrow of the world that works death"—eternal death. In the same chapter from which we have quoted, Paul gives the result of genuine reformation, in the following words: "For behold this selfsame thing, that you sorrowed after a *godly sort*, what carefulness it wrought in you; yea, what clearing of yourselves, yea, what indignation, yea, what fear, yea, what vehement desire, yea, what zeal, yea, what revenge! In all things you have approved yourselves to be clear in this matter."

These are the fruits of sincere and abiding reformation. These are fruits worthy of repentance. Men who cut off their sins by righteous acts—by obeying all the commands of God—are on their way heavenward and homeward. Having become "the sons of God" by being born into the family of God, they continue to honor that high and holy relation by a godly walk and a chaste conversation. Having become "the servants of righteousness," they have "their fruit unto holiness," and "the end, life everlasting."

THE GOOD CONFESSION.

A TRULY penitent believer is ready to confess faith in Christ as the Son of God and as his Savior. He is willing to confess publicly that Jesus of Nazareth is the Messiah of God. In making this public profession, the confessor accepts all the obligations which the name of Christ carries with it. If need be, in bearing the name of Christ, he accepts obloquy, reproach, persecution, imprisonment, and even death itself. He who receives Christ as Prophet, Priest and King, and as the Captain of his salvation, and as his Guide and Examplar, willingly assumes all the obligations which his public profession of the name of Christ involves. He is willing and ready to step at the command of his great Captain. He who is thoroughly persuaded by evidence incontrovertible that Jesus Christ is the Son of God, enlists in his service with a high and holy determination, and with no mental reservation, to follow him in every detail of duty, and to give the work of Christ a prominence above any other work he may engage in. Christ is very explicit in regard to those who confess his name. He says: " Whoever therefore shall confess me before men, him will I confess also before my Father who is in heaven. But whoever shall deny me before men, him will I also deny before my Father who is in heaven." (Matt. x. 32, 33.) Again he says: " Whoever shall be ashamed of me and my words, of him shall the Son of man be ashamed when he shall come in his own glory, and in his Father's, and of the holy angels." (Luke ix. 26.)

Paul says; "I am not ashamed of the gospel of Christ" (Rom. i. 16), and to his son Timothy he writes: "Be not thou ashamed of the testimony of our Lord, nor of me his prisoner; but be thou partaker of the afflictions of the gospel according to the power of God." (2 Tim. i. 8.) Again, quoting from Isaiah xxviii. 16, Paul says: "As it is written, Behold, I lay in Zion a stumbling stone and rock of offense; and whoever believes on him shall not be ashamed"—shall not be confounded. (Rom. ix. 33.) After exhorting Timothy not to be ashamed of the testimony of Christ, and after speaking of his own sufferings, Paul says: "For the which cause I also suffer these things; nevertheless, I am not ashamed, for I know whom I have believed [trusted], and am persuaded that he is able to keep that which I have committed to him against that day."

(2 Tim. i. 12.) And in the sixteenth verse he says, "and [I] was not ashamed of my chain." Hear Paul again: "For it became him for whom are all things, and by whom are all things, in bringing many sons unto glory, to make the Captain of their salvation perfect through sufferings. For both he who sanctifies and they who are sanctified are all one; for which cause he is not ashamed to call them brethren, saying, I will declare thy name unto my brethren, in the midst of the church will I sing praise unto thee. And again, I will put my trust in him. And again, Behold me and the children which God has given me." (Heb. ii. 10–13.) And of the righteous of all ages who trust in God and who walk by faith, Paul says that "God is not ashamed to be called their God." (Heb. xi. 16.)

The good confession only embraces one article of faith, but it is comprehensive of all that can be confessed concerning Christ, and here it is: "And many other signs truly did Jesus in the presence of his disciples, which are not written in this book; but these are written that you might believe that Jesus is the Christ, the Son of God; and that, believing, you might have life through his name." (Jno. xx. 30, 31.) An illustration of what confession means is seen in the conversion of the Ethiopian eunuch: "And as they went on their way, they came to a certain water; and the eunuch said, See . . . water; what doth hinder me to be baptized? And Philip said, If thou believest with all thine heart, thou mayest. And he answered and said, *I believe that Jesus Christ is the Son of God.*" (Acts viii. 36, 37.) What more can a man believe than to *believe with all his heart?* If a man believes with all his heart, he gives his whole heart to God; for the word "heart" is frequently used in the Scriptures to represent the entire man—body, soul and spirit—as for instance when God says, "Son, give me thine heart;" or, as Christ says, "Where your treasure is, there will your heart be also." When a patriot is asked, in time of war, to lay his heart upon the altar of his country, every one knows that it means the entire consecration of his life—money, time and influence, and even the offering up of his body—to the service of his country.

Any ordinary intellect can make the "good confession," and take in the full meaning of confessing the name of Christ, but no living soul can comprehend the Thirty-nine Articles which some of the orthodox creeds contain. These Articles confuse, and mislead, and make the word of God of none effect. The simplest soul, upon the testimony of the prophets and apostles, can say, and say it intelligently, "I believe that Jesus Christ is the Son of God." There is encouragement to a believer in this, but a man of reason and of intelligent faith will turn away in disgust, and in pardonable unbelief, from metaphysical and scholastic articles of faith —the production of fallible and foolish men. Paul writes to his son Timothy thus: "Fight the good fight of faith, lay hold on eternal life, whereunto thou art also called, and hast professed a good profession before many witnesses. I give thee charge in the sight of God, who quickens all things, and before Christ Jesus, who before Pontius Pilate witnessed a good confession; that thou keep his commandment without spot, unrebukable, until the appearing of our Lord Jesus Christ." (1 Tim. vi. 12-14.) The same Greek word which is here translated "confession," in verse twelve is translated "profession," and refers to the fact that the Lord Jesus, when standing at the bar of Pilate, who claimed to have power over his life, did not shrink from an open avowal of the truth. Timothy, no doubt, witnessed a good confession when he first espoused the cause of Christ, and made a public profession of it in the presence of the congregation and of the world, which, doubtless, was the practice in the primitive order of things. "Such a method," says Barnes, "of admitting members to the church would have been natural, and would have been fitted to make a deep impression on others. It is a good thing often to remind professors of religion of the feelings which they had when they made a profession of religion; of the fact that the transaction was witnessed by the world; and of the promises which they then made to lead holy lives. One of the best ways of stimulating ourselves or others to the faithful performance of duty, is the remembrance of the vows then made; and one of the most effectual methods of reclaiming a backslider, is to bring to his remembrance that solemn hour when he publicly gave himself to God."

Paul, in his epistle to the Romans, makes allusion to the good confession in these words: "The word is nigh thee, even in thy mouth, and in thy heart; that is, the word of faith, which we preach; that if thou shalt *confess with thy mouth* the Lord Jesus, and shalt believe in thy heart that God has raised him from the dead, thou shalt be saved; for with the heart man believes unto righteousness; and with the mouth *confession is made* unto [or in order to] salvation." (Rom. x. 8–10.) Even in the days of Christ's personal ministration on earth, it was deemed both unsafe and unpopular to confess his name. Hence the refusal of the parents to tell who it was that cured their son of his blindness; "because they feared the Jews; for the Jews had agreed already, that if any man did confess that he was Christ, he should be put out of the synagogue." (Jno. ix. 22.)

There are plenty of people at this present time who, like the man and woman referred to, would far rather deny the truth which brought Christ to the cross, and, if possible, avoid the consequences of following that truth, than to be cast out of orthodox synagogues, and thus lose caste in fashionable society. There are thousands of nominal Christians who follow Christ afar off, and who deem it safe and honorable to acknowledge a historical Christ; but the very moment you ask them to take up the cross, and to follow him through good and evil report—to humble themselves by obeying his commands—to go down into the water to be buried in the likeness of his death—then it is that they ask to be excused, and turn away from the despised Nazarene. They may not feel ashamed of the great historical character, in his glory and exaltation, in his triumphal march among the nations, and in his mighty conquests, which he accomplishes by unseen and providential agencies, but they are "ashamed of his words;" that is, individually, they are not willing to obey his "words," which, if obeyed, would humble them in the eyes of the world. He who receives the words of Christ, which he says will judge him in the last day, becomes an humble man, a godly man, a praying man, a self-denying man, a generous-hearted and philanthropic man. There are many people who, in synagogues of fashion, will pay tithes of anise and cummin and frankincense, and all sorts of highly flavored spices, but who, when called upon to deal out love and mercy and truth, which are the weightier matters of the law, will practically deny Jesus Christ. Many will follow him for the miracle of the loaves and fishes, but turn away from him the moment he inculcates truth and righteousness. Many are willing to adore Christ as King and Conqueror, and ready to "crown him Lord of all," and sing hallelujahs to him as "Prince of Peace," who, if called upon, would refuse to assist him in bearing his cross; would refuse to watch with him at the garden of Gethsemane; would refuse to follow him to the cross; would deny him in the presence of his persecutors; would desert him in the agonies of death. But the glorious Paul says, "*For me to live is Christ; for me to die is gain*"—the gain of the glory of God.

IMMERSION.

We use the term immersion, because that is the term that should be employed invariably by a people engaged in a reformatory movement, that has for its end and object the complete restoration of the apostolic order of things. The Bible does not speak of "modes of immersion," but speaks of "one immersion"—of one specific act which conveys only one distinct idea.

Among honest and educated men there is no controversy on the subject of immersion. The controversy rests upon the assertion that sprinkling or pouring will answer the same purpose, an assumption wholly unwarranted, and as such it must be regarded as a direct violation of the law of God, and therefore a grievous sin.

Immersion is a necessary element in the plan of salvation. It is ordained as one of the conditions upon which is suspended the salvation of the sinner. The command to be immersed emanates from the Head of the Church—from Jesus the Christ, who has all authority both in heaven and upon the earth. We find no "non-essentials" in the economy of divine grace; but we do find that wicked and designing men pronounce immersion a "non-essential," which they do at the peril of eternal reprobation. All the commands of Jesus

Christ are essential to salvation. If not, why should they be commanded? Immersion is a divine positive institution, authorized by the infinite God, for the ordination of which he presumes to give no reason to mortal men.

It is enough for us to know that God, through Jesus Christ, has ordained it, and that acceptance with God and remission of sins depend upon its observance. If Jesus Christ is the Son of God, as we verily believe, there is no escape from this conclusion.

If we believe that Jesus is the Christ, the Son of God, and that we have life through his name, then immersion into the name of the Father, and of the Son, and of the Holy Spirit becomes an act of faith. If we can reject one command we can reject all, because, in rejecting one, we not only show that we have no faith in the Son of God as our Savior, but we also insult the majesty of the law-maker. An inspired apostle says: "He who keeps the whole law, and yet offends in one point, is guilty of all." The very fact that the ordinance of immersion, or rather the *negative* of immersion, has been the source of endless controversy from the beginning of the apostasy down to the present time, not only shows the rebelliousness of the human heart in undertaking to change the ordinance of God, but also shows, with peculiar emphasis, what importance is attached to it. It is evident that the Lord intended immersion as a test to the carnal heart. It is intended as a radical test of faith and obedience. Some other test would accord with the divine government just as well, if the Lord had so ordained. Christ says, "Whoever humbles himself shall be exalted," and whoever denies himself and takes up his cross, may become a disciple of Christ; and we feel sure that there is nothing more wisely intended to humble the proud heart of the sinner, than his utter helplessness in the waters of baptism, while in the hands of the administrator. If the belief of a lie and the violation of a divine positive command—the eating of the forbidden fruit—in the garden of Eden, merited the disfavor of God, and was the cause of their banishment from his presence; certainly, by the same parity of reasoning, an antidote to that fatal sin is found in the gospel, where the belief of the truth and the honoring of a divine positive institution restore the penitent believer to the favor of God, who receives him back as a prodigal and remits all his sins. Christ says in the most positive language, "Except a man be born of water and of the Spirit he *can not* enter the kingdom of God." Preachers—"false teachers"—will brazenly stand up and tell the people that they *can* enter the kingdom of God without being born of water. When the Lord placed an interdict upon the tree of the knowledge of good and evil, he said to Adam and Eve, "In the day thou eatest thereof thou *shalt surely die*," or "dying thou shalt surely die." But Satan, transformed into an angel of light, comes forward and puts in a negative, and contradicts the Almighty by saying, "In the day thou eatest thereof thou shalt *not* surely die;" and that controversy between light and darkness has been going on ever since.

Just before Christ ascended into the heavens he placed in the hands of the apostles the great commission, which says: "All power is given to me in heaven and in earth. Go you, therefore, and make disciples of all nations, immersing them into the name of the Father, and of the Son, and of the Holy Spirit; teaching them to observe all things whatsoever I have commanded you." In harmony with this commission, and under the guidance of the Holy Spirit, the apostle Peter, in answer to three thousand convicted sinners on the day of Pentecost, said, by the authority of the coronated and glorified King:. "Repent, and be immersed every one of you in the name of Jesus Christ, for the remission of sins, and you shall receive the gift of the Holy Spirit." If the "Pharisees and lawyers rejected the counsel of God against themselves, being not baptized of him," what will the end of them be who reject the ordinance of the Son of God?

Thus have we briefly established the authority and the necessity of immersion. The man who is not disposed to be hypercritical and skeptical, and who is an honest and patient investigator of the written testimony, asks no further proof than that which is recorded by the sacred historians. The importance of the institution is shown by the fact that the word *immerse*, with its cognates, is used about one hundred times in the New Testament. It is used about eighty times in connection with the ordinance of immersion. We learn by the very best authorities—lexical, philological, archæological and historical—that the original word $\beta\alpha\pi\tau\iota\zeta\omega$ (*baptizo*) never means to sprinkle or to pour, not even metaphorically. Baptism is not an English word, but it is a Greek word *anglicized*; i. e., it has an English termination. As immerse, sprinkle and pour are three specific words, having three specific meanings, and, as such, can not be used interchangeably without making nonsense, the word *baptizo* must either mean specifically immerse, or sprinkle or pour. If it means specifically immerse, then sprinkle and pour can not be included. If it means specifically sprinkle, then immerse and pour can not be included; or if it means specifically pour, then the other two definitions can not be included. And if all these words with specific and distinct meanings are definitions of the word *baptizo*, then no man is baptized until he passes the three ordeals of immerse, pour and sprinkle, which is absurd and ridiculous. Especially is this made manifest in the fact that when an object is immersed the object is plunged beneath the water; that is to say, the subject is *applied to the element;* whereas, when sprinkling or pouring takes place, the water or the element is *applied to the subject.* In immersing, the subject is put under the water; in pouring or sprinkling, the water is *poured upon* or *sprinkled upon* the subject with the hand or with some kind of pot. In primitive times the people *went to the water* in order to bury subjects or candidates in the likeness of Christ's death. In modern times the water—a "teenty little" cup full—is conveyed *to the people!* In view of these facts and contrasts we ask, Which is the right way?

There is not a version of the Scriptures in existence, among all the nations, in which the original Greek word is translated either pour or sprinkle. No scholar dare risk his reputation in so translating the word. In a small volume entitled, "Baptism: Its Meaning and Use," published by the American Bible Union, the erudite editor, Dr. Conant, has traced out the meaning of the word in classic Greek literature, there being some one hundred and fifty occurrences of the word in all, and in each particular case he shows that the meaning of the word is uniformly the same, without one exception. No one, so far as we know, has ever attempted to contradict the statement of Dr. Conant. He triumphantly shows that in every instance it means immerse. Pedobaptist scholars concede that the word does usually convey this sense in classic Greek, while at the same time they assume that it sometimes signifies "wash," "die," "stain," etc. But it is a significant fact that in classic Greek they never translate it "pour" or "sprinkle." They also assume that in the New Testament it is not used in its classic sense. Some Greek lexicons give "wash," "dye," "stain" as meanings of the word, but generally as secondary meanings, some of them being so cautious as to say that it conveys such meanings *only by consequence;* notably, Bailey, who says that "baptism, in strictness of speech, is that *kind* of washing which consists in dipping, and when applied to the Christian institution so-called, it was used by the primitive Christians in *no other sense* than that of dipping." ("Lex. Theol.," p. 221.) A thing immersed may be washed, dyed or stained, as a consequence of immersion. Whether dyed, or washed, or stained, depends upon the character of the element in which the immersion takes place. By metonymy of speech, consequences of an action may be substituted for the action itself. In this way frequently the words wash, dye, stain, soil, etc., are put for the English word dip. As for example, when the dyer dips an article into the dye-stuff, it is said he dyes it, when, in exactness of language, he *dips* it, and, as a *consequence*, it is dyed. When, therefore, the washer dips the same article into water it is said that he washes it, when, in fact, the article washed is only a consequence of the dipping in water. Shall we, therefore, conclude that wash is the meaning of the word dip? By metonymy of speech, a person or thing may be said to be immersed, as an effect, by being thoroughly drenched in a rain shower. The effect is the same as though the person were immersed.

In translating words from one language into another, the rule is always to translate by the primary meaning of the word as given in the lexicons, unless the connection makes it necessary to use a word of secondary meaning, which has never yet been done in translating the word *baptizo*. In regard to rules of interpretation, Sir William Blackstone, an eminent authority in law and jurisprudence, says: "Words of a law are generally to be understood in their usual and most known signification, not so much regarding the propriety of grammar as their general and popular use."

We frequently hear persons say, "If ever I become a Christian, I will be immersed." Why do they say so? Because they prefer to take a certainty for an uncertainty, and because there is no controversy in regard to the validity of immersion. As sprinkle and pour have always been held in doubt, since they were introduced in the apostasy of the Church, wise and conscientious men discard the doubtful and choose that which is positively true.

Dean Stanley, one of the great modern lights of the Church of England, in tracing out the history and meaning of "baptism," says:

"What, then, was baptism in the apostolic age? It coincided with the greatest religious change which the world has yet witnessed. Multitudes of men and women were seized with one common impulse, and abandoned, by the irresistible conviction of a day, an hour, a moment, their former habits, friends, associates, to be enrolled in a new society, under the banner of a new faith. That new society was intended to be a society of 'brothers,' bound by ties closer than any earthly brotherhood—filled with life and energy, such as fall to the lot of none but the most ardent enthusiasts, yet tempered by a moderation, a wisdom and a holiness such as enthusiasts have rarely possessed. It was, moreover, a society swayed by the presence of men whose words even now cause the heart to burn, and by the recent recollections of One, whom 'not seeing they loved with love unspeakable.' Into this society they passed by an act as natural as it was expressive. The plunge into the bath of purification, long known among the Jewish nation as the symbol of a change of life, was still retained as the pledge of entrance into this new and universal communion—retained under the sanction of Him into whose name they were by that solemn rite 'baptized.' In that early age the scene of the transaction was either some deep wayside spring or well, as for the Ethiopian, or some rushing river, as the Jordan, or some vast reservoir, as at Jericho or Jerusalem, whither, as in the baths of Caracalla at Rome, the whole population resorted for swimming or washing. The water in those Eastern regions, so doubly significant of all that was pure and refreshing, closed over the heads of the converts and they rose into the light of heaven new and altered beings. It was natural that on such an act were lavished all the figures which language could furnish to express the mighty change: 'regeneration,' 'illumination,' 'burial,' 'resurrection,' 'a new creature,' 'forgiveness of sins,' 'salvation.' Well might the apostle say, 'Baptism doth even now save us,' even had he left his statement in its unrestricted strength to express what in that age no one could misunderstand. But no less well was he led to add, as if with a prescience of coming evils, 'Not the putting away the filth of the flesh, but the answer of a good conscience toward God.'" The article from which this is quoted appeared in the *Nineteenth Century* for October, 1879, only a short time before the author passed on to the final Grand Assize.

This he pronounces "*the* apostolic baptism." After showing what "*was* the apostolic baptism," he then traces "in detail" "its history through the next three centuries," and shows how the ordinance was abused, how it was perverted from its original design, and how by crafty men it was tortured into an object of superstition. Referring to the "second characteristic of the act of baptism," Stanley says in the same article:

"Baptism was not only a bath, but a plunge—an entire submersion in the deep water, a leap as into the roiling sea or the rushing river, where for the moment the waves closed over the bather's head and he emerges again as from a momentary grave; or it was the shock of a shower-bath—the rush of water passed over the whole person from capacious vessels, so as to wrap the recipient as within the veil of a splashing cataract [Here Stanley quotes from Dr. Smith's *History of Christain Antiquities*, vol. i. p. 169—ED. REVIEW]. This was the part of the ceremony on which the apostles laid so much stress. It seemed to them like a burial of the old former self and the rising up again of the new self. So St. Paul compared it to the Israelites passing through the roaring waves of the Red Sea, and St. Peter, to the passing through the deep waters of the flood. 'We are buried,' said St. Paul, 'with Christ by baptism at his death; that like as Christ was raised, thus we also should walk in the newness of life.'* Baptism as the entrance into the Christian society was a complete change from the old superstitions or restrictions of Judaism to the freedom and confidence of the gospel. It was a complete change from the idolatries and profligacies of the old heathen world to the light and purity of Christianity. It was a change effected only by the same effort and struggle as that with which a strong swimmer or an adventurous diver throws himself into the stream and struggles with the waves, and comes up with increased energy out of the depths of the dark abyss."

---

* Rom. vi. 4; 1 Cor. x. 2; 2 Pet. iii. 20, 21.

In all his statements made up to this point, he does not give out even an intimation that he believed that rantism or affusion—sprinkling or pouring—was practiced in the apostolic age. The Dean indulges in a good deal of rhetorical vaulting, and plays with tropes and figures of speech as a child with a rattle, but his testimony is not invalidated by his superfluous language. After noting the many changes that took place during the apostasy of the Church in the form, design and subjects of baptism, the erudite Dean stultifies history, philology and his own reasoning powers by what follows:

We now pass to the change in the form itself. For the first thrirteen centuries the almost universal practice of baptism was that of which we read in the New Testament and which is the very meaning of the word "baptize"*—that those who were baptized were plunged, submerged, immersed into the water. That practice is still, as we have seen, continued in Eastern churches. In the Western church it still lingers amongst Roman Catholics in the solitary instance of the cathedral of Milan, amongst Protestants in the austere sect of the Baptists. It lasted long into the Middle Ages. Even the Icelanders, who at first shrank from the water of their freezing lakes, were reconciled when they found that they could use the warm water of the Geysers. And the cold climate of Russia has not been found an obstacle to its continuance throughout the vast Empire. Even in the Church of England it is still observed in theory. Elizabeth and Edward the Sixth were both immersed. The rubric in the Public Baptism for Infants enjoins that, unless for special cases, they are to be dipped, not sprinkled. But in practice it gave way since the beginning of the seventeenth century. With the few exceptions just mentioned, the whole Western churches have now substituted for the ancient bath the ceremony of sprinkling a few drops of water on the

---

*It is also the meaning of the word *taufen* ("dip").

face. The reason of the change is obvious. The practice of immersion, apostolic and primitive as it was, was peculiarly suitable to the Southern and Eastern countries for which it was designed, and peculiarly unsuitable to the tastes, the convenience and the feelings of the countries of the North and West. Not by any decree of Council or Parliament, but by the general sentiment of Christian liberty, this great change was effected. Not beginning till the thirteenth century, it has gradually driven the ancient Catholic usage out of the whole of Europe. There is no one who would now wish to go back to the old practice. It had no doubt the sanction of the apostles and of their Master. It had the sanction of the venerable churches of the early ages, and of the sacred countries of the East. Baptism by sprinkling was rejected by the whole ancient church (except in the rare case of death-beds or extreme necessity) as no baptism at all. Almost the first exception was the heretic Novatian. It still has the sanction of the powerful religious community which numbers amongst its members such noble characters as John Bunyan, Robert Hall and Havelock. In a version of the Bible which the Baptist Church has compiled for its own use in America, where it excels in numbers all but the Methodists, it is thought necessary, and on philological grounds it is quite correct, to translate John the Baptist by John the Immerser.

Not as an honest historian, not as a faithful philologist, not as a profound linguist, and not as a conscientious interpreter of God's word, does he assert that "*this great change was effected*" "*by the general sentiment of Christian liberty,*" but as a churchman—a high churchman at that—as a sectarian, as a defender of infant baptism, as an apologist for sprinkling and pouring, and as a vindicator of "our Church," he makes these bold and indefensible and unwarranted declarations. With one sweep of his pen he places the Church of England—which originated with Henry VIII.—above the apostolic Church. Tradition above the written word, the authority of councils above the authority of Jesus Christ, and "the general *sentiment* of Christian liberty" above the facts of the New Testament! And thus these great expounders of "Christian liberty" become "blind leaders of the blind." If questions of salvation and of eternal life are to be decided and regulated by "the *general sentiment* of Christian liberty" then is the Romish Church "just as good as any other Church," because, judging by her numerical strength and wealth and worldly wisdom, she represents more of the "general sentiment of Christian liberty" than any other body of religious people.

Pedobaptists are very much perplexed over the question of baptism. The difficulty meets them at every turn, and will not down at their bidding. Lyman Abbott, editor of the *Christian Union*, a man of rare ability, and as free of prejudice as sectarianism will allow any man to be, in commenting on the recent acts of the Baptists in convention at Saratoga, and speaking of Judson's Burmese Translation, says:

There is a scholarly, an acceptable, an actually accepted version of Scripture in the language of the Burmese. This version is without competition, present or prospective. It is *the* Burmese Bible, at least for an indefinite time to come. The Burmese depend on it, on it alone, for their knowledge of the word of God. Such, on one side, is the state of the facts. But this Burmese version of Scripture renders the Greek word " baptize," with its cognates, by a vernacular equivalent meaning "immerse." No competent scholar will assert that this is an unscholarly rendering of the Greek original. This rendering, however, compels the Christian missionaries who do not practice immersion, and who, of course, do not teach immersion, to explain the terms involved. There is for such missionaries an obvious disadvantage in this. Still, in spite of the disadvantage, missionaries not Baptists do, as matter of fact, use this version, making the necessary explanation. Now the course taken by the American Bible Society is to refuse its aid in circulating this version of the Scriptures, which stands alone as the one means through which many millions of human beings may know the word of God and the way of salvation. The Bible Society should recede from this refusal. Now is an opportune time for it to correct its mistake. It can well afford to do so. Indeed, it can not afford not to do so. *Noblesse oblige.* Strength, wealth, prestige, involve responsibilities, create obligations.

. . . .

If the case were no other than it is; if it were a question of antecedent instruction to translators what kind of versions to produce, the case might be different. We might then say, Let "baptize" be transferred—that is, transliterated—into the heathen tongues, not translated at all. Missionaries of different views on the subject of baptism could then use one and the same Bible, applying their several explanations of the terms transferred. This is the course pursued in both the New and Old Versions of the Bible, and it is a wise one. But here is a version already in existence, already in possession, exclusive possession. It translates, indeed, instead of transliterating; but it translates truly enough so far as mere lexicography goes. Nobody can deny that, nobody at least whose denial would weigh. Nay, if non-Baptist Burmese scholars were to make a new version of their own, and in that version translate the terms in question, such scholars would not render those terms in a manner to *contradict* the version already existing. The utmost that they could do would be to render those terms by words or phrases of a general and indeterminate meaning. What would thus be gained? Why, against a version that gave what is certainly the general meaning of "baptize," there would be a version that did not give the meaning of that word at all. That is all. Would the gain be sufficient to warrant the American Bible Society in entering the field with a rival version? The Bible Society by its inaction has already answered that question. But either do this or do nothing is the alternative to which the American Bible Society is shut up if it refuses to help circulate Dr. Judson's Burmese version of Scripture. In this existing state of the case what is the duty of the Society seems to us very plain. The Society ought not to produce a rival version, and it ought not to do nothing.

The record of God stands fast, and the ordinances of God stand fast. And men—whether Papal or Protestant—can not remove them nor nullify them, unless they reject the word of God and crush down the Bible. And that is just what the so-called orthodox churches are doing and have been doing. And what is it done for, except it be, if possible, to popularize Christianity? The question still comes up, as in the days of the prophet Malachi, "What profit is there in keeping the ordinances?" And to please the people, time-serving preachers and priests admit that there is no profit in thus serving God. The "covenant of God is broken" and "the ordinance is changed" to please a gainsaying world; and hence, instead of reforming the world by teaching men of the world to fear God and honor his holy law, these miserable self-seekers compromise the truth of God and sell their souls for a mess of pottage.

IMMERSION—SPRINKLE—POUR. WHICH?

As we are not writing for Greeks and Latins, but for English readers—for the "common people"—we shall not impose upon our readers by appealing to dead languages of which many of them know comparatively nothing, except as we shall take the benefit of the latest versions of the New Testament, and as we shall avail ourselves of the benefits of some criticisms made by the best scholars of modern times. King James' Version, supplemented by the American New Revision, is plain enough for any ordinary man who is not a bigoted sectarian, nor a Pharisee of the deepest dye. Children who read the New Testament with minds unbiased, and illiterate negroes who hear the New Testament read aloud, never understand the word baptize as meaning either sprinkle or pour. The writer was sprinkled in infancy, and brought up in the Lutheran faith, and yet, during all this time, when reading the New Testament, he always believed in immersion as it reads in the apostolic commission and in parallel passages. It is our firm conviction that any rational man who reads the plain statements of Scripture, and then rejects immersion and substitutes sprinkle or pour, is morally dishonest, or does not believe the word of God as an inspired revelation. Let us recite a few passages.

"In those days came John the Baptist, preaching in the wilderness of Judea." (Matt. iii. 1.) *Baptistees* is the Greek of Baptist, and means "he who immerses." The passage never has, in any language, been translated either sprinkle or pour.

"Then went out to him Jerusalem and all Judea, and all the region round about Jordan, and were baptized of him in Jordan, confessing their sins." (Matt. iii. 5, 6.) If in the phrases, "*in Jordan*"—"*in the river Jordan*"—any one can, by stretch of the imagination, discover the idea of sprinkle, he is certainly beyond the pale of reason.

"I indeed baptize you with water (*en hudati—in water*), but he shall baptize you with the Holy Spirit" (*en pneumati hagio*—in the Holy Spirit, which actually took place on the day of Pentecost). (Mark i. 8.) The same Greek preposition is found in these passages: "*In* the wilderness—"*in* Jordan"—"in Bethlehem," and in very many other similar phrases in the New Testament. The American New Revision renders the passage just quoted, "*in water*," and "*in* the Holy Spirit;" and the English (Canterbury) Revision gives it that meaning in the margin of their work—a fact that forever annihilates all the petty quibbles of pedobaptists. The American revisers translate Matt. iii. 11, as follows:

"I indeed baptize you *in* water unto repentance: but he that cometh after me is mightier than I, whose shoes I am not worthy to bear: he shall baptize you *in* the Holy Spirit and *in* fire." Let it be distinctly noted that the American Revision is a pedobaptist work. This verse has been the puzzle, and the hiding-place, and the bamboozle of pedobaptists for the last fifty years. So far as this verse is concerned, their occupation is now gone. The great Lutheran commentator, Lange, a man of acknowledged scholarship, translates Matt. iii. 11 thus: "I indeed baptize you in (*en*) water, immersing you in the element of water, unto repentance." Let it be understood that *baptism* is not water, but that it is an *act of faith*—an *act of obedience*—whether the act takes place in water, or in some other fluid. Christ commanded the act to be done in water. Let us follow the record.

"And it came to pass in those days that Jesus came . . . and was baptized of John in Jordan, and straightway coming up *out of* the water, he saw the heavens opened." (Mark i. 9, 10.) How men can predicate sprinkle of such phrases as "in water"—"in Jordan"—"up out of the water," is a problem in ethics never understood by the writers of the New Testament. Such casuistry is worthy of the age of the mystics.

"And John also was baptizing in Ænon, near Salim, because there was much water there: and they came and were baptized." (John iii. 23.) John went where there was much water, or many streams, for the specific purpose of immersing the people, and not to water camels, and to assuage the thirst of the multitude. Neither the word "baptized" nor the circumstances denote or call to mind the idea of sprinkle or pour. These last two words are not in the premises.

"And as they went on their way, they came unto a certain water, . . . and they went down both into the water, both Philip and the eunuch; and he baptized him." (Acts viii. 36–38.) It will be noted that the parties first came *to* the water, then they *went down into the water*, and, having gone down into the water, then Philip *immersed* the eunuch. The idea of coming to the water, and then descending into the water, in order to sprinkle water upon the eunuch, is simply absurd as well as ludicrous. "A *certain* water," means one among a number of streams. By reference to Colman's "Map of the Holy Land" (a Presbyterian production), it will be seen that several rivers, emptying into the Mediterranean Sea, have their course in this part of the country. Now let us turn to the Epistles, and note how the allusions to baptism in them correspond with the practice of John, Christ and the apostles.

"Or are ye ignorant that all who were baptized into Christ Jesus were baptized into his death? We are buried, therefore, with him through baptism into death: that like as Christ was raised from the dead through the glory of the Father, so we also might walk in newness of life." (Rom. vi. 3, 4.)

"Having been buried with him in baptism, wherein ye were also raised with him through faith in the working of God, who raised him from the dead." (Col. ii. 12.) We have quoted from the American Revised Version. In all our researches we have never found one man of distinction who has denied that "buried" in both these passages refers to the ordinance of immersion, as practiced in the apostolic age; but, on the other hand, it is an indisputable fact that all lexicographers, commentators, reformers, historians, annotators and antiquarians affirm that these passages refer to immersion. Conybeare and Howson, both eminent critics in the Church of England, in the work entitled the *Life and Epistles of Paul,* translate thus: "With him, therefore, we were buried by baptism, wherein we shared his death when we *sank beneath the waters.*" To which this foot-note is appended: "This clause, which is here left elliptical, is fully expressed in Col. ii. 12. This passage can not be understood unless it be borne in mind that the primitive baptism was by immersion." (*Life and Epistles of Paul,* Vol. II., p. 169.) These same distinguished biblical scholars thus again speak of baptism:

It is needless to add that baptism was (unless in exceptional cases) administered by immersion, the convert being plunged beneath the surface of the water to represent his death to the life of sin, and then raised from this momentary burial to represent his resurrection to the life of righteousness. It must be a subject of regret that the general discontinuance of this original form of baptism (though perhaps necessary in our northern climates) has rendered obscure to popular apprehensions some very important passages of Scripture. (Vol. I., p. 439.)

Speaking of the conversion of Lydia, these authors say:

Lydia, being convinced that Jesus was the Messiah, and having made a profession of her faith, was forthwith baptized. The place of her baptism was doubtless the stream which flowed by the proseucha. The waters of Europe were "sanctified to the mystical washing away of sin." With the baptism of Lydia that of her "household" was associated. Whether we are to understand by this term her children, her slaves, or the work-people engaged in the manual employment connected with her trade, can not easily be decided. (*Life and Epistles of Paul*, Vol. I., p. 296.)

In a foot-note they remark as follows: "Meyer thinks they were female assistants in the business connected with her trade. It is well known that this is one of the passages often adduced in the controversy concerning infant baptism. We need not urge this view of it; for belief that infant baptism is 'most agreeable with the institution of Christ' *does not rest on this text.*" Italics ours.

Though these men, as the exponents of orthodoxy, and as prominent ecclesiastics in the Church of England, show amazing inconsistency by practicing what is not sustained by the word of God, and by practicing in the Church of England what was never practiced in the apostolic church; yet their testimony in regard to the literature of the New Testament, and their critical knowledge of the ancient languages, outweigh, in the court of public investigation, the smatterings and quibbles and cavilings of all the little sectarian pettifoggers of all the orthodox churches. Below we present the testimonies of some of the most celebrated church historians.

Mosheim, *Ec. Hist.* 1–87, says:

In this (the first) century baptism was administered in convenient places, without the public assemblies, and by immersing the candidate wholly in water.

In Stanley's *History of the Eastern Church* we have this language:

There can be no question that the original form of baptism—the very meaning of the word—was complete immersion in the deep baptismal waters; and that, for at least four centuries, any other form was either unknown, or regarded, unless in the case of dangerous illness, as an exceptional, almost a monstrous case. To this form the Eastern Church still rigidly adheres.

Philip Schaff, in his *History of the Apostolic Church*, says:

Indeed, some would not allow even this *baptismas clinicorum (baptism of the sick)*, as it was called, to be valid baptism, and Cyprian himself, in the third century, ventured to defend the aspersio only in case of a *necessitas cogens*, and with reference to a special indulgentia Dei (ep. 76 Magna). There were ecclesiastical laws which made persons baptized by sprinkling ineligible to church offices. . . . Not till the end of the thirteenth century did sprinkling become the rule and immersion the exception.

In the *American Cyclopedia* we have these words:

The form of baptism at first was, according to most historians, by immersion; but as Christianity advanced into colder climates, the more convenient mode of sprinkling was introduced.

All these are pedobaptists. Mosheim was a member of the Evangelical Lutheran Church; Dean Stanley was a member of the Church of England, and Schaff is a member of the Reformed (German) Church. But, like the Pope of Rome, the little Popes of the Protestant Church have assumed to "change" the ordinance of Jesus Christ. For instance, the following from John Calvin:

But whether the person who is baptized be wholly immersed, and whether thrice or once, or whether water be only poured or sprinkled upon him, is of no importance. Churches ought to be left at liberty, in this respect, to act according to the *difference of countries*. The very word *baptize*, however, signifies to *immerse;* and it is certain that *immersion was the practice of the ancient Church.* (*Christian Institute*, Chap. XV.)

And this from Luther:

First, the name *baptism* is Greek; in Latin it can be rendered immersion, when we immerse anything into water, that it may be all covered with water. And although that custom has now grown out of use with most persons (nor do they wholly submerge children, but only pour on a little water), yet they ought to be entirely immersed and immediately drawn out. For this the etymology of the word seems to demand. (*Luther on the Sacrament of Baptism.*)

In the Douay Bible (Romish translation), which contains Haddock's Notes, and especially approved by Pope Pius IX., with the sanction of many archbishops, we find the following confession:

Baptized.—The word baptism signifies a washing, particularly when it is done by *immersion* or by *dipping or plunging* a thing under water, which was formerly the ordinary way of administering the sacrament of baptism. But the Church, which can not change the least article of the Christian faith, is not tied up in matters of discipline and ceremonies. *Not only the Catholic Church, but also the pretended Reformed Churches have altered this primitive custom in* giving the sacrament of *baptism*, and now allow of baptism by pouring or sprinkling water upon the person baptized.

With such authorities as these, what further need have we of testimony? The practical question still remains: Shall we honor an institution of Jesus the Christ, which, besides the testimonies of the Scriptures, has the unequivocal approval of all scholars and all eminent men, or shall we practice a thing that rests entirely upon tradition and assumption?

THE HOLY SPIRIT.

God made promise in the gospel that the Holy Spirit should remain in the Church of Christ forever. The Spirit of God comes to the world and to the Church as a promise, not as a command, and not in answer to prayer. What God promises, he fulfills. When religious zealots pray God, and sometimes even command him, "to send down the Holy Spirit," they perform a thing that has no warrant in the Word of God. It looks like great irreverence, and betrays a wonderful ignorance of the mind of the Scriptures, to see men asking God to "send down" the Holy Spirit periodically, or as occasion may demand, or when sensational preachers are in a humor to get up a "big meeting," when, at the same time, the Spirit of God is ever present in his Church. When we read, "The Spirit and the Bride say, Come," is not that always in the present tense—ever present and never absent? When Christ said to his disciples that the Father would send them another Comforter (John xiv. 16), even the Spirit of truth, that he might *abide* with them and with the disciples of Christ *forever*, why irreverently and stupidly pray for that which we already possess? The Holy Spirit is ever present with the Word, as God and Christ are ever present in the Word. Some preachers act as though the Spirit of God, the greater part of the time, was roaming in infinite space, and that the Spirit made periodical visits to the earth, whenever some fanatic proposed to besiege the dominions of darkness.

God, in the beginning, revealed truth; Christ, as the Son of God, revealed the truth; the Holy Spirit confirmed the truth revealed; and these three agree in one —agree in character, agree in purpose, agree in action. God reveals law; Christ executes the law; the Holy Spirit confirms and gives finality to the law. In this, we have the legislative, the executive and the judicial. The apostles did not preach the Holy Spirit, but they preached as the Spirit gave them utterance—preached "Christ and him crucified," infallibly guided by the

Spirit. It is not the mechanical operations of the Spirit that change the moral nature of man, but it is the truth, as revealed by the Spirit—the truth being brought in contact with the mind and conscience of the sinner. We do not intend to discuss the possibilities and limitations of the Holy Spirit, but simply the sublime truths revealed by the Spirit. What the Spirit of God has power to do in the vast universe, above and beyond the revealed truth, we know not, nor is it our business to pry into the mysteries of the great Creator; but it is our privilege to harmonize and preach the truth which the Spirit has revealed. We shall scripturally analyze the following propositions:

(a) The baptism of the Holy Spirit.

(b) The impartation of the Holy Spirit by the imposition of apostolic hands.

(c) The gospel or the word as revealed by the Spirit.

(d) The confirmation of the word by attestations of miraculous power.

(e) The relation of the Spirit to the sinner.

(f) The relation of the Spirit to the child of God.

(g) The gift of the Spirit.

(h) Who quench the Spirit?

(i) Resisting the Spirit.

(j) The witness of the Spirit.

(k) The fruits of the Spirit.

(l) Personality of the Spirit.

There are only two cases on record of a visible baptism in the Holy Spirit, viz: the one which occurred on the day of Pentecost, when the gospel, *in fact*, for the first time was offered to the Jews, in the name of our risen Lord; and the one which took place in the house of Cornelius, at Cæsarea, when, for the first time, the gospel, *in fact*, was proclaimed to the Gentile world by the apostle Peter, who, with the "keys of the kingdom" of God as the *first* of the apostles in authority, but not *above* the other apostles in authority, opened the kingdom to both Jew and Gentile. (Acts, chapters ii. and x.) In both these places the gospel was introduced by visible miraculous manifestations, in harmony with the fact that in the inauguration of any new order of things, whether physical or religious, the Almighty made use of extraordinary power; but that, after the inauguration of the special order, by supernatural power, the Lord subsequently employed ordinary means in the accomplishment of his will. Spiritual creation is analogous to physical creation. In the physical creation, God created the first man a perfect man in stature, and not a babe in stature. Subsequent to that, every human being, including the Son of Mary, came up from babyhood, according to the laws of procreation. The first animal of every species, and the first bird of every species, and the first fish of every species, and the first flower of every species, was each made perfect according to its nature. After that, everything in the physical world must be reproduced through the medium of the seminal principle. The *giving* of the Ten Commandments on Mount Sinai by Moses, was through the interposition of a miracle. After this revelation, the Jewish people, in their religious worship and moral conduct, were to be educated and regulated by the precepts and principles which the constitution of the Jewish theocracy contained. Analogous to this was the Gospel Dispensation. To miraculously *reveal* the gospel was one thing; to induce the human family to live by its spiritual precepts and its moral power, is another thing. The law of Moses miraculously came down from Mount Sinai; "the law of the Spirit of life in Christ Jesus, which makes us free from the law of sin and death," came down miraculously from Mount Zion.

Certain results followed the baptism of the Spirit in the two cases mentioned: 1. A sound came from heaven like the rushing of a mighty wind. 2. Whatever that sound was, or the particular thing that produced the sound, it filled the room where the apostles were waiting the fulfillment of the promise of the Father. 3. Cloven or parted tongues, resembling fire, rested upon the heads of the apostles, symbolic of the fact that God intended to make use of human tongues in the dissemination of the glad tidings of salvation. Paul says (2 Cor. iv. 7): "We have this treasure [the preaching of the gospel] in *earthen vessels*, that the excellency of the power may be of God, and not of us"—the apostles. 4. The apostles were empowered by the guidance of the Spirit to speak in every tongue of the wonderful works of God.

On the self-evident principle that like causes, under like circumstances, produce like effects, we have this to say, that if any one in these modern times pretends to have been immersed in the Holy Spirit as were the apostles of Jesus Christ, he must produce the same credentials as those which appertained to the apostles. He must give assurance that at the time of his immersion in the Holy Spirit, there was (1) heard the rushing of a mighty wind coming down out of heaven; (2) that parted tongues as of fire stood upon his head; (3) that the house was filled with an unearthly sound, and (4) that he can speak in every man's tongue the gospel of Christ, without having learned the languages of all the tribes of the earth. Unless he can present such credentials as these, he is self-deceived as well as a deceiver of others.

The strange phenomenon which on the day of Pentecost and in the house of Cornelius-resembled fire, was but a *manifestation* of the presence of God; as was the fire that came down from heaven and licked up the first sacrifice upon the first altar reared by the command of Jehovah; as was the flaming sword placed at the entrance of the garden of Eden after the expulsion of Adam and Eve; as was the burning bush as seen by Moses in the land of Midian; as was also the shekinah in the most holy place of the tabernacle and temple worship of the Jews. When preachers, ignorant of the word of God—and sometimes willfully ignorant—call upon God to baptize the people "with the Holy Ghost and *with fire*," they do not seem to be aware of the fact that, since the organization of human society, and through all the generations of men, God has used fire as a symbol of his vengeance upon wicked nations, upon wicked families, and upon wicked individuals. When John the Baptist spoke of baptism in the Holy Spirit and in fire, he was addressing two distinct classes of men —the believing and the unbelieving, the righteous and the unrighteous. (Matt. iii. 11.) This statement is made clear by the fact that when Christ told his apostles that they "should be baptized in the Holy Spirit not many days hence," he said nothing about a "baptism in fire," for the reason that he was addressing *only believers*, and not unbelievers, as in the case of John, who had both classes before him. (See Acts i. 5.)

The apostles received the miraculous endowment of the Holy Spirit as the fulfillment of a special promise made by the Savior to them, but to no one else. Joel, the prophet, as well as John the Baptist, in general terms and in a certain sense, spoke of all nations as coming under the influence of the Spirit, just as, in a general sense, all families were to be blessed in Christ, or by the gracious influences of his gospel, according to the promise which God made to Abraham, or as quoted by Paul in these words (Gal. iii. 8): "And the Scripture, foreseeing that God would justify the heathen through faith, preached before the gospel to Abraham, saying: In thee shall all nations be blessed." But after Christ selects his apostles and educates them, and in anticipation of fitting them to carry out the great commission, he tells them, in specific terms, that they, as his accredited witnesses and embassadors, shall "receive the promise of the Father," and be endowed "with power from above." This promise Christ never made to the promiscuous multitude. There must be a limit somewhere, and Christ himself defines the limit: because if we embrace all mankind under the term "all flesh," as becoming recipients of the baptism of the Spirit, the proposition would include all sorts of men—believers, infidels and scoffers, and therefore, in proving too much, it would prove nothing.

THE BAPTISM IN THE SPIRIT.

It is one of the distinct offices of the Spirit to reveal the truth—not ordinary truth, which belongs to matter and force, but spiritual truth, which is born in heaven. In the city of Jerusalem, on the eventful day of Pentecost, when it was noised abroad that the apostles were speaking, in every man's tongue, the wonderful works of God, "as the Spirit gave them utterance," then "*the multitude came together*," and the multitude were "troubled in mind, because that every man had heard them speak in his own language." Here it is plainly seen that the multitude were not present to receive the endowment of the Holy Spirit, as the apostles received it. Christ never promised to immerse the "multitude" in the Holy Spirit, neither on the day of Pentecost nor on any subsequent period.

Christ, in his special charge to his apostles, says: "Nevertheless, I tell *you* the truth. It is expedient for *you* that I go away: for if I go not away, the Comforter will not come to *you;* but if I depart, I will send him to *you.* And when he [not *it*] is come, he will convince the world of sin, and of righteousness, and of judgment" —not convince the world by a *direct* agency, but through the *medium* of the apostles. (John xvi. 7, 8.) On the day of Pentecost, *after* "the multitude came together," the apostle Peter, standing up with the eleven, and speaking as the Spirit gave him utterance, without any thought upon his part, preached the good news of salvation to the assembled people, who, after being pierced to the heart by the words of truth uttered, cried out in great distress of mind, "Men and brethren, what must we do?" The answer to this will be given in another place.

We now come to the second case of the immersion in the Holy Spirit, that of the household of Cornelius, as recorded in the tenth and eleventh chapters of Acts of Apostles. Peter, in referring to the case of Cornelius and his house, after the immersion in the Spirit had taken place, in his rehearsal of the great event before his Jewish brethren, said: "And as I began to speak [began to preach the gospel], the Holy Spirit fell on them, *as* on us at the beginning. Then remembered I the word of the Lord, how that he said, John indeed baptized in [*en*] water, but you shall be baptized in [*en*] the Holy Spirit." The word of the Lord, under the reign of Christ, and therefore under the New Covenant, was first to be proclaimed in Jerusalem, as the *beginning* place. (See Isaiah ii. and Luke xxiv.) The Jewish brethren, who accompanied Peter to Cæserea as witnesses, "were astonished, because that on the Gentiles also was poured out the gift of the Holy Spirit. For they heard them [the first Gentile converts] *speak with tongues and magnify God*"—as the direct effect of this remarkable endowment. Peter, in his apology before his Jewish brethren, says: "Forasmuch then, as God gave them the like gift *as he did unto us* [apostles], who believed on the Lord Jesus Christ; what was I, that I could withstand God?" In those days of miracles, we must be careful to discriminate between the recipient of miraculous power and the recipient of the remission of sins through obedience to the gospel; for, in the case before us, we see that after the Holy Spirit "fell on all them who heard the word," Peter said, "Can any man forbid *water*, that these should not be baptized, who have received the Holy Spirit as well as we?" God evidently intended by this special miracle to convince the Jews that the "middle wall of partition" between Jews and Gentiles was now to be broken down, and that the boon of salvation through the gospel was also to be granted to the Gentiles.

From these facts, as well as from collateral testimony, we learn that the purpose of the immersion of certain characters in the Holy Spirit was not to change the moral nature of those persons, but that, as expressed in the language of Paul, tongues (the miraculous use of language) are for a *sign*, not to them that *believe*, but to them who *believe not.* (1 Cor. xiv. 22.) But "the gospel," as revealed by the Holy Spirit, "is the power of God unto salvation to them who believe" and obey. (Rom. i. 16.) God performed many miracles in the presence of Pharaoh, to give that hard and inexorable despot to understand that the Lord, by whom Moses was sent, was the Jehovah—the *I Am that I Am*—of the Israelites. Aaron's rod, metamorphosed into a serpent, swallowed up the rods of the Egyptian magicians, whose rods of divination also became serpents. But in that miraculous display of power there was nothing to change the moral character of the witnesses. The inspiration of the dumb beast on which Balaam, the heathen prophet, rode, and which brute beast rebuked the false prophet, did not affect the moral condition of that distinguished animal. Nor, so far as the facts are revealed to us, was the moral character of the prophet himself changed, who, mechanically guided by the Spirit of God, pronounced the richest of blessings upon the Israelites. The Corinthian Church possessed more gifts of working miracles than any church mentioned in the New Testament, and yet this church, above all the churches founded by the apostles, was the proudest and most corrupt, and one which was full of disorder and discontent, and against which Paul files no less than six distinct charges of immorality—all of which forcible facts go to show that inspiration does not by itself, as a mechanical agency of God, change the moral nature of man, nor the will-power of man. The Lord, as it were, dipped the apostles in a flood of inspiration, as men dip pens in ink, that by them, as pens in his hand, he might write upon the "fleshy tablets of the heart" "*the law* of the Spirit of life in Christ Jesus." Paul writes to the Corinthians: "Ye are our epistle written in our hearts, known and read of all men; forasmuch as you are manifestly declared to be the epistles of Christ ministered by us, written not with ink, but with the Spirit of the living God; not in tables of stone, but in fleshy tables of the heart." (2 Cor. iii. 3; Rom. viii. 2.) Here, figuratively, we have the pen, the ink and the written words: and the written or revealed words contain or convey the glad tidings of salvation.

IMPARTATION OF THE HOLY SPIRIT BY APOSTOLIC HANDS.

After his resurrection, and just before his ascension, Christ thus addressed the apostles: "But wait [at Jerusalem] for the promise of the Father, which," said he, "you have heard of me. For John truly baptized in water, but you shall be baptized in the Holy Spirit not many days hence." (Acts i. 4, 5.)

After rebuking some of the apostles for their unbelief, because they refused to believe that he had risen from the dead, thus Christ addresses them in connection with the Great Commission: "And these signs shall follow them that believe—*In my name* they shall cast out demons, they shall speak with new tongues, they shall take up serpents, and if they drink any deadly thing it shall not hurt them; they shall lay hands on the sick, and they shall recover." (Mark xvi. 17, 18.)

The subsequent history of the apostles shows conclusively that all these instructions of the Savior had direct reference to the miracles that should be wrought by the apostles and by those persons upon whom they should lay apostolic hands. Of course the apostles could lay hands upon a third party and the third party could perform miracles, as in the Corinthian Church; but it stands nowhere recorded that the power of working miracles ever transcended the third party; so that when the apostles left the stage of action, all this extraordinary power ceased entirely. Paul explicitly told the church at Corinth that prophecies should cease, and that speaking in other tongues and interpreting mysteries should vanish away; but, said he, "I show you a *more excellent way*" than working miracles; and that way is *"faith that works by love."* (See 1 Cor. chapters xii. and xiii.)

The imposition of apostolic hands was uniformly, if not invariably, attended by the working of miracles, and the act had no necessary connection with the remission of sins, which was alone effected by *obedience* to the gospel, or "the obedience of the faith." It is said of Stephen, after he had, in common with others, received the laying on of apostolic hands: "And Stephen, full of faith and power, did great wonders and miracles among the people." (Acts vi. 8.) "Now when the apostles, who were at Jerusalem, heard that Samaria had received the word of God, they sent them Peter and John; who, when they were come down, prayed for them and they received the Holy Spirit. . . . Then laid they their hand on them and *they received the Holy Spirit.*" (Acts viii. 14-17.) Here we see that after the apostles had received the Holy Spirit, as a miraculous endowment, they had power to impart the same miraculous gift to others. In the case of Cornelius the miracle occurred *before* baptism in water; in this case—in the case of the Samaritans—the miracle occurred *after* baptism in water; facts which go to show that God worked miracles in the days of the apostles when and where he pleased, without reference to the personal obedience of the sinner. Paul could not work miracles until he received the Holy Spirit. "And Ananias went his way [especially directed by the Lord] and entered into the house; and putting his hands upon him, said, Brother Saul, the Lord, even Jesus, who appeared to thee in the way, as thou camest, hast sent me, that thou mightest receive thy sight and *be filled with the Holy Spirit.*" (Acts ix. 15-17.) Here, again, baptism in water took place *after* the miracle of the Holy Spirit; for after Paul had received sight (being physically blind) he "arose and was baptized."

When Paul came to Ephesus he found certain disciples of John—probably converts of Apollos—to whom he thus spoke: "Have you received the Holy Spirit since you believed? And they said to him, We have not so much as heard whether there be any Holy Spirit. And he said to them, Unto what, then, were you baptized? And they said, Unto John's baptism. Then said Paul, John indeed baptized with the baptism of repentance, saying to the people that they should believe on him who should come after him, that is, on Christ Jesus. When they heard this they were baptized in the name of the Lord Jesus. And when Paul had laid his hands upon them, the Holy Spirit came on them, and *and they spake with tongues and prophesied*"—as a direct result of this miraculous impartation. (Acts xix.) Here the miracle occurred *after* the baptism in water. Paul himself had been miraculously called to be an apostle, that he might testify to the resurrection of Jesus the Christ, having both seen his glorified person and heard the voice of his mouth; but, in the meantime, in order to obtain the remission of his sins, he was obliged to do then what every sinner must do now. (Acts ix., xxii.)

If only religious teachers could see and appreciate this highly important distinction between the ordinary and the extraordinary—between what *officially* belongs to the apostles and what belongs to uninspired men, what a vast amount of mental perplexity and theological confusion and useless speculation might be saved. Why do not men discriminate between the age of miracles and the age in which we now live? If we, indeed, have indicated to us in "the gospel of our salvation" a "more excellent way" than the working of miracles, let us dismiss from our minds the idea of miraculous interposition, as having no direct connection with our own personal salvation, and let us, as wise and prudent men, abide the order of heaven. God *reveals* the truth; we *obey* the truth. God reveals our Savior; we believe Christ to be the Son of God, and submit to the conditions of salvation.

THE WORD AS REVEALED BY THE HOLY SPIRIT.

We know nothing of the secret counsels of God. We know nothing of unrevealed truth. But Paul says that "the mystery which has been hid from ages and from generations" is "now made manifest to his saints; to whom God would make known what is the riches of the glory of this mystery among the Gentiles; which is Christ in [among] you, the hope of glory." (Col. i. 26, 27.) Paul, in the close of his epistle to the Romans, says: "Now to him who is able to establish you according to my gospel, and the proclamation of Jesus Christ, according to the revelation of the secret, concealed in the times of the ages (but is now made manifest by the prophetic writings, and by the commandment of the eternal God is made known to all the Gentiles, in order to the obedience of faith) to the wise God alone, through Jesus Christ, to whom be the glory forever." (Rom. xvi. 25, 26, Macknight's translation.) Again to the Ephesians, Paul writes: "For this reason, I, Paul, the prisoner of Jesus Christ for you Gentiles, if, indeed, you have heard of the administration of the favor of God, which was given me for you, that by revelation the secret was made known to me . . . which in former ages was not made known to the sons of men, as it is *now revealed to his holy apostles and prophets by the Spirit.* . . . To me, the least of all saints, was this favor given, to publish among the Gentiles the unsearchable riches of Christ; and to make all see what is the administration of the secret, which had been hid from the ages by God who created all things." (Eph. iii. 1-9, Macknight's translation.)

By these and parallel passages, it will be seen that it was the office of the Holy Spirit to reveal the truth, and, in revealing the truth, to make known the plan of salvation. The Savior thus addressed himself to his apostles: "Nevertheless, I tell you the truth; it is expedient [or good] for you that I go away; for if I go not away, the Comforter will not come to you; but if I depart, I will send him to you. And when he is come, he will convict the world of sin, and of righteousness, and of judgment; of sin, because they believe not on me; of righteousness, because I go to my Father, and you see me no more; of judgment, because the Prince of this world is judged." (John xvi. 7-11.)

By this testimony we learn that the Holy Spirit revealed the plan of salvation to the sinner; and, by the power of gospel truth, we also learn, that the sinner would be converted to Christ. There is not the least intimation here of a special, direct, mystic operation upon the mind of the sinner; but, on the contrary, the language clearly indicates that the testimony of the Scriptures—the facts of the gospel—were intended to bear upon the understanding and conscience of the sinner, in order to the illumination of his mind, in order to convict him of sin, and also to make known to him the conditions of salvation. On the day of Pentecost the apostles spake as the Spirit gave them utterance. The tongue of the apostle Peter was guided by inspiration. An ungodly multitude—the "betrayers and murderers" of Jesus Christ—stood transfixed before the apostle.

He gave utterance to truth that caused the people to tremble with fear. He used human speech in conveying the truth to the hearts of the paralyzed people. The truth conveyed to their hearts was divine truth—the moral power of God. Three thousand were pierced to the heart *by the words spoken.* And being convicted by the words spoken, they cried out, "Men and brethren, what shall we do?" The answer of the apostle was direct: "Repent, and be immersed every one of you in the name of Jesus Christ for the remission of sins, and you shall receive the gift of the Holy Spirit." (Acts ii.) This gift of the Holy Spirit we shall notice under the same head further on.

We quote the language of Christ again: "If you love me, keep my commandments. And I will pray the Father, and he shall give you [apostles] another Comforter [the Paraclete], that he may abide with you forever; even *the Spirit of truth;* whom the *world can not receive,* because it sees him not, neither knows him; but you [apostles] know him, for he dwells with you, and shall be in you." (John xiv. 15-17.) Again: "But when the Comforter is come, whom I will send to you [apostles] from the Father, even *the Spirit of truth,* which proceeds from the Father, he shall testify of me (by means of language), and you shall also bear witness [testimony], because you have been with me from the beginning." (John xv. 26, 27.) From these utterances of Christ we discover that the *relation* which the Holy Spirit sustained to the apostles, and, we might say, to Christians, was entirely different from that which he sustained to the unregenerate world. Here it is positively asserted that the world *can not* receive the Holy Spirit in the same sense in which the apostles received him, and as the children of God receive him. But, for the enlightenment and conviction of the sinner, the Holy Spirit reveals the truth, presents the arguments of Scripture, and brings to bear the motive power of the gospel. The Spirit is the agent, and the word revealed is the instrument—the sword of the Spirit—whether wielded by apostles, evangelists, preachers or common disciples of Christ. And all this convicting power, as was manifested everywhere, in all the preaching of the apostles, was clothed in human language, through which medium alone the truth was communicated to the hearts of sinners. We dare not presume to limit the range and the power of the Holy Spirit; nevertheless, we are only authorized to proclaim to the world that which the Spirit of God has clearly revealed. "Revealed things belong to us and to our children; but secret things belong to God," and hence we dare not "rush in where angels fear to tread." Paul distinctly informs us that the Lord had committed the preaching of the gospel to "earthen vessels, that the excellency of the power may be of God, and not of us." The Holy Spirit revealed the message of salvation, but the message was to be *borne to men by men.* Hence Paul inquires: "How then shall they call on him in whom they have not believed? And how shall they believe in him of whom they have not heard? And how shall they hear without a preacher? And how shall they preach, except they be sent?" (Rom. x. 14, 15.) This one passage itself is sufficient forever to exclude the idea of an abstract operation of the Spirit on the sinner's heart.

But, if possible, to render this proposition still more explicit and conclusive we quote the language of Christ again: "These things have I spoken to you [the apostles], being yet present with you; but the Comforter, which is the Holy Spirit, whom the Father will send in my name, he shall *teach you all things*, anu bring all things to your remembrance, whatsoever I have *said* to you." Again: "Howbeit when he, the Spirit of truth, is come, he will *guide you into all truth:* for he shall not speak of himself [independently of, and contrary to the mind of the Father and the Son], but whatever he shall hear, *that shall he speak:* and he shall show you things to come." (John xiv. 26; xvi. 13.) If these apostles testified, they testified with their lips; and if they used their lips, they made use of language; and if they used language, this language, as the vehicle of inspired ideas, conveyed the glad tidings of salvation to the world.

On the day of Pentecost, when the apostles received "the promise of the Father"—the endowment of the Holy Spirit—"the law of the Spirit of life in Christ Jesus, which makes us free from the law of sin and death," was revealed; and this "law of the Spirit," which is "the gospel of our salvation," superseded the law of Moses—the law of condemnation, "the letter that kills." (Rom. viii.) In this "law of the Spirit," which is variously represented by the apostle as "the gospel," the "law of liberty," the "law of faith," etc., the conditions of salvation are found, as everywhere proclaimed in the apostolic age. If, in the conversion of a sinner, there is a power above and beyond the revealed truth necessary to intensify and consummate the process of the new creation in the image of Christ, the knowledge of such a fact is not recorded upon the pages of inspiration. When Paul emphatically declares that "the gospel is *the* power of God unto [or, in order to] salvation," which gospel consists in three fundamental facts—the death, the burial and the resurrection of Jesus Christ from the dead; and when we feel assured that faith in Christ as our personal Savior, and obedience to his gospel, positively and without doubt, secures our redemption from sin, and from all its fearful consequences, why perplex and delude ourselves upon mere matters of human speculation, and about which the revelation of God has nothing to say?

The apostle Peter understood this matter perfectly, when writing "to the strangers scattered throughout Pontus, Galatia, Cappadocia, Asia [Minor] and Bithynia," he said: "To whom [the prophets] it was revealed, that not to themselves, but to us [the apostles], they did minister the things which are now reported to you by them who have preached the gospel to you *with the Holy Spirit sent down from heaven.*" (1 Pet. i. 12.) And in the last verse of this same chapter, he emphasizes the declaration by saying, "But the word of the Lord endures forever. *And this is the word which by the gospel is preached to you.*" Such unmistakable and irrefutable testimony as this forever declares all modern systems of mystic regeneration unscriptural and false.

Paul sets the matter before the Corinthian Church thus: "For the preaching of the cross [the gospel] is to them who perish foolishness; but to us who are saved, it is *the power of God.*" In the same chapter, he declares "Christ to be the power of God and the wisdom of God." (1 Cor. i. 18, 24.) Thus he writes to the church at Rome: "Now to him that is of power to establish you according to my gospel and the preaching of Jesus Christ, according to the revelation of the mystery, which was kept secret since the world began, but *now is made manifest;* and by the Scriptures of the prophets, according to the commandment of the everlasting God, made known to all nations for the obedience of [the] faith." (Rom. xvi. 25-27.) Paul, speaking to the Corinthians of the things that are "prepared for them who love God," says: "God has *revealed them to us by his Spirit;* for the Spirit searches all things, yea, the deep things of God. For what man knows the things of a man, save the spirit of man which is in him? Even so the things of God knows no man, but the Spirit of God. Now we have received, not the spirit of the world, but the Spirit which is of God, that we might *know the things* which are freely given to us of God; which *things* [not abstractions] we speak, not in the words which man's wisdom teaches, but which *the Holy Spirit teaches* [through the gospel], comparing spiritual things spiritually." (1 Cor. ii. 10–13.) The apostle John accords with Peter and Paul when he thus expresses himself: "We are of God; he who knows God hears us; hereby *know we the Spirit of truth and the spirit of error.*" (1 John iv. 6.) If, then, all these things were brought to the recollection of the apostles, and they were guided by inspiration into *all the truth,* and all that truth is now in our possession as respects the scheme of redemption, what further need have we of testimony?

We intend a thorough investigation of this question, and hence the subject of the Spirit will be pursued.

THE CONFIRMATION OF THE REVEALED WORD.

Confirm means to make strong, to ratify, to make conclusive. That which was *legislated* into existence by the Almighty, and *executed* by the Son of God, was finally *confirmed* or ratified by the Holy Spirit. The word revealed was confirmed by attestations of supernatural power. After the apostles received the great commission, "they went forth and preached (Mark xvi. 20) everywhere, the Lord working with them, and *confirming the word with signs following.*" Paul says: "Wherefore tongues [miracles] are for a sign, *not to them who be-*

lieve, but to them *who believe not:* but prophesying [*teaching,* as is the meaning in this connection] serves not for them who believe not, but for them who believe." (1 Cor. xiv. 22.) Isaiah says: "*Bind up the testimony, seal the law among my disciples.* And I will wait upon the Lord, that hides his face from the house of Jacob, and I will look for him. Behold, I and the children whom the Lord hath given me, are for *signs* and for *wonders* in Israel from the Lord of hosts, who dwelleth in Mount Zion." (Isa. viii. 16–18.) According to Isa. viii. 19, 20, and Rom. x. 6–10, all men are prohibited from seeking after new revelations. In regard to the confirmation of the word, Paul says: "How shall we escape if we neglect [we Christians] so great salvation, which at the first began to be spoken by the Lord, and was *confirmed* to us by them who heard him. God also bearing them witness, both with signs and wonders, and with divers miracles, and gifts of the Holy Spirit, according to his own will." (Heb. ii. 3, 4.)

We shall now give some illustrations of what is meant by the confirmation of the word revealed. A few days after the preaching of the gospel in Jerusalem and after the establishment of the model Church, Peter, on his way to the temple, about three o'clock, cured a man who had been lame and helpless from his birth. The helpless man expected alms of Peter, but Peter, fastening his eyes upon him, with John, said: "Look on us. . . . Silver and gold have I none; but such as I have give I thee: in the name of Jesus Christ of Nazareth rise up and walk. And he took him by the right hand, and lifted him up; and immediately his feet and anklebones received strength. And he, leaping up, stood and walked and entered with them into the temple, walking, and leaping, and praising God." (Acts iii. 1–8.)

Here is an example of the confirmation of the word of the gospel revealed by the Holy Spirit. It was a physical miracle, and nothing is said which goes to show that Peter preached the gospel to the lame man at this time. If the lame man was converted to Christ, it took place after the miracle was performed, and by the preaching of the gospel.

We have a fearful illustration of the power of God, in those days of miracles, in the case of Ananias and Sapphira his wife, whom the Lord instantaneously struck down dead, because they lied to the Holy Spirit, by representing that they had laid the price of their entire possession at the apostles' feet, when, at the same time, they had "kept back part of the price." Surely, if, as some preachers boldly allege, God converts sinners to Christ by a miracle, this miracle produced a strange effect. In consequence of this wonderful display of the terrible power of God, "great fear came upon all the Church, and upon as many as heard these things. And by the hands of the apostles were many signs and wonders wrought among the people; . . . insomuch that they brought forth the sick into the streets, and laid them on beds and couches, that at least the shadow of Peter passing by, might overshadow some of them. There came also a multitude out of the cities round about to Jerusalem, bringing sick folks, and them who were tormented with evil spirits, and they were healed every one." (Acts v.) These miracles were a confirmation of the word, harmonizing with what Christ said to his apostles when he authorized them to go into all the world to preach the gospel, and making this promise to them—a promise which he never made to any other class of men: "And these signs shall follow them that believe [these miracles shall be reported to the credit of the apostles, endowed with the Holy Spirit]: In my name shall they cast out demons; they shall speak with new tongues; they shall take up serpents; and if they drink any deadly thing, it shall not hurt them; they shall lay hands on the sick, and they shall recover." And then we learn that "they went forth, and preached everywhere, the Lord working with them, and *confirming the word* with signs following." (Mark xvi. 16-20.)

"And there sat a certain man at Lystra, impotent in his feet, being a cripple from his mother's womb, who had never walked: the same heard Paul speak, who steadfastly beholding him, and perceiving that he had faith to be healed, said with a loud voice, Stand upright on thy feet. And he leaped and walked. And when the people saw what Paul had done, they lifted up their voices, saying, The gods have come down to us in the likeness of men. And they called Barnabas, Jupiter; and Paul, Mercurius, because he was the chief speaker." (Acts xiv. 8-12.) Here was a physical miracle, but not moral regeneration, which only can be accomplished by bringing the truth—the gospel—which is "*the* power of God," in contact with the understanding and conscience of the sinner.

While preaching in the streets of Philippi, Paul restored a certain woman to her right mind, by commanding, in the name of Jesus Christ, the evil spirit of divination to come out of her, but the miracle did not convert the woman to Christ. In connection with this same event, in the same city, while Paul and Silas were singing praises to God in the Philippian prison, where they had been imprisoned by their pagan persecutors, "suddenly there was a great earthquake, so that the foundations of the prison were shaken; and immediately all the doors were opened, and every one's bands were loosed." (Acts xiv. and xxi.) After this miracle, the Philippian jailer *heard the word of the Lord*, believed in the Lord Jesus Christ, and was immediately immersed, with all his house, who believed with him, and rejoiced with him. It is recorded that while Paul was in Ephesus, "disputing daily in the school of one Tyrannus, for the space of two years, that God wrought special miracles by the hands of Paul, so that from his body were brought to the sick handkerchiefs or aprons, and the diseases departed from them, and the evil spirits went out of them." (Acts xix.)

Paul, on his journey to Rome, having made his appeal to Cæsar, while crossing the Mediterranean Sea, was shipwrecked with other prisoners, and he and they cast upon the island of Melita. The record reads: "And the barbarous people showed us no little kindness: for they kindled a fire and received us every one, because of the present rain and because of the cold. And when Paul had gathered a bundle of sticks, and laid them on the fire, there came a viper out of the heat, and fastened on his hand. And when the barbarians saw the venomous beast hang on his hand, they said among themselves, No doubt this man is a murderer, whom, though he has escaped the sea, yet vengeance suffers not to live. And he shook off the beast into the fire, and felt no harm." (Acts xxviii. 1–5.) This miracle did not tell these barbarians who Jesus Christ was; from the miracle itself they learned nothing of the life and character of the Messiah; learned nothing of the revealed truth, and of the plan of salvation; learned nothing of the personal obedience to the gospel; did not even learn that they were without hope and without God in the world.

All the miracles recorded in Acts of the Apostles were intended to be confirmatory of the revealed word.

These divine attestations were necessary to fully establish the religion of Jesus Christ, and to give it precedence and superiority over all the religions of earth. But while all these miracles were performed with a view of opening the eyes of unbelievers, it required, at the same time, the power of the revealed truth to affect the heart, and to transform the spiritual nature of man. The Spirit ever speaks through the revealed truth, and never without intelligible language. The belief of the truth, and the obedience of the gospel, which saved and sanctified sinners in the apostolic days, will, by the same application, save sinners now. How dare we make the Holy Spirit contradict himself, by adding a supposed power to the gospel which God has never revealed, and which simply amounts to a priestly assumption? The apostles, guided infallibly by the Spirit, preached only "Christ and him crucified." When theologians and ministerial mountebanks torture the Spirit to testify to a mode of salvation, in the present day, which he never testified to under the direct supervision of the apostles, they are not only found guilty of committing an egregious blunder, but they are perpetrating a terrible sin. Let us illustrate. A case is tried in a civil court. A change of *venue* is called, and the case is transferred to another court. The same witnesses are called to testify on both occasions. Suppose the witnesses in the second trial contradict the testimony they gave on the first trial—what would be the verdict of the people? Would they not cry out that the witnesses had perjured themselves? Now, then, what disposition will God make of men—professedly leaders of the people, and professedly servants of Jesus Christ—who will make the Holy Spirit contradict his own testimony, by teaching a mode of salvation in the present age which was not taught in the apostolic age?

Let the people hear what "the Spirit and the Bride *say*"—in intelligible words, which all men can understand. While Peter was on the housetop in Joppa, and "thought on the vision, the Spirit *said* to him [in words to be understood], Behold, three men seek thee. Arise, therefore, and get thee down, and go with them, doubting nothing, for I have sent them;" and Peter, in rehearsing the conversion of Cornelius and his household, thus alludes to the case: "And he showed us how he [Cornelius] had seen an angel in his house, which stood and said to him, Send men to Joppa, and call for Simon, whose surname is Peter; who shall *tell thee words* whereby thou and all thy house *shall be saved."* (Acts xi. 13, 14.) "Now the Spirit *speaks expressly* that in the latter times some shall depart from the faith, giving heed to seducing spirits, and doctrines of demons," etc. (1 Tim. iv. 1.) Thus we see that when the Spirit spoke he used words; the words conveyed ideas—conveyed "the mind of the Spirit"—and the ideas were always tangible and intelligible.

THE GIFT OF THE HOLY SPIRIT.

We must distinguish between the gift of the Holy Spirit as the power of working miracles, and the gift of the Holy Spirit as the promise of God to his obedient and ever-faithful children. Paul says: "There are *diversities* of gifts, but the same Spirit. And there are differences of administrations, but the same Lord. And there are diversities of operations, but it is the same God who works all in all. But the manifestation of the Spirit is given to every man to profit withal. For to one is given by the Spirit, the word of wisdom, to another the word of knowledge, by the same Spirit. To another, faith, by the same Spirit; to another the gifts of healing, by the same Spirit; to another the working of miracles, to another prophecies, to another the discerning of spirits, to another divers kinds of tongues, to another the interpretation of tongues. But all these work that one and the self-same Spirit, dividing to every man severally as he will." (1 Cor. xii. 4–11.)

All these endowments evidently refer to the power of working miracles, and must not be confounded with "the gift of the Holy Spirit" as a promise made to the ordinary Christian, who is not expected to work miracles as they were worked in the apostolic age. And yet "the gift of the Holy Spirit," as promised on the day of Pentecost to the three thousand converts, may have included the working of miracles, while the apostles were present in person with the churches of Christ. Whether this "gift" to the ordinary Christian means the actual personal indwelling of the Spirit, or an abstract indwelling of the Spirit, or the indwelling of "the *mind* of the Spirit," are questions which have been the source of endless and perplexing talk. We do not believe in the "word alone" system, nor in the "Spirit alone" system; but we do believe that if the word of the Spirit is in the heart of the Christian the Spirit is present with the word; the *how* of it we do not know: we walk by faith. We can not conceive of an abstract principle, nor of the bare isolated word dwelling separately in the heart of a Christian. We confidently assert, because of the absence of rebutting testimony, that where the word or mind of the Spirit is not received into the heart, there the Spirit does not go.

Paul says: "Let this mind be in you, which was also in Christ Jesus." "Let the word of Christ dwell in you richly." (Col. iii. 16; Phil. ii. 5.) "The *word* of Christ" evidently is the same as "the *mind* of Christ."

Christ is certainly present with his own word wherever received, but in what metaphysical sense we can not explain, any more than we can explain how God in the physical world is present working in the seed which has been deposited in the ground. The body is represented as "the temple of the Holy Spirit," because it is by the truth which the Holy Spirit has revealed that the heart is sanctified, and the body consecrated to the service of the Lord. (1 Cor. vi. 19.) It is after the sinner obeys the gospel and not before he obeys that he receives "the gift of the Holy Spirit." Paul, in addressing Christians at Ephesus, says: "That we should be to the praise of his glory, who first trusted in Christ. In whom you also trusted, after that you heard the word of truth, the gospel of your salvation: in whom also after that you believed, you were sealed with the Holy Spirit of promise, which is the earnest [or pledge] of our inheritance, until the redemption of the purchased possession." (Eph. i. 13.) The promise of the Father is that the Spirit shall abide with the Christian forever, and through the word be the constant luminary of the Church, the temple of God, which is composed of living stones or regenerated men and women.

Christians are represented as "walking after the Spirit;" as "minding the things of the Spirit;" as being "in the Spirit;" as having the Spirit of Christ; as "mortifying the deeds of the body through the Spirit;" as being "led by the Spirit;" as having "received the Spirit of adoption;" and the Spirit is represented as "dwelling in our mortal bodies." (Rom. viii.) In the same chapter we learn that the "Spirit bears witness with our spirit [the mind of the Spirit bears witness with the mind of God's children] that we are the children of God;" that "the Spirit helps our infirmities," and that he "makes intercession for us"—the children of God. None of these beautiful and expressive terms apply to the ungodly and disobedient. They indicate the tender and intimate relations which exist between the promised Comforter and the adopted children of God. The final glorification of the saints depends on the fact that the Spirit of God dwells in their mortal bodies. Says Paul: "Now if any man have not the Spirit of Christ, he is none of his. And if Christ be in you [not literally], the body [or the passions in the body] is dead because of sin; but the spirit [of the man] is life because of the righteousness. But if the Spirit of him who raised up Jesus from the dead, dwell in you [Christians], he who raised up Christ from the dead, shall also quicken [make alive] your mortal bodies by his Spirit who dwells in you." From which premises we conclude that unless we receive and retain in our hearts "the mind of the Spirit" and are led by the words of the Spirit, we shall never be raised up to glory and immortality. They who are the "sons of God" are "led by the Spirit of God," and having received "the Spirit of adoption," they, as "new-born babes," are enabled to cry, "Abba, Father" (Rom. viii.). Paul writes in the same style to the Galatian Christians, when he says: "Because you are sons [once having been aliens] God has sent forth the Spirit of his Son into your hearts, crying, Abba, Father." He addressed them as the adopted sons of God, and not as unbelieving and disobedient aliens. The Spirit of God strives with the wicked world as in the days of Noah, *through the word of God*, which is "the sword of the Spirit," and which was wielded by prophets and apostles.

While it is true that sinners must be convicted by a Divine revelation, as revealed by the Spirit, and also be convicted and convinced by the arguments of the Scriptures, in order to the obedience of the faith, it is equally true that the children of God must "pray in the Spirit, and keep themselves in the love of God." (Jude 20, 21.) They must "pray always, with all prayer, and supplication *in the Spirit.*" (Eph. vi. 18.) "Where the Spirit of the Lord is, there is liberty," because it is "the Law of the Spirit of Life in Christ Jesus that makes us free from the law of sin and death." (2 Cor. iii. 17; Rom. viii. 2.) "But if you [Christians] are led by the Spirit" —the law of the Spirit, or "the Spirit of truth"—you are not under the law of sin and death. (Gal. v. 18.) "By one Spirit," both Jews and Gentiles have access to the Father, and "*through* the Spirit" the children of God are built together, for an habitation of God. (Eph. ii. 18-22.) "By one Spirit"—instructed by "the mind of the Spirit"—we have all been immersed (*ebaptisthecmen*) into one body, whether we be Jews or Gentiles, . . . and have been all made to *drink into one Spirit.*" (1 Cor. xii. 13, 14.)

The Spirit of God is said to "rest upon" his children in tribulation. "If you be reproached for the name of Christ, happy are you, for the Spirit of the glory of God rests upon you." (1 Peter iv. 12.) Christians are said to be sanctified by the Spirit. "Elect according to the foreknowledge of God the Father, through sanctification of the Spirit unto obedience and sprinkling of the blood of Jesus Christ." (1 Peter i. 2, 4.) God's people are sealed by the Spirit. "Now he who established us with you, in Christ, and has *anointed* us [typified by the anointing of kings under the Jewish dispensation], is God, who has also *sealed* us, and given the earnest [pledge] of the Spirit of our hearts." (2 Cor. i. 21, 22.) "Grieve not the Holy Spirit of God, whereby you are *sealed* to the day of redemption." (Eph. i. 13, iv. 30.)

"The allusion to the seal," says Bickersteth, "as a pledge of purchase, would be peculiarly intelligible to the Ephesians, for Ephesus was a maritime city, and an extensive trade in timber was carried on there, by the shipmasters of the neighoring ports. The method of purchase was this: The merchant, after selecting his timber, stamped it with his own signet, which was an acknowledged sign of ownership. He often did not carry off his possession at the time; it was left in the harbor with other floats of timber; and in due time the merchant sent a trusty agent with the signet, who, finding that lumber which bore a corresponding impress, claimed and brought it away for the Master's use. Thus, the Holy Spirit impresses on the soul now, the image of Jesus Christ; and this is the sure pledge of the everlasting inheritance."

We have already had something to say on the gift of the Spirit; but as it is a question of considerable perplexity, and, as a consequence, has given rise to much controversy, we shall further attempt to throw light upon it. We shall show that the gift of the Holy Spirit was peculiar to the apostolic age. First, we remark, that the Spirit, as a personality, is distinct from the *gift* of the Spirit. The gift of the Spirit is a *promise*, and not a command. On the day of Pentecost, Peter said to the penitent believers: "Repent, and be immersed every one of you in the name of Jesus Christ for the remission of sins, and you shall receive *the gift* of the Holy Spirit. For the *promise* is to you, and to your children, and to all who are afar off, even as many as the Lord our God shall call." In Peter's sermon, from which the above is quoted (Acts ii.), we have these words:

"Therefore, being by the right hand of God exalted, and having received of the Father the *promise* of the Holy Spirit, he has shed forth this, which you now see and hear." In a general sense, all who obey the gospel receive the gift of the Spirit by receiving the blessing of God through the gospel; for "the gift of God is eternal life through Jesus Christ;" but in a special sense, the gift of the Holy Spirit is the power of working miracles.

By reference to the words of Peter just quoted, it will be seen that the remission of sins was one thing, and the special gift of working miracles in the future altogether another thing, as may be seen by tracing out the work and preaching of the apostles, consequent upon whose preaching the work of performing miracles followed, in many places and by diverse methods. This "gift" on the day of Pentecost was similar to that bestowed upon the household of Cornelius, the first Gentile converts. The accompaniments of this special gift were not always the same; but, as in the Corinthian Church, it was given to every man by the same Spirit to profit withal; and because the Corinthians could work miracles, they were puffed up with pride. The gift of the Holy Spirit was not always bestowed in the same manner, nor for the same purposes; a full explanation of which may be found in 1 Cor. xii. The gift of the Holy Spirit is further explained in what took place in the household of Cornelius, in the city of Cæsarea. It is said that when the Holy Spirit fell on these Gentile converts, on that eventful occasion, that the Jewish brethren who accompanied Peter were astonished, "because that the gift of the Holy Spirit was poured out upon the Gentiles." When rehearsing this matter before his Jewish brethren, after his return to Jerusalem (Acts xi.), Peter said: "And as I began to speak, the Holy Spirit fell on them, even *as* on us [apostles] at the beginning, and I remembered the word of the Lord, how he said, John indeed immersed in water; but you shall be immersed in the Holy Spirit. Since then God gave them the *like gift* as he did to us [apostles] who believed on the Lord Jesus Christ, what was I, that I could withstand God?"

That this gift of the Spirit was for a special object, and limited to the apostolic period, and that it was diverse in its manifestations, can only be made clear by an appeal to the facts. Philip, who was only an evangelist, and not an apostle, had preached in Samaria, and there made a number of converts. This news having gone to Jerusalem, the headquarters of the apostles, the apostles sent down Peter and John, both apostles, who, on arriving at the place, discovered the fact "that the Holy Spirit had fallen upon none of them; only they were immersed in the name of the Lord Jesus," through whom they had received the remission of sins, and, of course, were now constituted members of the "one body." The apostles then prayed "that they might receive the Holy Spirit;" and, having "laid their hands upon them, *they received the Holy Spirit;*" in pursuance of which miraculous gift they were at once enabled to perform miracles, as did the apostles themselves. (Acts viii.) At another time, when Paul arrived at Ephesus, he found certain of John's disciples there, who had never heard of the wonderful demonstrations of the Holy Spirit, but knew only of the baptism of John; but who, after listening attentively to the preaching of Paul, "were immersed in the name of the Lord Jesus," in obedience to which command they obtained the remission of their sins, which was in strict harmony with the organic law of induction into Christ's kingdom, as announced in the great commission. Then "when Paul laid his hanas upon them [who were already Christians], *the Holy Spirit came upon them;*" and, as a result, corresponding with similar cases, *"they spake with tongues and prophesied."* (Acts xix.)

Paul, writing to the Corinthian Church, whose members grew proud by the working of miracles, thus writes: "But the manifestation [or gift] of the Spirit is given to every man to profit withal. For to one is given by the Spirit *the word of wisdom;* to another *the word of knowledge* by the same Spirit; to another *faith* by the same Spirit; to another the *gifts of healing* by the same Spirit; to another *the working of miracles;* to another *prophecy;* to another *discerning of spirits;* to another *divers kinds of tongues;* to another the *interpretation of tongues:* but all these work that one and the selfsame Spirit, dividing to every man severally as he will." (1 Cor. xii. 7-11.)

With the passing away of the apostles, these miraculous manifestations ceased. They all tended toward the perfection of the body of Christ. When the primitive Church came into "the *unity of the faith*, and of the knowledge of the Son of God, unto a *perfect man*, unto the measure of the stature of the *fullness* of Christ . . . making increase of the body to the *edification of itself in love,*" the special gifts of working miracles were dispensed with, to give way to *the more excellent way which works by love.*

THE WITNESS OF THE SPIRIT.

"The Spirit itself [himself] bears witness with our spirit that we are the children of God." This language was addressed specifically to Christians—to the children of God—and not to sinful and unconverted men. As God's faithful and believing children we receive the "mind of the Spirit;" this mind of the Spirit is the testimony of the Scriptures, for "the testimony of Jesus is the Spirit of prophecy." The *"mind* of the Spirit" contains the conditions of salvation. The gospel is the mind of the Spirit revealed. In the revelation made by the Spirit, we find the mind or the will of the heavenly Father. The apostles, under the guidance of the Holy Spirit, proclaimed the last will and testament of the great Testator. We receive the testimony; we believe the testimony; our faith is founded on testimony; we obey the conditions of the gospel and obtain the remission of our sins; consequently the mind of the spirit of the believer bears witness with the Spirit, or, which is the same thing, with the *mind* of the Spirit, that he is a child of God, because he has received, and believed, and obeyed the things revealed by the Holy Spirit. Hence also, the Christian is "*led* by the Spirit of God." The sinner must be *convicted* by the revealed facts of the Spirit, and *obey* the truth of the Spirit, before he can claim to be *led* by the Spirit. "For as many as are led by the Spirit of God [led by the *instructions* of the Spirit of God], they are the sons of God." (Rom. viii. 16.) Paul's admonition to Christians is this: "*Walk in the Spirit*, and you shall not fulfill the lust of the flesh." "But if you are led by the Spirit—'by the law of the Spirit'—you are not under the [Mosaic] law." (Gal. v.)

The "groanings" spoken of by Paul in Rom. viii. 22, 26, are not the "groanings" of the Holy Spirit, but the groanings of this flesh, under the dominion of sin. Hear Paul's explanation in verse 27: "And he who searches the hearts [by the truth] knows what is the *mind* of the Spirit, because he makes intercession *for the saints* [not for the sinners] *according to the will of God.*" Intercession, in behalf of the saints, is made through the revealed will of God. It is the promises of God that help our infirmities. Paul, in this chapter, is speaking of the redemption of the bodies of the saints. The body of the saint is in bondage, groaning and travailing to be "delivered from the bondage of corruption into the glorious liberty of the children of God." The hope of the Christian is the redemption of his body from the grave. Paul says distinctly: "Even we ourselves [we Christians] *groan within ourselves,* waiting for the adoption, viz., the *redemption of our body*" from the pains and penalties of physical death.

RESISTING THE HOLY SPIRIT.—The blessed Stephen, standing in the august presence of the Jewish Sanhedrim, after having given utterance to a most searching sermon, based on a long line of historical evidence, and deduced from their own Scriptures, and proving by them that this Jesus is the Christ, the Son of God, thus addressing them: "You stiff necked and uncircumcised in heart and ears, you do always resist the Holy Spirit: *as* your fathers did, so do you." And the *manner* of resisting the Holy Spirit is thus expressed in the succeeding verse: "Which of the prophets have not your fathers persecuted? And they have slain them who showed before of the coming of the Just One; of whom you have now been the murderers and betrayers; who have received the law by the disposition of angels, and have not kept it. When they heard these things [these words of burning truth] they were cut to the heart." (Acts vii.)

By reference to the ninth chapter of Nehemiah, we may ascertain how the Jewish fathers resisted the Spirit of God. The prophet, referring to the guidance of the Israelites through the wilderness, says: "Thou gavest thy good Spirit also to *instruct* them. . . . Nevertheless, they were disobedient, and rebelled against thee, and cast thy law behind their backs, and slew thy prophets who *testified* against them. . . . Yet many years didst thou forbear them, and testified against them *by thy Spirit in thy prophets;* yet they would not give ear; therefore thou gavest them into the hand of the people of the lands." God clothed the prophets with his Spirit. "The Spirit of the Lord clothed Gideon." "Then the Spirit clothed Amasai." "The Spirit of God clothed Zechariah." (Judges vi. 34; 1 Chron. xii. 18; 2 Chron. xxiv. 20.) God inspired the prophets; clothed with authority, the prophets bore the message of God to the people; by resisting the prophets the people resisted the words of the prophets; by resisting the words of the prophets the people resisted the Spirit of God which was in these prophets. In the same manner the Lord clothed the apostles with the Holy Spirit. Clothed with the Spirit, the apostles bore the message or the words of salvation to the nations of earth. By resisting the words of the apostles, ungodly men resisted the Spirit of God, who spoke through them. These were ministers extraordinary. Ministers ordinary now take up the same words, and bear them to the people. "The gospel is the power of God unto salvation," whether preached by the apostles or by uninspired men. All who resist the truth in the present day, resist the Spirit of God precisely in the same sense that wicked people did under the preaching of the apostles, because it was the Spirit of God that revealed the same truth. The word of God is the sword of the Spirit, and when rebels run against that instrument, they plunge against that which is sharper than any two-edged sword. (Heb. iv.)

While it is true that in this way sinners resist the truth, and therefore the Spirit that revealed the truth, it is equally true that Christians "quench the Spirit" by neglecting to be "led by the Spirit" wherever Christian duty has been pointed out. If any one produces the "fruits of the Spirit," we may know that such an one is under the power and influence of the Spirit. If any professed Christian produce not the fruits of the Spirit, but is sour and crabbed and petulant and ugly in disposition, and withal covetous and avaricious, though he professes to have been baptized in the Spirit, we may conclude at once that that person is not under the directing power of the Spirit.

PERSONALITY OF THE HOLY SPIRIT.—The Holy Spirit is not an abstraction, or a subtle influence, or a mystic effluence, or an ethereal intangibility any more than the Father is, any more than the Son is. The Holy Spirit is always represented as speaking by intelligible language. When the antediluvians resisted the Spirit of God, who spoke through Noah, and resisted the Spirit by *resisting the words of the Spirit*, God said: "My Spirit shall not always strive with man." (Gen. vi. 3.) "Wherefore, as the Holy Spirit *says*, To-day if you will hear *his* [not *its*] voice, harden not your hearts." (Heb. iii. 7.) "The Spirit and the Bride *say*, Come, and let him that hears say, Come; and let him that is athirst come; and whosoever will, let him take of the water of life freely." (Rev. xxii. 17.) "He that hath an ear, let him *hear* what the Spirit *says* to the churches." (Rev. ii. and iii.) "The Spirit *speaks* expressly that in the last days some shall depart from the faith." (1 Tim. iv. 1.) If we had space, and deemed the fact necessary to the argument, we could adduce an abundance of Scripture to show that the Holy Spirit, as a personal being, can be vexed, blasphemed, lied against, tempted, insulted. This can not be predicated of a mere influence; for an influence can not be vexed.

"Blessed are the dead that die in the Lord. Yea, *says* the Spirit, they rest from their labors, and their works do follow them."

THE LAW OF THE SPIRIT.

These expressions are found in the eighth chapter of Romans:

"The law of the Spirit of life in Christ Jesus has made me free from the law of sin and death."

"Who walk not after the flesh, but after the Spirit."

"For they that are after the flesh, do mind the things of the flesh; but they that are after the Spirit, the things of the Spirit."

"But you are not in the flesh, but in the Spirit, if so be that the Spirit of God dwell in you. Now, if any man have not the Spirit of Christ, he is none of his."

"But if Christ be in you, the body is dead, because of sin; but the Spirit is life, because of righteousness."

"But if the Spirit of him that raised up Jesus from the dead, dwell in you, he that raised up Christ from the dead shall also quicken your mortal bodies by his Spirit that dwelleth in you."

"For if you live after the flesh, you shall die; but if ye through the Spirit, do mortify the deeds of the body, ye shall live."

"For as many as are led by the Spirit of God, they are the sons of God."

"But you have not received the spirit of bondage again to fear; but you have received the spirit of adoption, whereby we cry, 'Abba, Father!'"

"The Spirit also bears witness with our spirit, that we are the children of God."

"Who have the first-fruits of the Spirit?"

"Likewise the Spirit also helps our infirmities."

"But the Spirit itself makes intercession for us."

"And he that searches the heart knows what is the mind of the Spirit."

In the first citation, we see at a glance that Paul is comparing the law of the Spirit—the gospel—with the law of Moses. It was the truth contained in the law of the Spirit, that made Paul free from the bondage of sin and death. That is, the conditions of salvation are found in that law, which, by the Holy Spirit, was sent down from heaven. (1 Pet. i. 12.) All the epistolary writings were addressed to Christians, and not to the world. Hence, these writings can not be applied to the world. Christians are not to follow after and be controlled by the instincts of the flesh; but they must follow the Spirit, or pay strict attention to the things revealed by the Spirit. Christians are not exhorted to look after the *nature*, the *essence* and the *origin* of the Spirit. Now "*the things* of the Spirit" are the facts and precepts and promises of God that are found in the gospel. The gospel contains the good news of salvation.

Christians can not walk literally in the Spirit, for since the Spirit is an intelligent Person, and not an essence, how could such a thing be? That which is flesh itself can not walk literally in the flesh, but the carnal man is subject to the laws of an animal nature. It is not conceivable that a Christian can *literally walk in the Spirit*, and the Spirit literally *dwell in him* at one and the same time. This would be a palpable contradiction in terms. A Christian can enjoy the Spirit of Christ, without the necessity of the actual presence of Christ. We receive the Spirit of Christ by receiving his words; for his "*words* are life and they are spirit." His words communicate eternal life to the children of God. "Let the word of Christ dwell in you richly *in all wisdom.*" The germinating power is in "the seed of the kingdom." The word of God is the seed of the kingdom. Without receiving the doctrine of Christ, we can not receive the Spirit of Christ. And, by parity of reasoning, we can not receive the Spirit, unless we accept "the law of the

Spirit." It is by living a life of righteousness that we secure to ourselves the Spirit of life.

The same Spirit that raised up Jesus from the dead, will also quicken our mortal bodies—raise them from the dead—if we retain in our hearts the germinating principle of life which, by the gospel, is communicated to us. If we follow the promptings of our animal desires, we shall surely die; but if, through the Spirit—minding the things of the Spirit—we mortify the base passions of our bodies, we shall live. Only those are the sons of God who are led by the Spirit of God. As the Spirit is not here in person to lead us, and we can not conceive of being led by an essence or an influence, we must conclude that we are led by the "mind of the Spirit," that we might know, by positive knowledge, the things that are freely given to us. (1 Cor. ii. 12.) Paul says: "I am crucified with Christ; nevertheless, I live; yet not I, but *Christ liveth in me;* and the life which I now live in the flesh, *I live by the faith of the Son of God,* who loved me, and gave himself for me." (Gal. ii. 20.) Do not all Christians live in the same manner? In Gal. iii. 2, he thus questions the Galatians: "This only would I learn of you, Received you the Spirit by the works of the law, or *by the hearing of faith?* Are you so foolish? having *begun in the Spirit,* are you now made perfect by the flesh?" These Christians were under the dispensation of the Spirit, not under the dispensation of Moses. In the same chapter, we read "that the blessing of Abraham might come on the Gentiles through Jesus Christ; that we might receive *the promise* of the Spirit through faith; which promise is the blessing of salvation through Christ." In Gal. v., we are represented as obtaining our liberty through Christ. In Romans, we are made free by "the law of the Spirit;" or, in other words, by the gospel of Christ. In the fifth verse, again, we read: "For we, through the Spirit, wait for the hope of righteousness *by faith*." These Galatians were exhorted to "walk in the Spirit"—in the dispensation of the Spirit, and not in the "lust of the flesh," as those under the law. "But if you be led of the Spirit, you are not under the law." This is Paul's argument throughout—running a parallel between the law and the gospel, for the benefit of those Judaizing Christians who troubled the churches.

We receive "the Spirit of adoption," and are made "fellow-citizens with the saints in light," by being "immersed into the one body," under the dispensation and direction of the "one Spirit." The Spirit, or "the *mind* of the Spirit," "bears witness with our spirit," or with the *mind* of our spirit, that we "are the children of God," which is predicated by the fact that we are led by the revelations of the Spirit. Consequently, wherever the mind or the words of the Spirit go, there the Spirit is present; but in what special sense we presume not to know, any more than we know how God is present in a grain of corn to cause it to grow. We pretend to know nothing about final causes. In all these operations we walk by faith, not by sight. The Spirit that helps our infirmities can not be an abstract, ethereal Spirit, or a subtle influence; and the Spirit therefore that intercedes in our behalf, must intercede through some medium; and, hence, to save ourselves from the bewilderment of all mysticism, we must conclude that "the mind of the Spirit" is that medium, and that the word of God is the mind of the Spirit. The consolations of the Spirit come to the child of God through the revelations of the Spirit. And the Spirit tells us by revelation, "That eye hath not seen, nor ear heard, nor hath it entered the heart of man, the things which God hath laid up for them who love him." If the consolations of the Spirit do not come to the Christian through the revelations of the Spirit, then the whole subject is wrapped in impenetrable mysticism. It is all summed up in a few words by Paul to Timothy: "Hold fast the form of sound words, which thou hast heard of me, in faith and love, which is in Christ Jesus. *That good thing* which was committed to thee, *keep*, by the Holy Spirit which dwells in us." Satan is ever trying to catch away that good thing—the word of God—out of our hearts, lest we should believe and be saved. (Luke viii. 12.)

THE END.

www.ingramcontent.com/pod-product-compliance
Lightning Source LLC
Chambersburg PA
CBHW030313240426
43673CB00040B/1151